THE SOCIAL PSYCHOLOGY OF
ROMANTIC RELATIONSHIPS

The Social Psychology of Attraction and Romantic Relationships

Madeleine A. Fugère, Ph.D.
Jennifer P. Leszczynski, Ph.D.
Alita J. Cousins, Ph.D.

First published 2015 by
PALGRAVE

Palgrave in the UK is an imprint of Macmillan Publishers Limited, registered in England, company number 785998, of 4 Crinan Street, London N1 9XW.

Palgrave Macmillan in the US is a division of St Martin's Press LLC, 175 Fifth Avenue, New York, NY 10010.

Palgrave is a global imprint of the above companies and is represented throughout the world.

Palgrave® and Macmillan® are registered trademarks in the United States, the United Kingdom, Europe and other countries.

ISBN 978-1-137-32482-5   ISBN 978-1-137-32483-2 (eBook)
DOI 10.1007/978-1-137-32483-2

This book is printed on paper suitable for recycling and made from fully managed and sustained forest sources. Logging, pulping and manufacturing processes are expected to conform to the environmental regulations of the country of origin.

A catalogue record for this book is available from the British Library.

A catalog record for this book is available from the Library of Congress.

For D. F. and R & R. Your daily love and support mean so much to me. Special thanks to Mom and Dad. M. A. F.

To my husband and children whose love and support inspire me every day. J. P. L.

To my children, who inspire me to write and provide me with many great stories. A. J. C.

Contents

Preface

Throughout my teaching career I have taught countless sections of Social Psychology. Throughout the course, I use so many examples related to human attraction and romantic relationships that the course could be subtitled "The Social Psychology of Attraction and Romantic Relationships." Over the past eight years I have also been fortunate to teach a variety of first-year, upper-level, and honors seminars on attraction and romantic relationships. When planning my first attraction course, my colleagues Alita Cousins and Jennifer Leszczynski (both professors of Social Psychology and experts in evolutionary theory and gender research, respectively), and I attended a faculty meeting. At this meeting we discussed my new attraction course and also discussed the possibility of writing a book on the Social Psychology of "Dating and Mating." Eight years later, we have written that book for readers interested in learning how social psychological theory and research apply to attraction and romantic relationships.

The purpose of this book is to synthesize the social psychological theory, research, and concepts that can be applied to attraction and romantic relationships. Principal themes of the current book include first impressions of physical and non-physical characteristics, attitude formation and attitude change, perceptions of the self and others, attraction research, relationship research, love, sex, evolutionary theory, and gender. In each of these areas, we discuss the research related to each domain and provide examples from the media and/or from real life to illustrate the concepts.

My interest in Social Psychology began when I took my first Social Psychology class with my favorite professor, Dr Susan Rakowitz, at Fairfield University. Dr Rakowitz was also the first to apply Social Psychology to "dating and mating" for me. In one of our in-class exams, she posited the following question (which I had the good fortune to find in an instructor's manual she authored), "Imagine that you are a fairly boring person. Somehow you manage to get someone to invite you out for dinner. According to cognitive dissonance theory, which would improve your chances of having a second date – getting your date to pay for a really expensive meal at a fancy French restaurant, or a cheap one at the local burger joint?" (Rakowitz, 1995, p. 204). I was hooked! In fact, I still use this question to begin discussion on the first day of my Social Psychology classes.

In preparing to write this book, I perused my favorite Social Psychology textbook (Kassin et al., 2011) and then researched all of the theories, research, and concepts that I illustrate using examples related to attraction and romantic relationships. That initial research led to a deluge of supporting research articles. (Every time I read an article I find at least three more articles I want to read!) I have compiled summaries of the most interesting and relevant research and how it can be applied to the realms of human attraction and romantic relationships. In some cases, I present more comprehensive detail about a particular study. Look for these more detailed summaries in the sections labeled "What the research says." These sections are intended to aid the reader in critically evaluating the research by reviewing both what the research *does* say and what it *doesn't* say. Throughout the book you will see that the results of research can change depending upon factors such as demographic variables (e.g. the age, gender, ethnicity or cultural background of the participant or the target person), hormonal variations (e.g. which phase of the menstrual cycle a woman is in), chemical factors (e.g. whether the participants are exposed to certain chemical compounds), or methodological modifications (e.g. how the researchers manipulated the independent variable, how they measured the dependent variable), etc. Keep these factors in mind as you critically evaluate the research that is described in this book.

In many cases I have provided summaries of the earliest social psychological research. Although some of the original research is quite old, I felt it was important to reference the original research for several reasons. First, I am hoping that you will become interested in the research and choose to examine some primary sources on your own. The original research is often (but not always) shorter and easier to read than some more recent research. (At the end of each chapter I present some suggestions for further reading.) Second, the original research often addresses more global issues rather than the more molecular issues typical in more current studies. Throughout this book you will find a nice balance between classic and current social psychological research.

A few caveats: first, this book is by no means an exhaustive summary of all the research related to attraction and intimate relationships. There is more relevant research available for those who are interested in delving deeply into the topics presented in this book. It was freeing to us to not begin with the goal of presenting an exhaustive summary of this research, in that way we were able to organize the book on the basis of social psychological theory and research, as well as to focus on the research that was the most interesting to us and the research that we thought would be the most appealing to readers. For this reason in this book you will see a slightly stronger focus on attraction than on romantic relationships. Second, you will find that the majority of research cited within this book addresses heterosexual attraction and relationships. As reviewed by Kassin et al. (2011), much of the research investigating attraction and romantic relationships among gay men and lesbians shows similar processes to those which operate in heterosexual relationships. However, in the future, more research is needed to specifically address attraction and romantic relationships among gay and lesbian adults as well as those adults who identify with alternative sexual orientations. Third, this book does not contain dating or relationship advice and some of it is written with the intent to be humorous, so please do not make any dating or relationship decisions based upon what you read in this book! Do feel free to interpret events in your dating life and relationships as consistent or inconsistent with the research reported in this book. Relating the theories and research to your own life is a great way to learn, understand, and apply the concepts.

Before you begin reading the content of this book, we should define a few of the terms that we use throughout the text. First, we talk a lot about "dating" and "mating." When we refer to dating, we usually mean the process through which potential romantic partners choose to get to know one another better and to court one another. When we refer to mating, we usually mean the process of choosing a "mate" or a partner, for either a long-term or short-term relationship. Although both dating and mating may involve the physical act of mating (i.e. sexual intercourse) when we discuss sexual relationships, we will refer to those specifically as such. Furthermore, the major emphases of this book are human attraction (although occasionally we review research related to other animals) and romantic relationships (although occasionally we present research related to friendships or other types of relationships as well).

In order to provide real-life examples of the social psychological phenomena we review in the text, you will find that my colleagues and I rely upon the experiences of our friends and relatives, and sometimes our own experiences as well. We refer to these anecdotes as "Personal moments" throughout the text. These anecdotes are not intended to be scientific evidence for a particular phenomenon; they are only intended to provide real-life illustrations of the theories and research presented in the book. I have found these anecdotes to be particularly helpful for my students in understanding, remembering, and applying the material. Similarly, we provide some media examples as well, referring to these as "Media moments" throughout the text. These anecdotes are also not intended to be evidence for these phenomena, merely illustrations presented in the media that are relevant to the particular theories and research. The real evidence of the phenomena described in this book is presented in the discussion of the empirical research cited throughout the book. Also, although I have presented the media portrayals faithfully, I have changed the names of my loved ones to protect those innocent friends and family members who have unwittingly appeared in this manuscript. (If you are a friend or relative of mine and you are reading this book, don't worry, if you don't like what you are reading, I'm not talking about you.) Dr Leszczynski is the primary author of the gender chapter and Dr Cousins is the primary author of the evolutionary theory chapter, therefore, all first person references in those chapters refer to the respective primary authors. Just to keep you on your toes, Dr Leszczynski and I co-wrote the chapter on sex and love. In that chapter we have indicated to whom the first person references refer.

Lastly, when presenting hypothetical examples or questions I often switch between the masculine pronoun (he) and the feminine pronoun (she) in order to avoid a gender bias and in order to avoid the grammatically incorrect "they" for the singular case.

I would like to thank my family, especially my amazing (and attractive, tall, slightly older, symmetrical, intelligent) husband, my mother, and my two wonderful boys. Without the support of my family I could never have accomplished the writing of this book. I would like to thank my father for all of his love, support, and encouragement throughout his lifetime; everyone should have a person like my father in their lives for unconditional love and support. I would like to thank my colleagues Alita Cousins and Jennifer Leszczynski for their invaluable contributions to the manuscript; my mentors Susan Rakowitz, Skip Lowe, and David Kenny for their inspiration in the classroom as well as their support and encouragement through the years hence; Eastern Connecticut State University for supporting this project through sabbatical leave as well as through research reassigned time; my research assistants (especially E.G. and J.P.). Most of all, I would like to thank Paul Stevens and Jenny Hindley for their interest in and support of this project. I couldn't and wouldn't have written this book without their support. In particular Paul's early feedback was essential to the development of this book.

By now I imagine you are dying to know the answer to the question about the restaurant and who should pay, so read on! And enjoy!

Part I
Attraction

Forming Attitudes toward Potential Partners: First Impressions of Physical Characteristics

1

First impressions

Imagine that you are ready to start dating (the process through which potential romantic partners get to know one another better) and/or mating (the process of choosing a "mate" or a partner, either for a long-term or short-term relationship). Where do you begin? When you meet a potential mate, you probably have an immediate reaction to that person, which we usually call a first impression. Much of social psychology is very intuitive and your intuition is probably correct on this topic; first impressions are very important.

Even though we can surmise that first impressions are important, a number of questions remain about the process. For example, how quickly do first impressions occur? Can you just look at a potential date and form an impression? Do you need to meet him in-person or will a photo suffice? Is physical attractiveness a necessity? Are first impressions accurate?

There are many ways to form first impressions, but there are a few commonalities across modalities. First, our impressions tend to form very quickly. Second, our impressions are often based on physical appearance, with some characteristics being more important than others. Third, our impressions tend to be fairly accurate, even when based upon very little information. In this chapter we discuss the research pertaining to first impressions of physical characteristics (for example, height, weight, and age). In Chapters 2 and 3, we discuss first impressions of non-physical characteristics (such as personality and behavior) as well as the importance of meeting in-person.

First impressions of physical appearance

A personal moment: A friend of mine, we'll call her Louise, is currently searching for a long-term mate. One day we talked about her experience with online dating. Louise recounts that on dating websites she can scroll through photographs of potential dates as fast as her computer will display them. There is often very little information displayed in the initial profiles she encounters, just a photograph, possibly the age of her potential date, and an area in which he lives. As Finkel et al. (2012) review, more detailed information such as education, profession, and religion is accessible in the extended profile. Louise routinely scrolls through and quickly chooses or passes over potential dates based primarily on physical appearance, and sometimes only on facial appearance. Is choosing or foregoing a potential mate based on physical appearance a good strategy? Are we making good dating decisions? Or are we missing out on some wonderful people? It seems likely that we are doing a bit of both. But when making our mating decisions, we do not just aim to find *any* potential mate; we want to find the *best* possible mate. Physical appearance cues may be important when selecting the best possible mate. Below I review the research in this area which suggests that physical appearance may be a useful tool to use when looking for an ideal partner.

In this chapter we will consider various physical characteristics and how they impact our attraction to potential partners. If you were searching for a partner, which aspects of a potential partner's physical appearance would be most important to you? In evaluating a potential partner's physical characteristics, you can probably quickly and accurately ascertain information about that person's physical attractiveness, height, weight, age, and even voice and scent. These physical characteristics may serve as an important basis for our attraction to potential companions. Making mating decisions based upon these physical features may actually lead us to choose better partners. In this chapter, we explore the often-hidden benefits to mating with a physically attractive partner, from more pleasing personalities to more potent sperm.

Physical attractiveness

When you see a photograph of a potential mate, what kind of information do you glean from the physical appearance of the person in the photograph? One of the first things you might notice is whether you consider the target person to be physically attractive or not. When I sat down with my friend Louise to browse through photographs of potential dates, we were both strongly influenced by the physical attractiveness of the men pictured in the photographs. We would stop to view a profile in more detail if we considered the man to be "attractive" or "good looking."

Stereotypically, people assume that physical attractiveness is more important to men than women, and indeed, some research suggests that men more often state that physical attractiveness is important to them than do women (e.g., Buss, 1989; Buss et al., 2001; Feingold, 1990; Lippa, 2007; Smith et al., 1990). Evolutionarily, the physical appearance of a potential partner may be more important to men because attractiveness in a female partner may be more strongly linked to reproductive ability than attractiveness in a male partner (Buss, 1989, see Chapter 4 for more information on evolutionary theory). Recent research investigating real-life and experimental preferences, however, suggests that physical attractiveness in a potential partner is equally important to both men and women (e.g., Eastwick et al., 2011; Eastwick & Finkel, 2008; Feingold, 1990; Luo & Zhang, 2009; Kurzban & Weeden, 2005; Sprecher, 1989; Thao et al., 2010; however, see also Li et al., 2013, as discussed in Chapter 4). Furthermore, research by Lenton and Francesconi (2010) suggests that when faced with a wide variety of potential partners (such as one might encounter on a dating website) both men and women are more likely to rely on physical attractiveness when making dating decisions.

The influence of physical attractiveness

Physical attractiveness is not perceived in isolation. When we perceive a potential partner as physically attractive, that might prompt other positive perceptions beyond perceptions of physical characteristics. In a classic study performed by Dion et al. (1972), the researchers manipulated the physical attractiveness of men and women presented in photographs. The researchers presented participants with photographs of attractive, average, and unattractive targets and asked the participants to rate the targets on a variety of traits. Consistent with the authors' expectations, they found that attractive targets were assumed to have more positive characteristics such as better personalities, better jobs, and more rewarding life experiences. Attractive targets were also expected to be happier. This tendency to expect positive qualities from attractive targets is equally evident in undergraduates from the United States and from Taiwan (Shaffer et al., 2000). Moreover, Zebrowitz et al. (2012) found these same expectations among Tsimané men living in an isolated area of Bolivia. This trend may be especially true for female perceivers: women who perceive male targets as physically attractive are more likely than their male counterparts to perceive other positive qualities in the target person (Levesque et al., 2006). So when we consider an attractive person as a potential date, we may be reacting favorably not only to his physical attractiveness, but also to the expectation that he may possess other positive qualities.

Dion et al. (1972) characterized their results as confirming the "what is beautiful is good" (p. 289) stereotype. A vast body of literature supports their findings (see Griffin & Langlois, 2006, for a review). Interestingly, Langlois et al. (2000) report that attractive individuals even rate *themselves* more favorably than unattractive individuals do. However, Griffin and Langlois question whether Dion et al.'s results actually indicate that those who are perceived as *attractive* are expected to have *positive* qualities or, rather, the results indicate that those who are perceived as *unattractive* are expected to have *negative* qualities. In Dion et al.'s research, unattractive targets were rated less favorably than their attractive and average counterparts in almost all categories. Indeed both processes of choosing an attractive mate and avoiding an unattractive mate may help us to make better mating decisions.

What the research says

In Griffin and Langlois's (2006) research, the researchers manipulated the physical attractiveness of women presented in photographs (no photographs of men were presented in this study). Photographs of young adult Caucasian women were pre-tested and selected to represent highly attractive, moderately attractive, and unattractive women. These photographs were rated by both young adults (college students) and children (elementary school students, between the ages of seven and nine) from the United States. Although the adults performed their ratings via computer while the children performed theirs on paper, both the adults and children made negative ratings of the unattractive women on attributes such as sociable, helpful, and smart relative to the moderately attractive women. However, the moderately attractive and highly attractive women only differed on the attribute "sociable." Therefore, the physical attractiveness of women does seem to enhance perceptions of sociability, but not necessarily other positive attributes. These results suggest that rather than attractiveness being advantageous per se, it might be particularly *disadvantageous* to be unattractive. Because the targets featured in this research were limited to Caucasian women, the authors stress that future research assessing "perceptions of male and ethnically diverse faces is essential" (p. 202).

Think critically

Griffin and Langlois (2006) critically examined the notion that "what is beautiful is good." Instead the authors posited that unattractive stimulus persons might be expected to possess negative qualities. Their sample involved both college-aged students and young children as participants, suggesting that these effects occur in perceivers of different ages. Do you think the same results could be expected if the authors used older adults as participants? How do you think the results might differ if the authors tested their hypotheses with a sample of older adults? (Hint: look for research cited elsewhere in this manuscript to inform your opinion.)

Facial attractiveness

When Louise and I perused photographs of her potential dates, most photographs included facial appearance. Indeed it was extremely rare to encounter a photograph of a potential mate that did not include his face; however, it was common to encounter a photograph of a potential mate that did not include the rest of his body. Obviously, facial appearance is an important determinant of physical attractiveness, perhaps even more important than other physical characteristics. So what kind of information does facial appearance convey? And what types of facial features are considered attractive?

First, we will consider perceptions of women's faces. Perceptions of the youth and femininity of a female face are significantly positively correlated with perceptions of women's attractiveness (Weeden & Sabini, 200. cross-cultural research assessing the preferences of participants fron United States, Brazil, Paraguay, Russia, and Venezuela, Jones and Hill (1_ ╵ ╵) found that across cultures men and women rated youthful, feminine women as more attractive. Similarly, in research assessing the preferences of respondents from the United Kingdom and Japan, Perrett et al. (1998) found that men and women from both cultures preferred more feminized female faces (both in Caucasian and Japanese target faces). Moreover, Cunningham et al., (1995) asked US and international students from both Western and Eastern societies to evaluate facial photographs of college-aged target women from the United States and other nations. These authors found that women's faces were rated as more attractive if they had "large eyes...small noses...smaller chins...higher eyebrows...larger smiles...full hair" (p. 268).

Preferences for male faces are a little less straightforward. Cunningham et al. (1990) reported that men were perceived as more attractive when they had large eyes, a small nose, a large chin, prominent cheekbones, and a broad smile. However, some studies show a preference for femininity in a male face, whereas some studies show a preference for masculinity in a male face (see Weeden & Sabini, 2005). For example, the cross-cultural research performed by Perrett et al. (1998) referenced above revealed that men and women from both Eastern and Western cultures preferred more feminized male faces. According to the authors, the more masculinized faces were perceived as more dominant and older, but less warm, honest, and cooperative. (See Chapter 4 for a longer discussion of preferences for feminized male faces.)

Other studies show that women's preferences for male facial characteristics change based upon their menstrual cycle. For example, Johnston et al. (2001) asked women (at different times throughout their menstrual cycle) to scroll through a video segment which changed from a masculine-looking face to a feminine-looking face. These authors found that women tended to choose a more masculine-looking face as most attractive during the most fertile phase of their menstrual cycles. Little et al. (2008) corroborated this result with photographs of real men. Once again, women preferred images of more masculine men when their chances of conception were the greatest.

Despite the findings, discussed above, suggesting that perceptions of attractiveness are not always consistent, there is widespread agreement about physical attractiveness, both within cultures and across cultures. Cunningham et al. (1995) showed cross-cultural consistency regarding perceptions of the attractiveness of women. The researchers asked US and international students to evaluate facial photographs of target women, some of whom had been involved in an "international beauty contest and, as such, had been selected by members of their own culture as being attractive" (p. 265). The results showed that regardless of the ethnic background of the participants or the targets, the raters tended to agree about the attractiveness of the female faces. Jones and Hill (1993) also found significant agreement across cultures in perceptions of attractiveness based upon facial photographs of men and women. Similarly, in a meta-analysis conducted by Langlois et al. (2000), these authors reported a great deal of agreement both within cultures, across ethnic backgrounds, and across cultures with regard to perceptions of physical attractiveness.

Preferences for attractive faces persist across the lifespan. In an intriguing study, Langlois et al. (1991) found that six-month-old infants from the United States preferred to look at photographs depicting attractive faces (versus unattractive faces) belonging both to other babies and to adults. Moreover, Zebrowitz et al. (2013) found that while older adults and undergraduates tended to agree with one another in their impressions based upon facial photographs, older adults generally rated the stimulus persons even more positively than did their younger counterparts.

Symmetry

In addition to facial attractiveness, photographs can reveal information about facial symmetry. Although people tend to prefer facial symmetry (the left and right sides of the face match one another) to asymmetry, this preference is not usually a conscious one. (I have never heard Louise mention that she is looking for a partner whose left and right sides of the face are identical.) Yet, facial symmetry does influence our perceptions of physical attractiveness; participants prefer both male and female faces that are more symmetrical (see Weeden & Sabini, 2005 for a review). For example, Japanese participants preferred modified symmetrical faces to naturally unsymmetrical faces (Rhodes et al., 2001). Similarly, Càrdenas and Harris (2006) found that men and women both preferred symmetrically manipulated faces to asymmetrical natural faces. Remarkably, Càrdenas and Harris also found that faces painted with symmetrical designs were judged as more attractive than faces painted with asymmetrical designs. Why is symmetry so attractive?

Perilloux et al. (2010) discuss the reasons why symmetry strongly influences attraction. The authors state that "most organisms are genetically programmed to develop identically on the right and the left. Thus, deviation from perfect bilateral symmetry is believed to reflect the degree to which an individual's genotype is unsuccessful at buffering it from the developmental assaults of parasites, pathogens, and other environmental stressors" (p. 34). The ability to withstand these environmental insults indicates better genetic quality. Not surprisingly, more symmetrical humans are also generally healthier, live longer, and are more intelligent (Perilloux et al.). In fact, Luxen and Buunk (2006) estimated that 20% of the variation in intelligence could be explained by symmetry (with the relationship between the two variables slightly stronger in men than women).

Likewise, Manning (1995) also suggests that facial symmetry may be attractive because it indicates that a target possesses "good genes." Manning found that symmetry in men (assessed in a variety of ways including symmetry of ear height) was positively related to body weight and size, suggesting a link between male symmetry and height. Manning states that "male body weight is condition-dependent in that it is only individuals with the best genes who are able to develop and maintain large size" (p. 145). Moreover, Manning also found that symmetry in women was negatively related to body weight. Therefore facial symmetry can signal not only that a partner is healthy but also that future offspring might be healthier as well if we choose symmetrical partners as mates.

Averageness

Another facial feature that can enhance perceptions of attractiveness is "averageness." This possibility sounds counter-intuitive; when we think of attractive exemplars (such as celebrities), we rarely think that those exemplars are average. However, like facial symmetry, the preference for averageness is another unconscious preference which may steer us toward better partners. Average faces are preferred by members of both Western and Eastern cultures. For example, Rhodes et al. (2001) showed a preference for average faces in Chinese and Japanese participants. The researchers manipulated photographs via computer to make them look more or less like an averaged composite face. Making the photographs look more average increased their attractiveness to both Chinese and Japanese participants, while decreasing their averageness decreased their attractiveness. Photographs of real faces with closer to average proportions are rated as more physically attractive by members of different cultures as well (Jones & Hill, 1993). Less distinctive faces are consistently perceived as more attractive, whether they are computer-generated or naturally occurring (Rhodes, 2006).

As with symmetry, averageness may also be a cue to a healthy mate. Rhodes (2006) states that average or typical faces may be seen as more attractive because they may signal good genes or optimal functioning (e.g., the author states that an "average" nose may be optimally shaped for breathing). Similar to the benefit of symmetry discussed above, Rhodes posits that average features may reflect the "ability to withstand stress during development" (p. 203). Rhodes et al. (2005) suggest that average faces may also be perceived as more symmetrical, youthful, and pleasant, thus explaining our attraction to them. Surprisingly, Halberstadt and Rhodes (2000, 2003) showed that averaged dogs, wristwatches, birds, fish, and automobiles were also rated as more attractive than individual stimuli. (I am assuming that at least the wristwatches and automobiles were not rated more favorably because they make better mates.) Rhodes et al. (2005) suggest that averaged stimuli may be seen as more attractive because they are also perceived as more familiar. (As we will discuss in Chapter 5, increased familiarity is associated with liking.)

Health

Both the research regarding symmetry and the research regarding averageness reviewed above suggest that facial attractiveness may be linked to good health.

Weeden and Sabini (2005) state that individuals tend to assume that both men and women with attractive facial features are healthier. However, according to these authors, the actual relationship between facial attractiveness and health is very small for women and not reliable at all for men. Interestingly, although men's facial attractiveness may not be related to their overall health, Weeden and Sabini review research by Soler et al. (2003) which suggests that ratings of male facial attractiveness are correlated with semen quality; more attractive men had sperm which were more likely to be able to fertilize an egg. (It is a little unsettling to think that Louise could be sorting through photographs of potential mates based upon facial attractiveness and what is really underlying her judgments may be whether the men have good sperm quality. I have decided not to share this bit of research with Louise; I do not want to distract her while she is perusing photographs of attractive men.)

Height

Height may be an important influence on initial human attraction, especially for potential male partners. Height may serve to indicate that men possess good genes, and tall men may be perceived as more physically dominant (Buunk et al., 2008). Interestingly, in most birds and mammals, the male mates are larger than the female mates as well, possibly due to females choosing to mate with larger males or due to males competing for access to females, with the larger males more likely to triumph (Stulp et al., 2012).

What the research says

In their research, Stulp et al. (2012) investigated the relationship between men's height and reproductive success (as measured by their total number of children as well as the number of children living to reproductive age). Their sample consisted of men over the age of 64 from the United States. These authors found a curvilinear relationship between height and number of surviving children. Men of average height (in this study, 179.21 cm or roughly 5 feet, 10½ inches tall) tended to have the most surviving children relative to both shorter and taller men. Stulp et al. also found that taller men tended to earn more money and attain a higher educational level (although the authors do acknowledge that their sample was collected from a population of high school graduates, and therefore biased toward a more educated sample). Moreover, although for this sample the effect of height was not as strong as the effect of income or education, the authors emphasized that the effects of education and income were not strong enough to make up for being too short or too tall in terms of reproductive success. Another important finding was that men of average height tended to marry at a younger age, potentially explaining that they might have more children because they began their reproductive "careers" earlier.

Think critically

Stulp et al. (2012) examined the relationship between height and reproductive success, as measured by the men's total number of children. Do you think that this is the best way to operationally define "reproductive success?" What are some problems with using the number of children as a measure of reproductive success? In what other ways could reproductive success be measured (for example: number of sexual partners)? Are there problems with the alternative measures as well?

Consistent with the research presented above, Kurzban and Weeden (2005) found that men who were taller were chosen more often as a potential future dating partner at a speed-dating event. (In accordance with previous research, another important predictor of men's dating desirability in Kurzban and Weeden's research was facial attractiveness.) Similarly, Pawlowski and Koziel (2002) found that men who were taller received more responses to their personal ads placed in a newspaper relative to men who were shorter. (Interestingly, the factor leading to the highest increase in responses to men's ads was education, with more highly educated men receiving more responses to their ads.) Likewise, Salska et al. (2008) analyzed height information as well as height preferences provided by individuals using an online dating site. These authors found that women preferred men who were taller than average.

Another potential advantage to height for men might be decreased jealousy. Buunk et al. (2008) found that taller men were less jealous. These authors suggested that because taller men are often perceived as more physically attractive, their partners might be less likely to cheat, thus reducing tall men's feelings of jealousy. Alternatively, the authors suggested that because taller men are also perceived as more physically dominant, these men may be more intimidating to potential male rivals, thus also reducing tall men's feelings of jealousy. Jealousy has been linked to partner violence (e.g., Kaighobadi et al., 2009, see Chapter 4) and thus avoiding a jealous partner may be particularly beneficial to women.

Relative partner height

Think about a few heterosexual couples you know. In each couple, who is the taller partner, the man or the woman? Do you know any couples in which the woman is the taller partner? Relative partner height can be another important influence on our mate preferences. Most research shows that men and women prefer romantic partnerships in which the man is taller and the woman is shorter (e.g., Re & Perrett, 2012; Salska et al., 2008). According to Re and Perrett, the preference for a taller male partner is clear (although women do not necessarily prefer an *extremely* tall partner), but the association between height and attraction for a female partner is less clear. Some men prefer shorter partners, some men prefer women of average height, and some men prefer taller partners (relative to other women, not relative to themselves). One exception to this tenet involves shorter men, who may be willing to consider women taller than themselves as partners in order to increase their overall pool of potential partners (Salska et al., 2008).

As one might expect, preference for a partner's height is related to one's own height (Fink et al.,2007; Mautz et al., 2013; Pawlowski and Jasienska, 2005) with shorter women preferring a relatively larger difference between her own height and her male mate's height, and taller women preferring only a slightly taller male mate. Evidence for this effect was found in four different Western countries (Poland, Germany, Austria, and the United Kingdom). Interestingly, according to Pawlowski and Jasienska, a woman's preference for height also varies along with her menstrual cycle. These authors found that taller men were preferred when women were more fertile. Women's preferences also varied by the type of relationship they were asked to consider. Women were more likely to prefer taller mates for a short-term relationship than for a long-term relationship (Pawlowski & Jasienska, 2005).

Weight

Weight may be another important determinant of the physical attractiveness of a potential partner. Most of the research in this area focuses on women's weight, and more specifically, women's Body Mass Index (BMI) and waist-to-hip ratio (WHR), although a few studies have investigated perceptions of men's bodies (e.g., Swami et al., 2007; Swami & Tovée, 2008). Body Mass Index refers to a measure of body fat and can be calculated in different ways, but a simple method for calculating BMI is to divide weight in kilograms by height in meters squared (Carmalt et al., 2008). To measure waist-to-hip ratio, measure the circumference of the waist and divide by the circumference of the hips (Furnham et al., 2005). Body weight may impact our perceptions of women's physical attractiveness because both BMI and WHR are related to women's health and fertility (Perilloux et al., 2010; Singh et al., 2010).

Much of the research on body weight reveals that individuals prefer mates with average weight. For example, Yanover and Thompson (2010) asked undergraduates from North America to rate the perceived health and attractiveness of drawings of both male and female body figures. This research revealed that for both male and female figures, individuals of average weight (compared with underweight and overweight) were perceived as the most attractive and healthy. Interestingly, these authors found that heavier, more muscular individuals were rated as more attractive and healthy as well. Paying attention to physical cues such as weight and muscularity may help us to identify a strong and healthy mate.

Perceptions of women's body size and shape

In their research investigating men's ratings of women's bodies, Furnham et al. (2005) manipulated drawings of female figures which varied in BMI and WHR simultaneously. These authors discovered that the female figure of average weight (rather than underweight or overweight) with a waist-to-hip ratio of 0.7 was considered most attractive and healthy by a sample of undergraduate men and women from the United Kingdom. (Other research also suggests that a WHR of 0.7 is rated as the most attractive, both by men, Dixson et al., 2011, and women, Cohen & Tannenbaum, 2001). Furnham et al. also reported that BMI was perceived as a stronger indicator of health and fertility than WHR.

Consistent with these findings based on drawings of hypothetical female figures, Kurzban and Weeden (2005) found that thin women with a lower BMI were rated as more desirable by their male counterparts at a speed-dating event. Correspondingly, women with a higher BMI as well as overweight and underweight men were less discriminating (more willing to say yes to potential dates) than their counterparts at a speed-dating event (Kurzban & Weeden). Moreover, Smith et al. (1990) found that men were more likely to request that thin or slim women respond to their personal ads. Body weight may therefore be a more important determinant of men's interest in women than women's interest in men.

Swami and more than 50 colleagues (2010) collected data regarding men's and women's perceptions of the ideal female body weight from individuals living in 26 different countries and 10 different global regions. The participants included more than 7,000 college students as well as non-student community members. In this research, although both men and women participated, men were asked to choose the drawing of the female figure that they found most attractive, and women were asked to choose the drawing they thought would be most attractive to men. The authors suggested that the current "ideal" body size for women is thin and possibly even underweight, especially in more socioeconomically developed nations. However, across cultures, men preferred a figure displaying a heavier body weight than women *thought* men would prefer.

Interestingly, Swami et al. (2010) also found the largest effects of body weight on perceptions of physical attractiveness within countries with both high and low socioeconomic status locations. The authors noted that in the more impoverished areas, both men and women seemed to prefer heavier body sizes, "possibly because of the association between body fat and resource security" (p. 319). Consistent with these results, Swami et al. (2011) found that men from a poorer socioeconomic environment in Indonesia (Lombok) preferred a heavier female figure than did men from a more affluent area in Indonesia (Bali) and men from the United Kingdom. Residents of Lombok also considered a larger range of body figures as attractive versus their more affluent counterparts. Perceptions of the ideal female body weight or shape may change not only with culture, but with socioeconomic status, with women of larger body sizes preferred in less affluent areas.

Perceptions of men's body size and shape

Although men's weight and body shape may not be as important a determinant of physical attractiveness as women's (see Kurzban & Weeden, 2005), Swami et al. (2007) investigated women's ratings of men's physical attractiveness in a cross-cultural study involving participants from Greece and the United Kingdom. The women were asked to rate a series of photographs depicting real men wearing form-fitting clothing and varying in waist-to-chest ratio (WCR) as well as BMI and WHR. In this research the faces of the men were obscured in order to isolate the effects of body size and proportion and to eliminate the potential confound of facial attractiveness. The authors stated that WCR was the strongest determinant of physical attractiveness ratings for both the Greek and the British samples. BMI was also significantly related to ratings of physical attractiveness, but less so than WCR, indicating that "men's upper-body shapes are more important for male attractiveness to women than overall body masses" (p. 23). Waist-to-hip ratio was not a significant predictor of women's ratings of men's physical attractiveness. The authors also specified that the Greek women seemed to find a more V-shaped torso (lower WCR) as more attractive than did their British counterparts while simultaneously preferring a slightly lower BMI than did their British counterparts. (The authors note the limitation that the men pictured in the stimulus images came from the United Kingdom and thus may not represent the body sizes of Greek men as well as they represented British men.)

Waist-to-chest ratio may be an important factor in men's physical attractiveness because it may signal increased physical strength, dominance, masculinity, or even heightened testosterone levels (Swami et al., 2007). Although waist-to-chest ratio may be one influence on women's perceptions of men's physical attractiveness, it does not appear to be as strong an influence as women's waist-to-hip ratio or BMI is for men's perceptions of the physical attractiveness of women.

Gay men's and lesbians' preferences for body size and shape

A personal moment: When I was in college one of my friend's boyfriends, Kyle, began seriously body-building. He became very muscular and he occasionally participated in body-building competitions. As a result of one of these competitions, he was invited to model for the magazine *Muscle Fitness*. While in the airport waiting for an international flight, I found the magazine with Kyle's layout. I purchased the magazine and talked with Kyle about it after I returned to the United States. Kyle told me that the magazine was targeted toward gay men, who tended to prefer more muscular men. Years later I found out that Kyle's assertion was supported by research (see below).

Swami and Tovée (2008) investigated the weight and waist-to-chest ratio preferences among gay and heterosexual men (in this study, the preferences of men indicating a bisexual orientation were not analyzed). Most of the men involved in this project were Caucasian university students from the United Kingdom. The men evaluated photographs of real men varying in WCR as well as BMI. Although BMI was significantly related to men's ratings of the physical attractiveness of male targets, the data revealed that WCR was the most important predictor of the physical attractiveness ratings. Furthermore, the data also suggested that gay men prefer a lower WCR than their heterosexual counterparts, indicating that gay men's perceptions of physical attractiveness are more strongly influenced by a muscular upper-body.

Cohen and Tannenbaum (2001) explored perceptions of attractiveness for female figures varying in weight and waist-to-hip ratio among both lesbian and bisexual women. Respondents to this online survey were asked to rate drawings of the female figure for their physical attractiveness as well as other factors. These authors found that although lesbian and bisexual women tended to prefer the WHR of 0.7 as most attractive (similar to the findings discussed above for men and women whose sexual orientation was not specified; see Furnham et al., 2005), these women tended to rate the heavier figure (rather than the slender figure) as more attractive. Cohen and Tannenbaum posit that lesbians may prefer a heavier body weight because they themselves tend to be heavier than their heterosexual counterparts, thus preferring a partner resembling their own body weight. Alternatively, the authors suggest that lesbians may be more comfortable (or less dissatisfied) with a heavier body weight than heterosexual women.

Similarity of weight

Similar to the results with regard to height discussed above, preference for weight in a partner may be related to one's own weight; however, the results in this literature are mixed. For example, Swami et al. (2010) found a positive correlation between men's BMI and the body size they chose as most attractive; men with a higher BMI also preferred figures portraying a heavier female body weight. However, Kurzban and Weeden (2005) found that men preferred women with a dissimilar BMI to their own at a speed-dating event. Future research will be necessary to determine the strength and relationship of one's own body weight to an ideal partner's body weight. Future research should also examine whether this relationship changes across cultures or with variations in socioeconomic status.

Breast size and penis size

Breast size may be a relatively observable feature, whether conveyed through photographs or through an in-person meeting. In fact, in research recording men's eye movements, Dixson et al. (2011) found that men were more likely to look at a woman's breasts or waist first and spent more time looking at the breasts than any other body regions, including the face. (Of course, this research involved a photograph of the front of a naked woman as a stimulus, not a clothed woman, as would usually occur in *most* in-person first meetings or photograph sharing.) Interestingly, recent research conducted by Furnham et al. (2006) suggests that women preferred larger breast sizes (as presented via drawings of the female figure) than men did. Likewise, Cohen and Tannenbaum (2001) found that lesbian and bisexual women preferred drawings of the female figure with larger breasts (vs. smaller breasts). Furnham et al. also found that the presence of larger breasts heightened perceptions of physical attractiveness for heavier figures with higher waist-to-hip ratios. In contrast, Dixson et al. found in their research that waist-to-hip ratio was a more important determinant of sexual attraction than breast size.

Although penis size is not usually presented via photographs or upon meeting someone for the first time, we address the research on penis size in conjunction with the research on breast size. Current research conducted by Mautz et al. (2013) suggests that women rated male figures as more sexually attractive when the figures displayed larger penis sizes (as well as a larger shoulder-to-hip ratios and a taller height). Interestingly, the effect of penis size was more pronounced for taller men. Furthermore, for shorter men, having a larger penis did not enhance their perceived sexual attractiveness.

A media moment: In an episode from the HBO series *Sex and the City*, a character named Samantha is talking with her friend Carrie about a man she is currently dating whose penis is so large, she cannot have sex with him. She refers to him as "Mr. Too Big." In a previous episode, Samantha had dated a man named James whose penis she described as too small. In response to Samantha's current complaint, Carrie quips "You broke up with James because he was too small. This guy's too big. Who are you, Goldi-cocks?" Samantha answers, "Yep! I'm looking for one, that's just right."

Age

Imagine you were looking for a romantic partner, would you want your partner to be older or younger than you? Or would you prefer a partner of the same age? Would you consider dating a partner who was much older or much younger? Although the age of a potential partner may not always be objectively evident based upon a photograph or through an in-person meeting, we can estimate age based upon the physical appearance of a potential partner.

As reviewed by Buss (1989), men and women seem to prefer partners of different ages, but in a complementary fashion. Buss found that across cultures, men prefer women as mates when they are slightly younger, while (conveniently for heterosexual partnerships) women prefer men as mates when they are slightly older. In the same research, Buss reviews marriage records which indicate that across cultures, men tend to marry women who are between two to five years younger than themselves. Buss concludes that "preferred age differences between spouses are indeed reflected in actual age differences at marriage" (p. 9). This relative age preference persists across the lifespan. As men age, they tend to prefer even younger female partners, while as women age, they continue to prefer older male partners (until they reach their 70's, when they become willing to consider younger partners, see Alterovitz & Mendelsohn, 2009).

Age preferences may also be related to the search for an ideal mate. Buss (1989) states that men tend to prefer and marry younger women because younger women are more likely to be fertile. Buss also posits that women may prefer older men because of the relationship between men's age and income; older men might be better able to provide for a partner or a family. Buss further speculates that older men might be more dominant or mature and suggests that future research explore women's motivations for preferring older partners.

A personal moment: My friend Louise reports in her online profile that she is willing to consider a mate who is a few years younger or a few years older, though she has told me privately that her ideal mate would be close to her own age. You may notice that her preferences seem inconsistent with the results of the research reported above suggesting that women prefer mates who are slightly older than themselves (e.g., Buss, 1989). Personal anecdotes that contradict research findings should not necessarily be construed as evidence against the research findings. The research summarized in this book is usually based on group results, not individual results. Therefore, within each group there may be variation in individual preferences. For example, some women may prefer younger mates, some may prefer mates of their own age, and some may prefer older mates, but across individuals, women as a group tend to prefer slightly older mates. Individual anecdotes which seem to contradict research results may actually be consistent with individual variation in the group results.

First impressions of voices

Hearing the voice of a potential mate may enhance or diminish perceptions of attractiveness. What types of vocal characteristics sound attractive to you? A high or low pitch? Monotone or lots of pitch variation? Vocal attractiveness is often associated with physical attractiveness.

Perceptions of men's voices

Women seem to find lower-pitched voices as more masculine as well as more vocally attractive (Saxton et al., 2006; Simmons et al., 2011). Interestingly,

Simmons et al. also found that men with lower-pitched voices had lower sperm concentrations. (The authors speculated that this negative relationship might be driven by increased testosterone, and stated that this effect was small and was unlikely to impact the men's ability to have children.) Curiously, Saxton et al. also explored girls' perceptions of the vocal attractiveness of men, finding that young girls' preferences did not match the preferences of adult or even adolescent women.

What the research says

Saxton et al. (2006) asked young girls (aged 7–10), female adolescents (aged 12–15), and adult women (aged 20–34) to evaluate male voices and photographs of faces. The researchers recruited 12 male native English speakers from the United Kingdom between the ages of 23 and 28 to record vocal samples. The participants' vocal samples were recorded while the men counted from one to five. Photographs of the men were taken showing neutral facial expressions. The photographs were also cropped so that hairstyle and clothing could not be seen. All female participants were unaware that the photographs of the faces and the recordings of the voices belonged to the same men. The authors found that the adult female participants tended to agree about which faces and voices they preferred. Furthermore, perceptions of vocal attractiveness were positively correlated with perceptions of facial attractiveness for the adult sample (that is, vocal samples rated as attractive were produced by targets whose faces were also perceived as attractive). Finally, the authors also showed that adult women preferred men with lower-pitched voices. Interestingly, the judgments of the adolescent girls mimicked those of the adult women. However, although the young girls agreed with one another about which faces were attractive, in contrast to the older samples, they did not choose the same voices as the most attractive, and they did not prefer the lower-pitched voices. The authors highlight these differences in preferences based upon age and suggest that "a period of maturation and learning may be required...in order to fully develop optimal judgments for mate choice" (p. 1184). The authors do acknowledge the potential confound of age difference between the female raters and the male speakers, and they posit that younger girls may be more adept at rating vocal stimuli produced by boys of their own age rather than by older men.

Think critically

Saxton et al. (2006) showed that the age of the female perceiver was an important determinant of perceptions of the attractiveness of men's voices. However, their adult sample included only women between the ages of 20 and 34. Do you think that post-menopausal women would show the same preferences as women of reproductive age? The authors speculate that younger women may need to mature and learn before they can make optimal mating decisions. Once women have matured, will they retain their vocal preferences? Or will those vocal preferences disappear when they cease to impact reproductive possibilities?

Perceptions of women's voices

Consistent with the research reviewed above regarding men's voices, women's voices may also influence perceptions of their attractiveness. Collins and Missing (2003) found that men preferred women with higher-pitched voices (and also expected women with higher-pitched voices to be younger). Interestingly, the authors also showed that women with lower-pitched voices also tended to be heavier. Furthermore, consistent with the research on women's preferences, the men also agreed about which female faces and voices they preferred. These authors showed that women with more attractive voices were also perceived as having more attractive faces.

Fraccaro et al. (2011) performed an interesting research project suggesting that women speak in a higher pitch when speaking to someone they consider attractive. These authors "asked women to read a scripted message as if they were leaving a voicemail message to arrange a date with each of two pictured men" (p. 59). The men's faces were manipulated to represent a more masculine-looking face as well as a more feminine-looking face. The authors then analyzed the pitch of women's voices on the two voicemail messages. The researchers found that women tended to speak in a higher-pitched voice to the man whom they found more attractive. Specifically, women who preferred masculine faces (and rated them as more attractive) spoke in a higher-pitched voice when leaving the voicemail message for the more masculine-looking man and vice-versa for the more feminine-looking man. The authors posited that because men seem to prefer higher-pitched voices in a female partner, "speaking with higher voice pitch to men that they find particularly attractive may function to increase women's attractiveness to preferred potential mates" (p. 64).

Conversely, Farley et al. (2013) found that women spoke in a lower-pitched voice to a current opposite-sex romantic partner than they used with a same-sex friend. These authors asked female and male undergraduate students from the United States who were in heterosexual romantic relationships for less than one year to call both their romantic partners and a same-sex friend (in a random order). Independent raters rated the women's and men's voices for sexiness, pleasantness, and the perceived degree of romantic interest. The raters also guessed whether each participant was talking to a friend or a romantic partner. The researchers found that the independent raters were able to identify whether men and women were speaking with a friend or romantic partner at better than chance levels, even when only coding the two-second phrase "how are you?". They also rated men's and women's voices as more pleasant, sexier, and exhibiting more romantic interest when individuals were speaking with their romantic partners rather than their same-sex friends. Interestingly, women spoke in a lower-pitched voice and men spoke in a higher-pitched voice when talking to their romantic partners. The authors speculate that men and women might be trying to match their partner's vocal pitch when talking to one another.

Correlates of vocal attractiveness

In addition to being associated with physical attractiveness, attractive voices are associated with bodily symmetry. Both men and women judged as having attractive voices are also more symmetrical (Hughes et al., 2002). Recall from our earlier discussion of symmetry that symmetry may indicate that a potential partner possesses good genes or the ability to withstand pathogens during development (Manning, 1995; Perilloux et al., 2010). Interestingly, men and women with attractive voices tend to have sex earlier, have more sex partners, and are more likely to be sexually unfaithful (Gallup & Frederick, 2010). Likewise, Hodges-Simeon et al. (2011) found that men who spoke with less frequency variation (more monotone) and used more dominant language also reported having more sexual partners within the past year. Taken together, this research suggests that partners with attractive voices may make better short-term partners than long-term partners. Future research should investigate this possibility.

Vocal personality information

Similar to the research reviewed above regarding physical attractiveness (Dion et al., 1972), vocal attractiveness may also be related to positive personality perceptions. As reviewed by Zuckerman et al. (1991), targets rated as having more attractive voices were likewise perceived to have more pleasing personalities. Interestingly, these results occurred when raters judged both voices alone as well as voices and photographs of faces rated together. Moreover, the authors reported that the effect of vocal attractiveness was sometimes stronger than the effect of visual physical attractiveness.

Vocal information may be particularly useful for discerning certain personality traits. For example, Zuckerman et al. (1990) found that vocal information was more informative when judging traits such as neuroticism, while visual information was more informative when evaluating traits such as extroversion. Also, Zuckerman et al. found that the effects of vocal information and visual information are stronger alone than when presented together. So if you meet someone over the telephone and do not have a photo, or if you see a photo of someone but never hear her voice, the effects of the vocal or visual attractiveness will be more pronounced than if you meet her in-person and experience both types of information simultaneously.

Further, Zuckerman et al. (1990) found that visual and vocal information are particularly important when forming first impressions. These authors collected ratings of physical and vocal attractiveness from strangers and from targets' same-sex roommates. They found that although ratings of physical and vocal attractiveness were related to personality perceptions among strangers, neither ratings of physical nor vocal attractiveness were related to personality perceptions among roommates. Interestingly, in support of mere exposure theory (which we discuss in Chapter 5, see Zajonc, 1968), the authors found that targets were rated more favorably by those perceivers who were more familiar with them.

Body scent

You were probably expecting to read about a potential mate's physical attractiveness, height, or weight influencing attraction, but were you expecting to read about a potential mate's scent? The preference for a partner who smells good may be another unconscious preference, similar to that of the preference for symmetry and averageness. And, yet, scent may convey more information about whether you have chosen a "good" potential mate than do other physical characteristics. Have you ever encountered a person whose scent disgusted you? Would you consider dating that person under any circumstances?

Research on body scent shows that it is an important indicator of attraction, perhaps even more important for women searching for a male partner. Herz and Inzlict (2002) asked men and women to rate the importance of different factors in a mate. The authors found that the scent of a potential partner was rated as more important by women than men. Furthermore, women rated a male partner's scent as more important than men's physical attractiveness or vocal attractiveness. In a study linking body scent to nonverbal behavior, Roberts et al. (2011) asked women to evaluate the body scent (from pads worn beneath men's arms while sleeping) and the attractiveness of men's nonverbal behavior presented in videos. These authors found that women who liked a man's body scent also rated his nonverbal behavior as more attractive (based on short silent videos). In experimental research, Saxton et al. (2008) exposed some women to the scent of androstadienone, a compound which humans naturally secrete in the underarm area. The authors found that women exposed to androstadienone rated men as more attractive at a speed-dating event.

A companion who possesses a pleasing natural odor may also be a "good" partner in other ways. In an intriguing study performed by Thornhill et al. (2003), the researchers asked primarily Caucasian and Hispanic men and women from the United States to sleep in a t-shirt for two nights. (The participants were also required to wash their sheets with unscented detergent, refrain from using scented soaps or perfumes, avoiding eating particularly pungent foods, refrain from smoking or drinking alcohol, and refrain from sleeping next to or having sex with a partner during those two days and nights.) The participants contributed a blood sample and were measured to assess symmetry. Men and women then smelled the t-shirts worn by members of the other sex and rated the "pleasantness" and "sexiness" (p. 671) of the smell of the t-shirts. Independent raters judged the facial attractiveness of the participants.

The results revealed many fascinating results. First, women who were in the fertile phase of their menstrual cycle preferred the scent of men who were more symmetrical. Men, however, did not find the smell of symmetrical women as more pleasing or sexy. Second, men rated the scent of women as more attractive when the women did not share the same immune genes as the men (as the authors posit, potentially providing future offspring with enhanced immunity). Women, however, did not show this same preference in the present study. Third, men preferred the scent of women who were independently rated as more facially attractive. Women, however, did not prefer the scent of more facially attractive men. Fourth, men preferred the scent of women who were at the most fertile point of their menstrual cycle. These findings all suggest that a pleasing scent may be indicative of a good potential mate. Although women may be more likely than men to express the sentiment that scent is more important (Herz & Inzlict, 2002), scent is an important indicator of the quality of a mate for both male and female partners. However, you may need to ask all of your dates to wash their sheets, shower with unscented soap, avoid pungent foods, etc. in order to detect these mating advantages.

Chapter summary

In this chapter we have reviewed research suggesting that first impressions of potential romantic partners can be based upon characteristics such as physical and facial attractiveness, height, weight, age, vocal characteristics, and body scent. These features may be attractive to us because of the other benefits associated with pleasing physical features. Physical attractiveness is often associated with a pleasant personality and a happier disposition. Facial attractiveness as well as facial cues such as symmetry and averageness may indicate that a potential partner is healthy and has "good genes." Preferences for the height and weight of a potential partner may also be related to health or potential reproductive fitness. Vocal attractiveness seems to be related to perceptions of physical attractiveness as well as perceptions of positive personality characteristics. Finally, an attractive body scent may signal that a partner possesses good genes or different immune genes than our own. First impressions of physical characteristics may help us to find the best possible mating partners.

Suggested reading

Alterovitz, S. S., & Mendelsohn, G. A. (2009). Partner preferences across the life span: Online dating by older adults. *Psychology and Aging, 24*(2), 513–517. doi:10.1037/2160-4134.1.S.89
  This article is interesting and easy to read. Students might enjoy critically evaluating the way the authors measured the desired age of potential partners relative to participants' own ages.
Griffin, A. M., & Langlois, J. H. (2006). Stereotype directionality and attractiveness stereotyping: Is beauty good or is ugly bad? *Social Cognition, 24*(2), 187–206. doi:10.1521/soco.2006.24.2.187

I recommend this article because the authors critically evaluate the previously accepted finding that beauty is associated with other positive characteristics.

Saxton, T., Caryl, P., & Roberts, S. (2006). Vocal and facial attractiveness judgments of children, adolescents and adults: The ontogeny of mate choice. *Ethology, 112*(12), 1179–1185. doi:10.1111/j.1439-0310.2006.01278.x.

This article is interesting both due to the intriguing findings as well as the inclusion of women and girls of different ages as participants.

Stulp, G., Pollet, T. V., Verhulst, S., & Buunk, A. P. (2012). A curvilinear effect of height on reproductive success in human males. *Behavioral Ecology and Sociobiology, 66*(3), 375–384. doi:10.1007/s00265-011-1283-2

Although the statistics presented in the result section of this article may be challenging to comprehend, this article is interesting and explores a number of potential variables related to height.

Weeden, J., & Sabini, J. (2005). Physical attractiveness and health in Western societies: A review. *Psychological Bulletin, 131*(5), 635–653. doi:10.1037/0033-2909.131.5.635.

This article presents a thorough review of the literature outlining the potential benefits to mating with a physically attractive partner.

Forming Attitudes toward Potential Partners: First Impressions of Non-Physical Characteristics

First impressions of personality

Although physical characteristics such as height, weight, and physical attractiveness strongly influence our first impressions, non-physical characteristics such as personality, intelligence, and behavior can play an important role in our impressions as well. In this chapter we discuss first impressions of personality and behavior derived through methods other than meeting in-person. In the first part of the current chapter, we will consider first impressions formed on the basis of *ascribed* characteristics (i.e., someone tells you that a potential date possesses certain characteristics). In the latter portion of this chapter, we will focus on impressions created through *inferring* personality information from different sources (other than meeting in-person) such as photographs, videos, and Internet profiles. In Chapter 3 we will examine the speed and accuracy of first impressions of non-physical characteristics formed through in-person meetings. As with our first impressions of physical characteristics, our first impressions of other characteristics are formed surprisingly quickly and accurately, and based upon minimal information.

First impressions based on ascribed traits

Have you ever heard a potential date described by a friend? (Or worse, a relative?) Which traits did your friend use when describing this potential date? Did you form an impression based upon the list of traits your friend provided you? Research suggests that we can and do form impressions based solely upon trait information provided to us by others. My graduate school professor and mentor, Skip Lowe, described this impression process as "starting with a trait." When we form an impression based on ascribed traits, (e.g., someone tells you "this person is nice and kind") we start with trait-based information and form an impression based upon those traits. See if you can form an impression of my friend Danny: Danny is handsome, funny, smart, generous, honest, kind, and single. (Now you know that Danny is a made-up guy, right? Otherwise I would have fixed him up with my friend Louise from Chapter 1 and she would not be searching the Internet for her next date.) But you did form an impression of Danny from that list of traits, right? You probably formed a positive impression and thought he sounded like a nice guy. The more important question is not whether you can form an impression based upon what a friend or relative tells you, but whether you can trust the person providing you with the list of traits!

> A personal moment: One summer one of my favorite cousins from California visited my family. He travelled with a friend of his named Dave, who was also visiting his family. My cousin brought Dave to meet my parents one night, and my mother subsequently told me "you have to meet your cousin's friend Dave. He is really nice and very attractive." Considering the source of this information I immediately concluded that I had no interest in meeting Dave, and that if I ever had the misfortune to meet him, I would not like him at all. You will be surprised (and so was I) to hear that I did eventually meet Dave and found that my mother's impression was very accurate. Dave was very nice and very attractive. (I ended up marrying him.) But I have to caution you: all the other men that my mother thought I should meet were completely incompatible with me. Parents and their adult offspring may not share corresponding views of potential partners because they do not tend to agree about the important characteristics of potential mates (at least as reported by adult offspring, see Buunk & Solano, 2010). According to Buunk and Solano, parents tend to place more emphasis on a partner's religious beliefs and ethnic background while adult children tend to value a partner's sense of humor and creativity.

Disagreements between parents and children aside, the research in this area suggests that we can and do form impressions based upon lists of traits. Some of the first research on impression formation was performed by Solomon Asch (1946), who showed that people formed impressions of hypothetical target persons based upon lists of traits. He also found that not all traits are equally weighted when forming an impression.

Asch (1946) performed some of the first "first impressions" research. He asked participants to form an impression of a person with the following traits: "intelligent, industrious, impulsive, critical, stubborn, envious" or "envious, stubborn, critical, impulsive, industrious, intelligent" (p. 270). He found that the target person described by the first list of traits was perceived more positively than the target person described by the same traits listed in the reverse order. In essence, the first trait served as a first impression through which the subsequent traits were interpreted. As Asch notes, "when the subject hears the first term, a broad, uncrystallized but directed impression is born. The next characteristic comes not as a separate item, but is related to the established direction" (p. 271–272). Furthermore, Asch's research also showed that even if a particular trait is not learned first, some traits can exert a stronger influence on our overall impressions than others.

What the research says

Asch (1946) asked two groups of participants to provide their impressions of a person with the following traits: "intelligent, skillful, industrious, *warm*, determined, practical, and cautious" or "intelligent, skillful, industrious, *cold*, determined, practical, and cautious" (p. 262). Not surprisingly, the results of this research showed that varying one trait (warm versus cold) had a large impact on overall impressions. People had a more favorable impression of the target described as "warm" rather than "cold" (even though these traits were presented in the middle of the list). Asch referred to these very important traits that have a large impact on our impressions as "central" traits. Further, when Asch varied the lists of traits slightly: "intelligent, skillful, industrious, *polite*, determined, practical, and cautious" or "intelligent, skillful, industrious, *blunt*, determined, practical, and cautious" (p. 266), he found that other traits (for example polite versus blunt) are less important to our overall impressions. He called these traits "peripheral" traits. Asch notes that those who were described as "polite" were viewed more positively, but the impact on the overall impression was weaker than that of the central trait of "warm."

Think critically

Asch (1946) found that traits such as warm and cold had a large impact on our impressions. What other traits might be strong enough to be considered central traits? Are central traits more likely to be positive or negative? Do you think that the difference between targets described as warm or cold is due to the positive valence of the term *warm* or the negative valence of the term *cold*?

Similar to Asch's (1946) research, Nisbett and Wilson (1977) varied whether a professor answered questions in a warm way or in a cold way. Participants who saw the warm version tended to rate the professor as more physically attractive and to rate his mannerisms as more appealing. Participants who saw the cold version tended to rate the professor in the opposite manner. These authors interpreted the results as showing a "halo effect" (p. 255) in which positive overall evaluations of the professor also enhanced perceptions of his other attributes. The halo effect persists even when "there is sufficient information to allow for independent assessments" (p. 250) of these other attributes (e.g., physical appearance could be evaluated independently of warmth). Furthermore, the participants seemed to be unaware that the professor's warmth or coldness affected their other evaluations.

In Asch's (1946) research as well as in Nisbett and Wilson's (1977) research, participants derived very different impressions of stimulus persons described as having negative or positive traits (or shown exhibiting negative or positive traits). Think back to the research described in Chapter 1 by Dion et al. (1972) as well as Griffin and Langlois (2006), showing positive associations with physical attractiveness and negative associations with unattractiveness. Do you think that positive traits cause more positive overall perceptions, or that negative traits cause more negative overall perceptions?

Negativity bias in first impressions

Just as first impressions and central traits may be more important than other information that we learn about a potential partner, negative information seems to be more important than positive information. Consider the example I give to my students when I teach Social Psychology: Imagine that I told you I had a friend who was waiting out in the hallway to meet you. Imagine that I told you a lot of positive things about this friend. For example, my friend is very nice and very generous. He is kind to his mother and he donates a lot of money to charity. He is smart and is also a talented artist. He has a good job and a nice home. He has been praised by his brothers and sisters as the best of the bunch, and his cat adores him. But then imagine that I told you that this friend also has a tendency to kick puppies when he gets angry. Would you come away feeling positively about this friend because I told you so many positive things and only one negative thing about him? Or would you feel negatively about him despite the lengthy list of positive attributes? Research on the negativity bias suggests that you would view my friend negatively. Negative information tends to be weighted more strongly than positive information, even when the positive information is more abundant.

Baumeister et al. (2001) review some of the first research to explore integrating positive and negative traits into a holistic impression (originally performed by Anderson in 1965). According to Baumeister et al., this research was meant to show that participants considered equally valenced positive and negative information similarly (e.g., a trait with a +2 rating presented along with a trait with a –2 rating would yield a neutral overall impression). According to Anderson, male undergraduate students were asked to review short lists of personality traits that had been rated earlier for positivity/negativity by a previous set of respondents. For example, two positive traits were "reasonable" and "truthful" while two negative traits were "spiteful" and "abusive" (p. 395). The men participating in this research project were expected to form overall impressions generally commensurate with the average of the individual positive and negative trait ratings. As Baumeister et al. review, however, the negative adjectives exerted a stronger influence on the overall impressions of the second group of participants than did the positive adjectives. Baumeister et al. state that "the unfavorable ones lowered the global impression rating more than a simple additive or averaging model would predict, unlike the favorable traits, which did not exert an influence beyond averaging" (p. 345).

A variety of reasons explain why negative information is weighted more heavily than positive information when forming impressions of individuals. First, think back to a few of your experiences when meeting new people. Do you recall learning more positive or more negative information about those people? Negative information occurs more rarely when forming impressions, but it is more salient when it does occur, which can help to explain why this information carries more weight (Rozin & Royzman, 2001). Negative events may also elicit stronger physiological responses than positive events (Rozin & Royzman, 2001; Cunningham et al., 2003). For example, Cunningham et al.

(2003) found that negative stimuli caused greater activation of the amygdala than positive stimuli.

Negative information may be more important because of the survival value associated with avoiding negative events (Baumeister et al., 2001; Rozin & Royzman, 2001). From an evolutionary perspective "organisms that were better attuned to bad things would have been more likely to survive threats and, consequently, would have increased probability of passing along their genes" (Baumeister et al., 2001, p. 325, see Chapter 4 for a discussion of evolutionary theory). In a particularly poignant example of negativity bias, Rozin and Royzman pose the rhetorical question of how many lives a murderer would have to save in order to "neutralize one act of murder" (p. 299). The research reviewed above on the negativity bias may reflect our efforts to make better mating decisions by avoiding individuals with negative qualities.

A media moment: In a real-life illustration of the negativity bias, a news organization reported on a local baseball coach who decided to retire after a long career during which his baseball teams had won several national championships in their division. Directly before he announced his retirement, the coach was accused of using profanity and throwing a helmet into the stands during one of his team's games. According to the Associated Press (2013) the coach alleged that the news media had failed to see "the hundreds of thousands" of positive things he accomplished during his career, implying that the media was unduly influenced by one negative incident.

Implicit personality theory

A personal moment: One day my friend, Todd, called me and said that he would love for me to meet his new girlfriend, Sandy. He described Sandy as cute, enthusiastic, and friendly. I immediately said that I would love to meet her. I expected to like Sandy and I wondered what other positive traits she was likely to possess. I thought she might be funny and outgoing and a good long-term partner for Todd. Later I realized I was using an implicit personality theory in forming my impression of Sandy.

Perceivers tend to use implicit personality theories when forming impressions (Schneider & Blankmeyer, 1983). That is, we have and use ideas about which types of traits usually go together. So, if you learn that Sandy is enthusiastic, you might also expect her to be talkative and sociable. Or, if Todd told you that Sandy was kind and generous, you might also expect her to be polite and charitable. Implicit personality theories might also help to explain the halo effect referenced above (Nisbett & Wilson, 1977). The professor's warm manner might lead one to believe that he also possesses other positive qualities. Similarly, implicit personality theories might also explain why negative information is weighted more strongly than positive information. Perhaps when we hear that a person has one negative trait, we assume that person will have other negative traits as well. These perceptions may help to guide our mate preferences, so that we prefer others whom we believe possess numerous positive qualities.

Not only do we expect certain traits to go together, but once we have those expectations, they might color our subsequent interactions with that person (Schneider & Blankmeyer, 1983). If we expect Sandy to be cute and enthusiastic, we might specifically look for behaviors which confirm her extroversion, or if we expect her to be polite and generous, we might be more willing to interpret her behavior as selfless. This possibility also provides a potential explanation for the negativity bias. Perhaps when we hear that a person has negative traits, we are more likely to notice negative behaviors performed by that person or even to elicit negative behaviors from that person (see the discussion of self-fulfilling prophecy in Chapter 7).

Although cross-cultural research on implicit personality theories is rare, one study assessed implicit personality theories in samples of college students from the Philippines and from the United States (Guthrie & Bennett, 1971). These authors suggested that in different cultures we might have different ideas about which traits are usually paired together. For example, although the Filipino students tended to have similar perceptions to those of the American students regarding the trait of extroversion (sociability or friendliness), they tended to view emotional stability differently. The authors noted that although the American students typically associated emotional instability with anxiety as well as with physical symptoms, the Filipino students tended to separate anxiety from physical symptoms and were less likely to assume that the presence of one would imply the presence of the other. Given that the research assessing cross-cultural differences is so rare and somewhat dated, future research in this area is essential.

Inferring traits from observations

In the first portion of this chapter, we discussed impressions formed on the basis of ascribed traits, If you start with trait information, how do those traits influence your impressions? We will now transition to impressions based upon observations. My graduate school professor, Skip Lowe, used to refer to this situation as "ending with a trait." When we create an impression based on observations (e.g., we see a man helping an older person cross the street), we start with an observation of a person or a behavior and conclude with a trait inference (e.g., "that man must be very kind and helpful").

First impressions based on photographs

In addition to gleaning information about physical attributes from facial photographs (see Chapter 1), we can garner some personality information such as perceptions of warmth or honesty from photographs of faces (Hassin & Trope, 2000). For example, research by Stirrat and Perrett (2010) demonstrates that facial width might be an important indicator of the trustworthiness of male targets; suggesting that people are more likely to trust and cooperate with men with narrower faces. However, we do not just want to know whether we can form impressions based on photographs; we want to know whether those impressions are *accurate*. Although the accuracy of personality impressions is difficult to objectively assess (see Kenny, 1994), different types of evidence suggest that we can accurately perceive targets' personality characteristics. For example, both younger and older adults tend to agree in their judgments regarding the competence, aggressiveness, and trustworthiness of facial photographs, suggesting accuracy in their impressions (Zebrowitz et al., 2013). Furthermore, Willis and Todorov (2006) showed that judges can accurately discern a great deal of personality information from extremely short exposures to photographs of faces as compared with judges allotted an unlimited amount of time to form their impressions. Agreement among observers is one criterion that can be used to assess the accuracy of personality impressions (typically referred to as consensus, see Kenny, 1994). In this chapter, as well as in Chapter 3, we discuss the problem of an accuracy criterion for personality judgments.

What the research says

Willis and Todorov (2006) showed undergraduate students from the United States photographs of actors displaying neutral facial expressions, and asked the students to judge whether the actors seemed to be attractive, likable, trustworthy, competent, or aggressive. In the first iteration of this research project, undergraduate students had an unlimited amount of time to consider the photographs and make their judgments. In the second iteration of the project, a new group of undergraduate students were exposed to the facial photographs for either 100, 500, or 1,000 milliseconds. The authors found that the participants' judgments regarding the aforementioned traits after 100 ms exposures were significantly positively correlated with judgments made after longer exposure intervals. (However, the authors also found that participants' confidence in their trait judgments increased as exposure intervals lengthened.) Willis and Todorov's research suggests that 100 ms is enough time to form an accurate personality impression.

Think critically

Willis and Todorov (2006) assessed the accuracy of first impressions by measuring agreement among observers who evaluated the target photographs for different time intervals. Is this a good way to assess whether the observers formed accurate impressions? What are some other criteria the authors could have employed to assess accuracy? Are there problems associated with the other criteria as well?

Personality impressions are remarkably consistent across cultures. For example, Zebrowitz et al. (2012) compared personality impressions based on male facial photographs between men from the United States and men from an isolated culture in the Bolivian rainforest. These authors found that men from each culture tended to agree in their ratings of targets' personality characteristics such as intelligence, dominance, and warmth. Although agreement for faces from one's own culture was stronger, men across cultures also agreed with one another about the personality traits of the targets. Once again, this research suggests that we can very quickly and accurately form impressions of a target person's traits, even if that person hails from a different culture. If we were inaccurately perceiving an individual's characteristics, we might expect perceptions to vary widely across observers as well as across cultures.

In addition to facial photographs, full body photographs also reveal personality characteristics (Naumann et al., 2009). Rather than merely examining whether perceivers agreed in their impressions of the targets (as done in the research cited above) in this research, observers' impressions of targets' traits (such as agreeableness, likability, extroversion, and religiosity) were consistent with reports made by the target persons themselves as well as reports made by three people who knew the targets well. Self-reports of personality as well as the reports of those who know the target well are also frequently employed to assess the accuracy of observers' personality impressions. Additionally, Naumann et al.'s research showed that observers formed even more accurate impressions of the targets when the targets were allowed to strike any pose they liked and convey any facial expression they liked (versus a condition in which the poses and facial expressions were standardized). It is likely that photographs of themselves which people choose to share with others are photographs which will convey more personality information because they are likely to be photos that the target person likes and/or sees as representative of herself.

In addition to quickly forming accurate impressions of personality, we are also able to quickly and accurately discern a target's sexual orientation from photographs. We can be fairly confident using a target's self-reported sexual orientation as an accuracy criterion. (Presumably an individual is the only one who can accurately identify his or her own sexual orientation.) In Rule and Ambady's (2008) research on the accuracy of judgments of sexual orientation, observers' judgments were directly compared to participants' self-reported sexual orientation. Rule and Ambady obtained photographs of gay and straight men from online personal ads for men seeking male or female relationship partners. The photographs were presented for varying durations (from 33 ms to 10,000 ms) or with no time constraints. The authors found that participants could accurately classify men's sexual orientation as gay or straight after only 50 milliseconds' exposure to a photograph. Furthermore, accuracy did not improve significantly with increased exposure to the photographs. The authors posit that it may be evolutionarily advantageous to be able to quickly and accurately classify sexual orientation in order to determine which individuals might be prospective mates or rivals (see Chapter 4 for more information on evolutionary theory).

Rule et al. (2009) replicated these effects with lesbian and straight target women, showing that these targets could be accurately classified as lesbian or straight with an even shorter exposure time of 40 milliseconds.

Sexual orientation may be an important characteristic to be able to deduce quickly and accurately. The faithfulness of a potential partner may be equally important. Rhodes et al. (2012) found that women could accurately judge a man's likelihood of being unfaithful from facial photographs. Women's judgments of a man's likelihood of being unfaithful were significantly related to his prior reports of cheating on a partner and having sex with a partner who was in another relationship. Once again, although men's self-reports may not be entirely truthful, the researchers did encourage the men to be honest and made sure that the men's responses were contributed anonymously. This research suggested that facial masculinity was an important cue in assessing the likelihood of unfaithfulness. Men who had more masculine facial features were also more likely to report being unfaithful in the past. Although women were moderately accurate in their perceptions of men's faithfulness, men were much less accurate in their ability to detect infidelity in women. (This finding is potentially at odds with the finding that men view women's sexual infidelity as more upsetting than women view men's sexual infidelity; see Chapter 4.)

Although intelligence may not be entirely accurately measured through intelligence tests, these tests can provide a relatively objective criterion for assessing the accuracy of observers' intelligence judgments. Zebrowitz et al (2002) investigated whether perceivers could accurately estimate the intelligence of individuals shown in photographs. The photographs of targets consisted of children, adolescents, "middle adulthood" (ages 30–40), and "later adulthood" (ages 52–60, p. 241). College student raters were most accurate when judging the intelligence of children and early adolescents (age 13 for girls, age 15 for boys). They also accurately judged the intelligence of the "middle" adults. (The perceivers could not accurately estimate the intelligence of the older adults.) Interestingly, perceived attractiveness was positively correlated with perceived intelligence across all age groups. Perceived attractiveness was also significantly correlated with scores on the intelligence tests, suggesting that attractiveness may be an important cue to intelligence. Importantly, the samples used in Zebrowitz et al.'s research were representative samples from two cities in the United States and therefore represented a more robust range of IQ scores than might be found using college student samples.

First impressions based on video clips

Video clips may convey more information than photographs because you can see glimpses of behavior in videos rather than in "static" photographs (Hassin & Trope, 2000, p. 838). Below, we review evidence suggesting that from short video clips we can accurately form impressions of targets' sexual orientation, sociosexuality, romantic interest, intelligence, and even teaching ability.

In one of the early studies to investigate the ability to use short video clips to form accurate impressions, Ambady and Rosenthal (1993) conducted a research project which suggests that even very brief exposure to nonverbal behavior enables us to form accurate impressions. These researchers asked students to rate short, silent video clips of teachers (they call these video clips "thin slices" of behavior, p. 431). The students rated unfamiliar teachers after seeing three video clips of either two seconds, five seconds, or ten seconds each. The ratings of the teachers made by the student participants correlated strongly and positively with the ratings made by the teachers' real students on their teaching evaluations completed at the end of the semester. So it seems that very little nonverbal behavioral information tells us a lot about a target person, perhaps even as much as we might learn if we spent a few months with a target person. Once the researchers established the accuracy of students' ratings based on these "thin slices" of behavior, they extended this paradigm to investigate other behaviors as well.

Consistent with the research on still photographs (see Rule & Ambady's 2008 research, as well as Rule et al., 2009, as reviewed above), observers can accurately determine sexual orientation based upon short video clips. Ambady et al.(1999) found that participants could accurately judge the sexual orientation of target persons who were videotaped while discussing their academic and extracurricular activities. The perceivers discerned the sexual orientation of the targets at better than chance levels. Intriguingly, some targets were classified correctly almost all the time while some targets were more difficult to classify. Moreover, some perceivers were better judges of sexual orientation than others. Further, perceivers who were gay or lesbian themselves were much more accurate than their heterosexual peers at discerning sexual orientation from the shortest video clips and could even accurately categorize sexual orientation based upon still photos. Similarly, Valentova et al. (2011) explored perceptions of gay and heterosexual male targets in the United States and the Czech Republic. They found that participants were able to accurately classify gay and straight targets based on ten-second video clips, both within their own culture and between cultures. In this research project, accuracy was slightly better when participants judged targets from their own cultures, suggesting that some culture-specific cues may be used when evaluating sexual orientation.

A media moment: In the short film *Gaydar* (Ray & Lafond, 2002), male and female co-workers both have a crush on the same man, but they cannot figure out whether the desired man is gay or straight. In this movie the co-workers' "gaydar" (the ability to quickly and accurately judge whether someone is gay; the term comes from a combination of "gay" and "radar") is not functioning. However, the research above suggests that we can quickly and accurately discern a target's sexual orientation. My colleague (Alita Cousins) and I informally polled some of our gay and lesbian friends for anecdotes about gaydar. One friend believed that his gaydar only worked for men who were good looking. Could something like gaydar really exist? Are gay men and lesbians more likely to possess this ability? Could romantic interest improve one's gaydar?

Men and women are also able to accurately perceive women's sociosexuality through silent video clips. Stillman and Maner (2009) videotaped single women trying to solve a Rubik's Cube with a male confederate for five minutes (a confederate poses as another participant but is really hired by the researchers). These videos were then shown to independent raters who rated the women on a variety of personality characteristics as well as on their perceived sociosexual orientation. Sociosexual orientation was defined for the raters as "individual differences in the preference for unrestricted sex (without the necessity of love) or restricted sex (in the context of a long-term relationship)" (p. 126). Similar to the results discussed above, the raters accurately perceived the participants' levels of sociosexuality (such that the raters' perceptions were consistent with the women's self-reports of their own sociosexuality). Furthermore, the authors found that behaviors such as "eyebrow flashes, glancing at the confederate and paying little attention toward solving the puzzle" (p. 127) were strong indicators of the women's levels of sociosexuality. (Other research suggests that men's levels of sociosexuality can be discerned through smiling, laughing, and flirtatious glances as well, see Simpson et al., 1993.)

In addition to sociosexuality, short videos may also be useful for discerning romantic interest. In a cross-cultural study involving ten-second video clips of heterosexual German speed daters, Place et al. (2012) found that college student observers from the United States and China as well as adults from Germany were equally adept at identifying whether the speed daters were romantically interested in one another. Consistent with the research described above (Ambady et al., 1999), these authors also noted that some targets were easier to judge than others. However, targets whose romantic interest was deemed difficult to judge remained difficult to judge across cultures, with German observers only slightly advantaged, even though these video clips were presented in their native language. The authors interpreted these results as suggesting that romantic interest might be important to discern in both members of the pair, stating that it may be "adaptive for one to know not only the interest of potential suitors but also that of potential same-sex competitors" (p. 550).

Videotaped behavior can also be useful for evaluating the intelligence of a potential mate. In Prokosch et al.'s (2009) research, women accurately perceived men's intelligence based upon video clips of approximately four minutes in length. The researchers asked men to all perform the same behaviors while they were videotaped. In the videos the men were shown performing a variety of verbal and nonverbal behaviors such as reading news headlines and throwing a Frisbee. These authors showed that women's ratings of men's intelligence were strongly positively correlated with men's actual intelligence (based upon the men's performance on an intelligence test). Furthermore, intelligent men were preferred by women as both long-term and short-term mates. (See Chapter 3 for a further discussion of this research.)

Some online dating sites use video clips, video chats, and even virtual dates via avatars to introduce potential partners to one another (Finkel et al., 2012).

According to some Internet sources, the popular video-sharing website YouTube started as a dating website (Elliot, 2011). Given the wealth of information that can be conveyed by very short video clips (such as personality, intelligence, romantic interest, sociosexuality, sexual orientation, etc.), future research should assess whether online video clips result in more accurate impressions of potential dating partners than do static photographs, as well as whether video clips or online face-to-face chats convey as much information as an in-person meeting.

First impressions of personality as displayed by targets via the Internet

Have you ever tried to form an impression of a person based upon information gathered via the Internet? Do you think you would be as confident in these impressions as you would be if you met that person face-to-face? Perhaps surprising to some, most of the research in this area shows that we can form very accurate perceptions of a target through information gathered via the Internet. For example, research performed by Vazire and Gosling (2004) suggests that people can form accurate perceptions of targets based on the targets' personal websites (note that this research involved personal websites and not profile information posted on dating websites). Participants who viewed targets' personal websites rated them similarly to the targets' own ratings as well as similarly to ratings made by the targets' friends. Likewise, a recent study assessing the accuracy of personality information gleaned from Facebook profiles shows that people tend to present accurate personality information on their Facebook sites as well (Back et al., 2010). Back et al. suggest that, because these websites are typically seen by others who know them well, individuals may be motivated to present accurate information about themselves in these venues.

Similarly, Gill et al. (2006) found that participants easily garnered accurate impressions of targets' extroversion from their emails. In this project, judges rated emails of approximately 300 words written by different target participants. In their emails, the target participants described "their previous week, and plans for the next week, written as if to a good friend" (p. 501). The target participants also made ratings of their own personalities. The results showed that the judges tended to agree with one another about how extroverted the target participants were. The judges' ratings were also consistent with the target participants' own self-ratings of their degree of extroversion. However, the researchers found less agreement among judges as well as agreement with the target participants' own self-ratings concerning personality traits other than extroversion.

Cross-modalities

If given the choice, would you prefer to meet a potential mate in person or via the Internet? Some research shows that participants like one another more when they meet via the Internet first (rather than face-to-face). McKenna et al. (2002) found that men and women who interacted first in an Internet chat room (without exchanging photographs with their partners) liked one another more after their first online interaction and after their first face-to-face meeting than did pairs who met in-person on both occasions. Despite the differences in initial meeting style, impressions were consistent across modalities. That is, participants who tended to like one another online also liked one another in-person.

Similarly, Ramirez and Zhang (2007) found that undergraduates who performed a variety of tasks (such as planning a trip) either online, face-to-face, or via some combination of both modalities, also liked their partners better if they had interacted via email prior to their face-to-face meetings. However, Ramirez and Zhang's research also suggests that long delays in communicating only via computer before meeting in-person (e.g., six weeks in this research) tended to dampen the positive effects of meeting online first.

Importantly, in the research described above (McKenna et al., 2002; Ramirez & Zhang, 2007), physical attractiveness information was not conveyed during or prior to the Internet interactions. In real-life online meeting scenarios in which visual information is conveyed (usually via the exchange of photographs) and couples tend to like one another during an initial Internet interaction, this increase in liking after meeting online might be even stronger because physical attractiveness levels are already known. Future research may address this possibility. We should also note that both McKenna et al.'s research and Ramirez and Zhang's research involved undergraduates participating in research and not individuals who were actively seeking romantic partners. Future research should examine whether initially meeting online or meeting in-person facilitates liking among individuals who are actively seeking romantic partners. Furthermore, this research involved participants of college age, who are more comfortable with computers and with the concept of meeting online. Future research should investigate whether individuals of other ages also like one another more if they meet online first.

One reason that we may like others more when meeting via the Internet is because we project positive qualities onto our interaction partners. Bargh et al. (2002) suggest that because some information is not conveyed via email or via the Internet (as it is in in-person interactions), we may replace the missing information with positive information. Bargh et al. state that individuals may project "the characteristics of their ideal close friend onto their interaction partners" (p. 44). This explanation is supported by Norton et al. (2007), who suggested that when we first meet someone a lack of information about that interaction partner leads to the assumption of similarity which, in turn, leads to increased liking. Bargh et al. further speculated that these more positive projections may actually lead to self-fulfilling prophecies upon meeting in-person, leading individuals to elicit favorable behavior from their interaction partners (see Chapter 7 for a discussion of self-fulfilling prophecies).

Much of the research reviewed above suggests that individuals are generally successful at presenting their "true selves" via the Internet (Bargh et al., 2002,

p. 33; Back et al., 2010; McKenna et al., 2002). Conversely, a study of individuals who used online dating services revealed that eight out of ten participants admitted to lying about some part of their dating profile (Toma et al., 2008).

What the research says

Toma et al. (2008) obtained the online dating profile pages from 80 individuals in the New York City area who were actively using these services to search for mates. The researchers asked participants about the veracity of their profiles and also verified participants' height and weight and obtained their age from their driver's licenses. Toma et al. found that men tended to lie about their height (desiring to appear taller than they actually were) while women tended to lie about their weight (desiring to appear lighter than they actually were). Both men and women lied about their age at similar rates, although most participants only slightly underestimated their age. In terms of non-objectively judged criteria, men indicated a greater willingness than women to lie about their occupation, education, and relationship status. Both men and women indicated that they were least honest about their photographs. The authors note that the magnitude of deception involved in participants' objectively evaluated characteristics was small, perhaps due to the potential for future in-person interaction. Research by Cornwell and Lundgren (2001) corroborates these results, also showing that participants involved in romantic relationships conducted via the Internet reported that they were more likely to lie about their age and physical characteristics than those involved in "realspace" relationships (p. 208).

Think critically

In the research discussed above, both men and women admitted they were least honest about their photographs. In what ways could online daters be dishonest in presenting photographs of themselves? Do you think this dishonesty would be apparent upon meeting in-person? How could one evaluate the accuracy of photographs presented on dating websites?

A personal moment: A few nights ago while visiting my mother, I met one of her friends, Maggie, who asked me how work was going. After I told Maggie that I was writing this book, she took out her mobile phone and proceeded to show me her new app, a dating app for individuals over 50 years old. She showed me the profiles of a few men she was dating and expressed doubt about the truthfulness of those men who listed high salaries in their profiles. She also related that one man had stated in his profile that he was 5 feet 8 inches tall but when she met him in-person he was only about 5 feet 3 inches tall (and importantly, shorter than Maggie). I immediately told her about the research described above, at which point she admitted to me that in her online profile she had lied about her age.

Chapter summary

In this chapter we have reviewed research suggesting that we can and do form impressions based upon lists of traits ascribed to targets. Additionally, some traits, especially those learned first and negative traits, exert a stronger influence over our impressions. Most of the research reviewed in this chapter suggests that accurate first impressions of personality, sexual orientation, and intelligence can be gleaned promptly from photographs, short videos, and even through online profiles and Internet interaction. Humans are adept at forming accurate impressions based on a paucity of information. Although individual accuracy criteria may not actually indicate that we have accurately perceived a target's characteristics, a variety of criteria can strengthen our confidence that we are indeed forming accurate impressions. We present suggestions for future reading below.

Suggested reading

Ambady, N., Hallahan, M., & Conner, B. (1999). Accuracy of judgments of sexual orientation from thin slices of behavior. *Journal of Personality and Social Psychology*, 77(3), 538–547. doi:10.1037/0022-3514.77.3.538.
This research is very well designed and controls for potential confounds. Students will enjoy the topic and be interested in the results.

Asch, S. (1946). Forming impressions of personality. *The Journal of Abnormal and Social Psychology*, 41(3), 258–290. doi:10.1037/h0055756.
This article is long and not easy to read, but it is one of the classics in social psychology. It is interesting to read the myriad ways that Asch investigated impressions.

Baumeister, R. F., Bratslavsky, E., Finkenauer, C., & Vohs, K. D. (2001). Bad is stronger than good. *Review of General Psychology*, 5(4), 323–370. doi:10.1037/1089-2680.5.4.323
This article presents a thorough review of why negative information is more important to impression formation.

Buunk, A. P., & Solano, A. (2010). Conflicting preferences of parents and offspring over criteria for a mate: A study in Argentina. *Journal of Family Psychology*, 24(4), 391–399. doi:10.1037/a0020252
I really like this research because it contrasts the perceived preferences of parents and children. Students will also enjoy critically evaluating the way the parents' preferences were measured.

Rhodes, G., Morley, G., & Simmons, L. W. (2012). Women can judge sexual unfaithfulness from unfamiliar men's faces. *Biology Letters*, 9, 20120908. http://dx.doi.org/10.1098/rsbl.2012.0908
This article was short as well as easy to read. Students may enjoy critiquing the inaccuracy of men's impressions of women's faithfulness and reconciling this result with the predictions of evolutionary theory.

Willis, J., & Todorov, A. (2006). First impressions: Making up your mind after a 100-ms exposure to a face. *Psychological Science, 17*(7), 592–598. Retrieved from SPORTDiscus with Full Text database.
This article is fairly easy to read and presents an interesting continuity between limited and unlimited time to form impressions. Students will enjoy critiquing the criteria used to determine whether those impressions are accurate.

First Impressions of Non-Physical Characteristics: Levels of Acquaintance and the Importance of Meeting in Person

3

In Chapter 2 we noted that humans are capable of forming impressions based upon lists of traits, photographs, videos, or Internet interactions. Although impressions formed in this manner may be accurate, the impressions that we draw in this fashion might be qualitatively different from the impressions we form based upon meeting in person (Eastwick et al., 2011; Finkel et al., 2012). An in-person meeting can afford an opportunity to judge a target's actions and also interactions. Therefore, in this chapter we examine first impressions created through in-person meetings. In this first portion of the chapter we highlight impressions created in person under different levels of acquaintance (i.e., zero acquaintance, short-term acquaintance). In the latter portion of this chapter, we consider which traits are most important to us when making dating and mating decisions. Contrary to what we may believe, mate characteristics that seem indispensable to us may matter less than we realize in our real-life, in-person interactions.

Personality assessments at zero acquaintance

When you are able to observe a potential mate in person, but before you interact with that person (on any level, even via email or telephone), your level of acquaintance is termed "zero acquaintance." Kenny (1994) provides an example to illustrate zero acquaintance, depicting the scenario of a target sitting at a table in a restaurant while the perceiver observes the target from across the room. This situation may happen in real-life if you plan to meet a potential mate and are able to observe that person before actually interacting with him. As Kenny (1994) reviews, our impressions based upon zero acquaintance may actually be quite accurate, especially for certain personality traits.

As discussed in Chapter 2, although it is difficult to *objectively* determine whether an impression is accurate, evidence for the accuracy of a perceiver's observations of a target can be obtained from several sources. For example, a perceiver's ratings may be compared with the target's self-report ratings, with ratings made by other perceivers, or with behaviors performed by the target (Kenny, 1994). Research using these three criteria indicates that we can accurately perceive the extroversion of a target person, even at zero acquaintance. According to Kenny, there is consistency between self-ratings and other-ratings for the trait of extroversion; others do tend to see us as we see ourselves. Using the criterion of comparing one perceiver's ratings with the ratings of other perceivers, among observers there is widespread agreement, or "consensus" (p. 59), for the personality trait of extroversion (and slightly less consensus for conscientiousness) when assessed at zero acquaintance. Furthermore, Levesque and Kenny (1993) explored the relationships among perceivers' trait predictions and targets' behavior during a brief social interaction. This research showed that perceivers' trait predictions (e.g., nervousness, talkativeness) for women at zero acquaintance were strongly positively correlated with behavior during their subsequent brief social interactions with one another.

What the research says

Levesque and Kenny (1993) recruited groups composed of four unacquainted women to participate in a study of interpersonal perception. All of the women in the sample (undergraduates from the United States) did not know one another but they did introduce themselves by stating their names and hometowns before making ratings of one another. Each participant rated the other individuals (as well as herself) on a series of traits such as "shy-not shy" and "talkative-silent" (p. 1181). Each participant also made predictions about the anticipated behavior of each individual when interacting with herself as well as when interacting with the others. All of the women then participated in five-minute dyadic (two-person) interactions with every possible interaction partner. The interactions were videotaped, and behaviors such as body lean and gesturing were coded by two independent coders. The results of this study showed that observers tended to agree about how extroverted an individual was, even at zero acquaintance (referred to as consensus). Additionally, when the women tended to agree in their predictions about whether an individual would be nervous, that individual also rated herself as more nervous. Moreover, predictions about extroverted behavior across partners were confirmed by the videotaped behaviors displayed by the participants. For example, if the women tended to agree that a given individual was predicted to be talkative, that individual actually was more talkative with her interaction partners. The authors concluded that "people's snap judgments of extraversion are remarkably accurate" (p. 1185).

Think critically

Levesque and Kenny's (1993) research "challenges the notion that generally, person perceivers are biased and inaccurate" (p. 1186). However, there is no reason to assume that these participants were biased in any fashion. Might the results differ if the researchers deliberately biased the participants, leading them to believe that some individuals were shy or introverted? Do our expectations affect the accuracy of our observations?

Similar to the results discussed above, Marcus and Lehman (2002) assessed agreement between the observers' ratings and the participants' self-ratings of sociability. They also found strong agreement among observers (consensus) about ratings of a target person's sociability at zero acquaintance. Taken together, these findings indicate that we can quickly and accurately form impressions of a target's friendliness or sociability, but the findings related to the trait of extroversion may not extend to other personality characteristics. Behaviors associated with extroversion (smiling, gesturing, leaning forward) may be more quickly and easily discerned than more indirect behaviors associated with other traits (for example, emotional stability, see Levesque & Kenny, 1993; Kenny et al., 1992). Interestingly, as reviewed in Chapter 1, Zuckerman et al. (1990) suggest that vocal information may be more useful when judging traits such as neuroticism, while visual information may be more useful when judging traits such as extroversion.

In a cross-cultural investigation of the accuracy of personality perceptions at zero acquaintance, Albright et al. (1997) investigated consensus in the personality impressions of Chinese students. In this research, male and female undergraduates from Beijing were tested in groups of five unacquainted individuals. The experimenters asked the participants to look at one another but not talk to one another. The participants then made personality (e.g., sociable, intelligent, honest, etc.) as well as other ratings (e.g., physical attractiveness, neatness, smiling, etc.) of one another and of themselves. Similar to the results reviewed above for US samples, the authors found that Chinese students also agreed with one another in their ratings of individuals' personality characteristics as well as in their ratings of other characteristics, such as physical attractiveness. Furthermore, in a second study, photographs of the Chinese students were subsequently shown to students from the United States and vice versa. Although members within one culture rated one another in person while members from different cultures rated one another via photographs, the results showed strong consensus, both within cultures and between cultures. The authors concluded that people from different cultures not only show consensus in their personality perceptions within their cultures but also show consensus for people of other cultural backgrounds.

Ratings of extroversion might be particularly important to our perceptions of physical attractiveness because perceptions of extroversion tend to positively correlate with ratings of physical attractiveness (Kenny et al., 1992; Meier et al., 2010). In sum, although we may be able to quickly form accurate impressions of a potential mate's sociability and physical attractiveness, we may be unable to form impressions of a potential mate's other personality characteristics as expediently.

Short-term acquaintance

We may be able to form relatively accurate impressions based upon observing, but never interacting, with a partner; however, most real-life scenarios will include at least a short interaction with a potential romantic partner. Short-term acquaintance is defined as interaction between individuals for a few minutes or a few hours (Kenny, 1994). This interaction length might be typical for a first in-person meeting. As long as a target's behaviors are relatively consistent, "increasing acquaintance leads to increasing target accuracy" (Kenny, p. 141) in personality perceptions. Increasing acquaintance might lead to increased accuracy in perceptions of a target because longer acquaintance might provide more chances to observe a partner or because people who know one another well may be more willing to disclose information to one another (Kenny & Acitelli, 2001).

Indeed, some research supports the idea that increasing acquaintance leads to increased accuracy in person perception. For example, Letzring et al. (2006) found that students who interacted for 50 minutes or 3 hours were more accurate in their judgments of one another's personalities than students who did not interact at all (as compared to self-ratings, ratings of two others who knew them well, and a clinical interviewer's ratings). This research also highlights that not only the length but the type of interaction may influence the accuracy of person perception. Students who were specifically given the instruction to get to know one another as well as possible were more accurate in their judgments than students who were instructed to answer trivia questions together.

Similarly, Paulhus and Bruce (1992) found that in undergraduate peer-discussion groups, individuals' personality ratings of their group members became more accurate over the course of seven weeks (when compared with group members' self-ratings). Interestingly, Paulhus and Bruce's research also showed that although ratings of some characteristics became more accurate over time (for example, ratings of agreeableness); some characteristics remained hard to judge (for example, ratings of neuroticism). Moreover, consistent with the zero acquaintance literature reviewed above, some characteristics were perceived accurately from the time of the first meeting (for example, extroversion).

A media moment: I recently saw an amazing musical performance by Sharon Jones and the Dap Kings. One of my favorite songs was called "100 Days, 100 Nights," (written and produced by Bosco Mann in 2007). In this song, Jones sings the lyrics, "100 days, 100 nights to know a man's heart … and a little more before he knows his own." This song suggests that a long-term acquaintance might be necessary to know whether a partner loves you. Although Kenny's (2004) research does not address love specifically, his *PERSON* model suggests that not 100 *days*, but 100 *acts* can be enough to accurately judge a target person. Kenny's (2004) model predicts that increasing acquaintance is associated with modest increases in accuracy. Furthermore, these improvements generally occur over a very short-term acquaintance of just a few hours (required to observe roughly 100 acts completed by a target) when assessing the accuracy of personality and behavioral impressions. Future research will be necessary to determine whether 100 days and nights are indeed sufficient to determine whether a companion loves you.

Speed dating

The speed-dating paradigm presents a real-life scenario in which potential romantic partners get to know each other at a level that can be described as short-term acquaintance. In-person speed dating allows one to assess both physical appearance as well as personality in a short period of time, often just a few minutes.

> A media moment: In the HBO series *Sex and the City*, a character named Miranda attends a speed-dating event and finds that her potential dates are not interested in her when she reveals that she is an intelligent lawyer. However, when she pretends to be a flirty flight attendant, she is rewarded by the interest of a man who pretends to be a doctor. Needless to say, their relationship fails when Miranda cuts her finger and discovers that her partner is not actually a doctor. (She never reveals to him that she is not a flight attendant, though.) This anecdote seems to suggest that intelligence and occupation might be important factors when looking for potential partners at a speed-dating event. However, research conducted at real-life speed-dating events (see below) suggests that physical characteristics (and not education and occupation) exert the strongest influence over speed-dating preferences.

Although short-term in-person interactions allow the possibility of simultaneously evaluating physical and non-physical characteristics, in speed-dating research, physical attributes tend to exert a stronger influence on attraction than personality characteristics. For example, Kurzban and Weeden (2005) analyzed data from several speed-dating events involving adults living in major cities throughout the United States. Consistent with the research reviewed throughout Chapter 1, Kurzban and Weeden's research revealed that men were more attracted to women who were thin, while women were more attracted to men who were tall. Both men and women tended to be attracted to potential partners who were young, physically attractive, and of the same racial background. Interestingly, a potential date's education and income level did not impact men's or women's preferences during the speed-dating event. (However, men with higher incomes were more discriminating when choosing potential female partners.) Similarly, Todd et al. (2007) also found that German men based their speed-dating preferences on the physical attractiveness of their female counterparts. Moreover, research conducted by Luo and Zhang (2009) involving undergraduate students from the United States also suggests that both men and women prefer speed-dating partners who are physically attractive.

Consistent with predictions based on evolutionary theory (see Chapter 4), Kurzban and Weeden (2005) and Todd et al. (2007) found that women were more discriminating than men in their decisions about whether to say "yes" to a potential date. These findings may reflect the biological processes underlying men's and women's reproductive strategies. Although men can produce more children by mating with more women, the number of children that women can produce would not necessarily be enhanced by mating with multiple men. Alternatively, these results may be related to women's tendency to underestimate the degree of sexual interest displayed by their male interaction partners, as well as men's tendency to overestimate the degree of sexual interest displayed by their female interaction partners (Levesque et al., 2006; Perilloux, Easton, & Buss, 2012).

Although similarity is thought to be an important influence on attraction (e.g., see Byrne, 1961a; Byrne & Blaylock, 1963; Feingold, 1988 as reviewed in Chapter 5), the preference for self–partner similarity in speed-dating research is mixed. Todd et al. (2007) found evidence for self-reported similarity preferences, showing that participants who rated themselves positively on variables such as family commitment, physical appearance, attractiveness, and healthiness also strongly desired those traits in a potential partner. Luo and Zhang (2009), however, failed to find any influence of self–partner similarity on stated partner preferences in their speed-dating research. The difference between these two studies may hinge on the way similarity was measured. In Todd et al.'s research, self-reported *similarity preferences* were measured, while in Luo and Zhang's research, in-person *partner preferences* were measured. Although similarity seems to be important to us on paper, in our in-person interactions, physical attraction seems to dominate our dating and mating decisions. Intriguingly, cross-cultural research by Gebauer et al. (2012) suggests that similarity may be more important in countries where residents are less heavily influenced by physical attractiveness.

The strong reliance on physical attractiveness in speed-dating situations may be an artifact of "information overload" related to quickly meeting and evaluating large numbers of potential partners. Research by Lenton and Francesconi (2010) suggests that at larger speed-dating events (24–31 potential partners), individuals were more likely to base their mate choices on traits that were easily discernible, such as height and weight, while at smaller speed-dating events (15–23 potential partners), individuals were more likely to consider characteristics that required more time to evaluate, such as a partner's occupation and educational background. The authors interpreted these results to suggest that too many partners at a speed-dating event could drain limited cognitive resources and therefore force speed daters to use heuristics in their speed-dating decisions.

Accurate perceivers and "easy" targets

Whether we meet a potential partner for a few minutes or hours or whether we observe her from afar, some of us may more accurately perceive a partner's personality characteristics, and some targets may be more easily understood. Ambady et al. (1995) explored whether characteristics of particular perceivers might make them more accurate judges, as well as whether characteristics of particular targets might make them "easier" targets to judge at zero acquaintance. Their results reveal an interesting dichotomy. Ambady et al. found that both men and women who tended to be more accurate perceivers also tended to be more reserved (i.e., less expressive and less sociable). Conversely, but intuitively, Ambady et al. found that participants who were more outgoing and sociable (and less shy) were more accurately judged by perceivers. A review by Human and Biesanz (2012) suggests that targets who are well adjusted and more expressive tend to be more accurately perceived as well. These authors also speculate that people from more interdependent cultures may be more difficult to perceive accurately.

Women also seem to be more accurate person perceivers than men (Ambady et al., 1995; Stillman & Maner, 2009). In Stillman and Maner's (2009) study involving judgments of targets' levels of sociosexuality, women tended to more accurately discern levels of sociosexuality from the video clips than did men. Moreover, Rule et al. (2011) found that women in the most fertile portion of their menstrual cycle were more accurate at perceiving the sexual orientation of men (but not women). Gay and lesbian perceivers also more accurately judge the sexual orientation of target persons than do their heterosexual peers (Ambady et al., 1999), suggesting that both being a woman and potential romantic interest in a target may enhance the accuracy with which we judge sexual orientation.

Not only are women more accurate in their impressions, but they tend to derive more positive impressions from their interactions as well. In Marcus and Lehman's research (2002), women were more likely to report positive impressions of their partners (regardless of whether the partners were men or women), especially on the traits of sociability and cheerfulness. This finding is consistent with previous research demonstrating the "female positivity effect" (Winquist, Mohr, & Kenny, 1998, p. 370). Winquist et al. reviewed several data sets as well as conducting their own research involving within-gender and across-gender interactions. These authors found that across a variety of personality factors, women rated others (regardless of target gender) more positively than did men. The authors also found that women who exhibited more traditional sex roles (e.g., nurturance) rated their partners most positively, while men who exhibited more traditional sex roles (e.g., assertiveness) rated their partners most negatively.

Recall that the research discussed in Chapter 1 suggests that older adults also tend to rate others more positively than their younger counterparts (Zebrowitz et al., 2013). Future research will be necessary to determine whether positivity and accuracy are linked in older adults as they are in women or whether older adults derive more positive impressions because they less accurately process negative cues (Zebrowitz et al. 2013).

Consistent with the finding that men tend to be less accurate in their personality impressions, men are also more likely to overestimate women's sexual interest. A variety of studies show this effect in different ways. For example, Levesque et al. (2006) found that in pairs of unacquainted undergraduates, men perceived their female partners' behavior as more sexual than women perceived their male partners' behavior. Stillman and Maner's (2009) research showed that men were more likely than women to rate female targets as sexually unrestricted. Perilloux et al. (2012) found that during a speed-dating study men were more likely to overestimate their female partners' levels of sexual interest in them.

Although Overall and Hammond's (2013) research involved long-term romantic partners, rather than unacquainted partners, their research revealed that a perceiver's depressive symptoms might increase the accuracy with which one perceives his/her own romantic partner. Heterosexual romantic relationship partners who were more depressed more accurately perceived their partners' commitment to their relationships as well as their partners' behavior (when their perceptions were compared with their partners' self-reports). Future research is necessary to determine whether individuals with depressive symptoms are more accurate person perceivers in zero acquaintance or short-term acquaintance paradigms.

Intriguingly, our own romantic involvement may diminish the accuracy with which we perceive others' romantic relationships. Aloni and Bernieri (2004) recruited undergraduates from the United States to review 60-second video clips of heterosexual couples discussing shared activities such as going to a restaurant or doing household chores together. The participants were asked to judge separately the love of each partner for the other. The participants' judgments were then compared with the couples' self-reported love scores for one another. Undergraduates who were "in love" themselves were more confident in their judgments about others' love relationships, but were actually less accurate in their judgments. The authors suggested that participants who were in love themselves might be biased by their own love experiences and therefore less accurate when attempting to discern love in others.

The above research suggests that the most accurate person perceivers tend to be women and tend to be less sociable. Romantic interest may also increase the accuracy with which we perceive sexual orientation but hinder the accuracy with which we perceive the loving relationships of others. When judging our own romantic partners, those of us who are more depressed may also be more accurate in our perceptions. Interestingly, the research reviewed below suggests that our accuracy in judging a particular target may be enhanced if we find the target to be particularly attractive.

Accurate perceivers and attractive targets

In some intriguing research investigating first impressions of physical attractiveness and personality, Lorenzo, Biesanz, and Human (2010) examined whether physically attractive individuals might be perceived more accurately.

What the research says

Lorenzo et al. (2010) asked unacquainted male and female undergraduate students to participate in three-minute interactions with each group member. After the interaction the participants indicated how physically attractive they found their partners and rated their partners' personalities as well. Supporting Dion et al.'s (1972) results (reviewed in Chapter 1), Lorenzo et al. found that targets who were considered more physically attractive were also viewed more positively. Additionally, targets who were perceived as more physically attractive were also viewed more accurately (compared with both the individual target's self-report as well as the group's consensus view of the target). Perhaps the most interesting results of this research are that perceivers who viewed a specific target person as particularly attractive were more accurate at detecting that target's unique personality characteristics. The authors interpreted these results to indicate that attractive people may be accurately understood more easily and that perceivers may pay more attention to targets who are particularly attractive. This is good news for those of you who are actively dating and mating, suggesting that you will more precisely comprehend the personalities of potential partners who are particularly physically pleasing to you.

Think critically

Lorenzo et al. (2010) found that participants who were perceived as more physically attractive were more accurately perceived. Do you think these same results might apply to vocal attractiveness? If you perceived a partner as having a very pleasing voice (in the absence of visual information), might you be able to more accurately discern her personality characteristics as well? Which personality characteristics might be most accurately deduced through vocal information?

The importance of certain traits in mate selection

Given that a potential mate's characteristics can have a large impact on our first impressions and that we can readily perceive whether a potential partner exhibits those desired traits, it is particularly important to explore which traits are generally valued in a potential partner. In the final portion of this chapter, we consider: how trait preferences are typically measured; the difference between self-reported and actual mate preferences; and, finally, we consider in detail the traits of intelligence, sense of humor, and a good personality. Although the research reviewed thus far suggests that physical characteristics drive our mate preferences, research by Buss, Shackelford, Kirkpatrick, and Larsen (2001) suggests that, when participants are considering selecting a marriage partner, personality traits – such as a "pleasing disposition," "dependable character," "emotional stability and maturity," "mutual attraction and love," and "education and intelligence" – are rated as more important than "good looks" (p. 497). What people look for in a potential partner may also differ depending upon whether they are looking for short-term or long-term partners (Stewart et al., 2000). For example, Stewart et al. found that both men and women valued physical attractiveness in short- and long-term partners, but women rated financial earning potential as more important for a long-term partner and men rated the desire for children as more important for a long-term partner. (see Chapter 4 for more information on men's and women's short-term versus long-term mating strategies.)

Measuring trait preferences

Historically, researchers have investigated mate preferences by asking participants to rank order the importance of certain traits in a potential mate (e.g., Buss, 1989; Buss et al., 2001; Lippa, 2007). Although we discuss mate preferences in more detail in Chapter 4, we introduce the topic now in order to highlight the fact that people do not always identify on paper the same "important" traits as those that appear to influence them during in-person interactions. As reviewed above, in mate selection research involving lists of traits, participants tend to say that traits such as intelligence, a good sense of humor, honesty, and kindness are important in a potential mate (Lippa, 2007). Furthermore, a common finding consistent with evolutionary theory is that men tend to value physical attractiveness more than women do, while women tend to value ambition or wealth more than men do (Buss, 1989; Buss et al., 2001).

What the research says

Lippa (2007) investigated trait preferences in a huge sample of over 200,000 men and women who responded to an online survey posted on the website of the British Broadcasting Corporation (BBC). Although the respondents came from a variety of different nations and geographical regions, the bulk of the respondents were from the United Kingdom, the United States, Canada, and Australia (which is not surprising given that the survey was presented in English). One of the interesting features of Lippa's research is that he was able to obtain a large sample of heterosexual as well as gay and lesbian participants. These participants ranked their top-three trait preferences from 23 different traits presented by the researchers, such as ambition, facial attractiveness, honesty, social status, teeth, and values. Lippa found that mate preferences tended to vary more by gender and less by sexual orientation. He did find, similar to Buss's (1989) earlier research cited above, that men valued good looks and facial attractiveness more than women did and that women valued ambition more than men did. He discovered that gay men expressed similar preferences to straight men, ranking traits such as good looks, facial attractiveness, and fitness as the most important traits in a potential partner. He also found that lesbians and straight women tended to value similar traits, such as honesty, humor, and kindness.

Differences between heterosexual and gay and lesbian participants were evident on rankings for characteristics such as religiosity, parenting ability, and desire for children. Gay men also valued appearance-related attributes more strongly, such as hands and teeth, while heterosexual men tended to value intelligence and domestic skills more than their gay counterparts. Furthermore, lesbians tended to emphasize the intelligence of partners more than their heterosexual counterparts, while straight women tended to value ambition and wealth more so than lesbians did. Lippa also reported differences related to culture: members of more individualistic cultures tended to value factors associated with personality and agreeableness more than members of collectivistic cultures, who were more likely to value responsibility and dependability in a partner.

Lippa (2007) reported some limitations regarding his research project, including important characteristics that were not presented on the list, such as "chastity, loves me, acceptable to parents and friends, shares my interests, and exciting sex partner" (p. 207). It is possible that people's preferences would change if respondents generated their own "top-three traits" or if other possibilities were presented by the researchers. Lippa also recognized that the sample may have been skewed toward "young, well-educated, and affluent" participants (p. 207). It is possible that respondents who did not have access to the Internet would report different preferences than those with Internet access, or that those who were intelligent themselves would also prefer a more intelligent mate (Lippa, 2007). Furthermore, some of the "traits" listed in Lippa's article were "hands" and "teeth." Different participants could have interpreted these attributes in different ways. For example, "hands" could be taken to mean nice hands, clean hands, large hands, skilled hands, or the presence versus absence of hands.

Think critically

In Lippa's (2007) research, as in most research measuring the importance of traits in mate selection, the traits are presented outside of the context of a particular mate. Therefore participants may have assumed that a certain minimum level of physical attractiveness had been met. Do you think the results would differ if participants were presented with photographs of attractive, moderately attractive, or unattractive individuals and asked to imagine that the stimulus persons were their potential mates? Which traits would you rate as the most important for an attractive mate? An unattractive mate?

Self-reported versus actual mate preferences

Using self-report to indicate which traits are important may not be the best way to measure mate preferences. Although we may believe that certain traits are essential in a mate, our real-life partners may or may not match our stated preferences. Fortunately, we have the good sense to downgrade our previously essential preferences if our mates do not possess those traits, and to upgrade the positive traits which our mates do possess (see Fletcher, Simpson, & Thomas, 2000, Chapter 6). Eastwick et al. (2011) conducted research showing that participants' trait preferences had a *large* impact on their ratings of a potential partner's profile *prior* to their face-to-face interaction; however, *after* their face-to-face interaction the trait preferences appeared to have *no* influence on partner ratings. Participants in this research project were romantically unattached undergraduate students from the United States. The researchers created, "for confederate interaction partners," fake profiles specifically designed to corre- spond with participants' self-reported three most desirable or least desirable traits. Before the interaction, participants thought they would prefer those partners whose profiles matched their top-three traits. During the in-person interactions, the confederates provided standardized, scripted remarks. After the in-person interaction, the participants reported equal romantic interest to their partners, regardless of whether their partners' profiles appeared to match the participants' ideal traits or not. These results suggest that traits may not be as important as in-person interactions in determining liking.

However, because the interaction partners were confederates who delivered standardized scripts, real-life partners who actually display behavioral evidence for the three most important traits might remain more positively evaluated following a face-to-face interaction. Indeed, another study reported in Eastwick et al.'s (2011) article suggests that for current relationship partners, matching of ideal preferences with a partner's actual characteristics on a variety of traits is associated with greater relationship satisfaction and commitment. Nevertheless, the findings reviewed above raise the interesting possibility that even traits we consider to be very important in a potential mate might not matter much after meeting a potential partner face-to-face.

Furthermore, research by Sprecher (1989) and Eastwick and Finkel (2008) questions the repeated finding that physical attractiveness is more important to men than to women. Sprecher conducted research involving trait preferences and experimental vignettes. Although men stated that physical attractiveness was a more important trait in a female partner, and although women stated that earning potential was a more important trait in a male partner, men and women responding to experimental scenarios were equally influenced by both physical attractiveness and earning potential. Similarly, Eastwick and Finkel (2008) recruited undergraduate men and women to participate in a study of romantic attraction. The students completed an online questionnaire evaluating their stated preferences for a partner who was physically attractive, personable, ambitious, trustworthy, friendly, and had good career prospects. Then the participants met in person for a series of four-minute speed dates. Consistent with Sprecher's findings, Eastwick and Finkel also found that men reported that the physical attractiveness of a potential partner would be more important to them than women did, and women reported that the future earning capacity of a potential partner would be more important to them than men did. However, the real-life preferences of the participants failed to show any gender differences on those variables.

Interestingly, in their discussion of their research Eastwick and Finkel (2008) distinguish between mate characteristics that are "necessities" as opposed to "luxuries" (p. 261). These authors suggest that essential traits ("necessities") may be those that show the strongest sex differences. For example, the authors state that "if women consider earning prospects to be a necessity in a mate, they may be especially unwilling (compared with men) to consider a potential partner who falls below some acceptable threshold on this trait" (p. 261). The authors suggest that all of the men attending the speed-dating event (because they were all university students) may have already achieved the necessary financial status threshold. The same suggestion can be applied to women's physical attractiveness, perhaps all (or most) of the women in the sample exceeded the necessary physical attractiveness threshold. As Eastwick and Finkel state, this interpretation is supported by research performed by Li et al. (2002) suggesting that, for men, physical attractiveness is a necessity and, for women, social status is a necessity. Furthermore, recent research by Li et al. (2013) shows that when a full range of physical attractiveness and status partners are presented, people's ratings and actual mate choices more closely correspond (see Chapter 4 for a more detailed explanation of this research).

The research performed by Sprecher (1989) and Eastwick and Finkel (2008) suggests the possibility that we may not be aware of what attracts us to others or which characteristics are most important to us. Additionally, the criticisms suggested by Sprecher and Eastwick and Finkel can apply to Lippa's (2007) findings. Although respondents may self-report that humor or kindness is more important than teeth, I would challenge those participants to consider their reactions to a potential partner with *really* bad teeth (or no teeth) who is extremely kind and funny.

A personal moment: Anecdotal evidence also suggests that self-report may not always be the best way to measure mate preferences. When I was a child I was very fond of watching the original *Dukes of Hazzard* television show. Even from a young age, I always preferred blond Bo (played by John Schneider) to brunette Luke (played by Tom Wopat). If you had asked me to describe my ideal partner, I would have told you that he should have blond hair and blue eyes. This preference continued into adulthood when I preferred Brad Pitt to George Clooney in the movie *Oceans 11*. However, in real life, I rarely dated men with blond hair; almost all of my serious relationships involved boyfriends with brown hair, and I married a partner with dark brown hair and brown eyes.

Intelligence

In Buss et al.'s (2001) research, as well as in Lippa's (2007) research, both men and women ranked intelligence as more important than good looks in a potential long-term partner. However, in the "real-life" speed-dating research reviewed above (e.g., Kurzban & Weeden, 2005) physical appearance had a stronger impact on attraction than intelligence. Whether physical attractiveness or personality is more important when forming an impression of a potential partner may depend in part upon how the pair meets and what kind of information is available during their first encounter. If physical attractiveness information is conveyed right away (either through a photograph or an in-person meeting) that information will probably have a large impact on one's impression of her potential partner.

For example, in Prokosch et al.'s (2009) research (see Chapter 2), women watched videos of men reading news headlines, answering researchers' questions, and throwing and catching a Frisbee. Although not pictured in the video, each man also completed an assessment of his verbal intelligence. Importantly, women's ratings of men's intelligence strongly positively correlated with men's scores on the verbal intelligence measure, showing that women accurately perceived men's intelligence through these videos. However, it seems that women's attraction to the men was more heavily influenced by physical attractiveness than intelligence. (Their ratings did indicate that intelligence was an important factor in the women's preferences for both long and short-term mates, but it was not as strong a predictor as physical attractiveness.) Conversely, if personality information is salient, and physical attractiveness information is absent (such as meeting via the telephone or email), physical attractiveness information may take a backseat to personality impressions even upon meeting later in person (e.g., McKenna et al., 2002).

Unfortunately for men, if intelligence is important to women, it might be better for men to try to display their intelligence via video (as in Prokosch et al.'s 2009 research) rather than in person. Research performed by Karremans et al. (2009) shows that men's cognitive performance is impaired when they interact with women, especially attractive women. In this research project, the samples consisted of heterosexual undergraduate men and women from the Netherlands. The participants engaged in a conversation with a member of the same sex or other sex about "neutral" (p. 1042) topics for seven minutes. Cognitive performance was assessed by the researchers both before and after the conversation via a demanding working memory or attention task. As stated above, men's performance on this task declined after interacting with a woman (relative to the same-sex condition), and declined even more so after interacting with an attractive woman. Interestingly, women's performance on the task was unchanged regardless of whether they interacted with a same-sex or other sex individual. The authors suggest that men of other ages be tested to see if the effects generalize beyond men of college age (who might be particularly preoccupied with mating opportunities).

Although intelligence in a potential mate is valued across cultures, Lippa's (2007) research suggests that the importance of intelligence in a mate may vary with the gender equality of a culture. In societies with more egalitarian gender roles, men valued intelligence in women more. The meaning of intelligence may also vary with culture. For example, Zebrowitz et al. (2012) reported that the "abstract concept of intelligence is less culturally relevant" for the Tsimané men who inhabit the Bolivian rainforest than is the more concrete knowledge of "plants, animals, weather, soils, and diseases" (p. 123).

Sense of humor

Research conducted by both Lippa (2007) and Buunk and Solano (2010) suggests that a good sense of humor is valued as one of the most important traits in a potential mate (however, it may be less important in Eastern cultures;

see Toro-Morn & Sprecher, 2003). In order to evaluate the effect of sense of humor on attractiveness, McGee and Shevlin (2009) asked each participant to read a short vignette concerning a potential partner. The authors varied the sense of humor of the target person depicted in the vignettes. In perhaps the least surprising results detailed in this book, these authors found that both men and women who were described as having a great sense of humor were perceived as more attractive than those who were described as having an average sense of humor or as having no sense of humor.

Although McGee and Shevlin did not find gender differences in the importance of a sense of humor, most other comparable research suggests that a sense of humor is more important to women than men. An analysis of personal ads placed in magazines showed that a good sense of humor was more likely to be requested by women than men (Smith et al., 1990). Likewise, Lippa's (2007) research revealed that women ranked humor as the most important trait in mate selection while men ranked this trait as third most important. Correspondingly, women find men to be more attractive when those men are also perceived as humorous (although women were not rated as more attractive by men when they were perceived to be humorous, Bressler & Balshine, 2006). Similarly, Lundy, Tan, and Cunningham (1998) also reported that attractive men were rated as more attractive when they were humorous. Although humor may not enhance attractiveness for women, Li et al. (2009) found that both men and women reported that they would be more likely to use humor if they were attracted to a new potential romantic partner.

The relationship between attractiveness and sense of humor may be bi-directional, with a better sense of humor enhancing perceptions of attractiveness and with attractiveness enhancing perceptions of humor. For example, in Li et al.'s (2009) research, both sexes found attractive targets to be funnier than less attractive targets.

In an ironic turnabout, although men and women state that both intelligence and a good sense of humor are important to them, in research assessing both characteristics humorous individuals tend to be perceived as *less* intelligent (Bressler & Balshine, 2006; Lundy et al.,1998). In fact, in Bressler and Balshine's research, women were likely to choose humorous individuals as dating partners even though those individuals were also perceived as less intelligent. These findings may reflect the type of humor used in these research projects. Bressler and Balshine admit that the humorous statements used in their study were not particularly sophisticated (a sample humorous statement was "Why do toasters have a setting on them that burns the toast to a horrible crisp that no one would eat?" p. 32). Lundy et al. employed self-deprecating humor which "directly involved putting the self down" (p. 316) possibly leading to more negative evaluations with regard to intelligence. In their discussion of their research, Lundy et al. offer the possibility that "non-deprecating humor could enhance perceptions of intelligence" and that "it may not be the case that everyone who tries to be funny is seen as stupid" (p. 322). Let us hold fast to that little glimmer of hope!

A great personality

Imagine you hear about a potential mate from a friend and, instead of describing him as attractive, she describes him as having a "great personality." What type of partner would you expect to encounter? In US culture, there is anecdotal evidence to suggest that having a "great personality" is considered code for "physically unattractive." Unfortunately, I have been unable to find any research addressing the impact of the "great personality" description on expectations for physical attractiveness (this dearth provides a great opportunity for future research).

A few interesting studies do show that positive personality information can enhance perceptions of attractiveness. For example, in Swami et al.'s (2010) research, positive personality information enhanced the range of body sizes that men perceived to be physically attractive. These researchers asked male university students to indicate which women's figure was most attractive to them as well as the largest and smallest figures they considered physically attractive. Although the personality information did not impact the *one* figure that men chose as most attractive, it did impact the *range* of figures they perceived as attractive. Men receiving vignettes containing positive personality information (e.g., friendly, energetic, cheerful) indicated the largest range of figures as physically attractive. Negative personality information (e.g., shy, quiet, private) was associated with the opposite effect: men who read vignettes containing negative personality information considered a narrower range of figures as physically attractive.

Similarly, learning that positive personality characteristics were associated with a target presented in a photograph also enhanced the physical attractiveness of that target (Lewandowski, Aron, & Gee, 2007). In this research undergraduates rated photographs of members of the other sex during a pre-test, then performed a mathematical distractor task, then re-rated the same photographs which were now accompanied with positive, negative, or no personality information. Lewandowski et al. found that attractiveness and dating desirability ratings increased when photos were presented along with positive traits, and decreased when photos were presented with negative traits. Ratings stayed stable for photographs presented without any personality information. In this project, interestingly, women's ratings were more strongly influenced by the personality information than men's ratings.

In accordance with the research discussed above, Kniffin and Wilson (2004) found that non-physical features, such as liking and respect, enhanced perceptions of physical attractiveness for well-known targets. These authors asked individuals to rate people they knew (either targets presented in their own high school yearbooks, rowing team-mates, or archaeology class members) for physical attractiveness, and also for how well each target was known, how much each target was liked, how much each target was respected, and how physically attractive each target was perceived to be. The ratings of the participants were compared with the physical attractiveness ratings of those who did not know the targets (or, in the case of the archaeology class, ratings made on the first day of class when the classmates did not know one another well). In all three studies the data revealed that individuals who liked and respected the targets also rated them as more physically attractive than strangers did. Conversely, at a speed-dating event, Kurzban and Weeden (2005) found that having an attractive personality enhanced men's dating desirability only slightly and did not enhance women's desirability at all. Perhaps the positive impact of personality requires more than a few minutes to influence one's perceptions of the physical attractiveness of a real-life target person.

A personal moment: During my first year in graduate school, I was invited by one of my classmates who played the piano in a rhythm and blues band to attend one of his performances. My best friend and I attended the gig and (because we were both single at the time) we lamented the fact that we did not find any of the band members to be particularly attractive (sorry, band guys, that was just my first impression). However, I ended up joining the band as a vocalist, and through the more than ten years that we played together, I came to find each of the band members as more attractive versus my impression during that first gig. Perhaps the fact that they were all nice guys, talented musicians, and intelligent men motivated my increased attraction toward them. (Hmmm … maybe I can introduce my friend Louise from Chapter 1 to one of the band members? Of course it will take her ten years to find them as attractive as I do!)

Correspondingly, positive personality information may influence attraction in other ways. Quist et al. (2012) examined the impact of the characteristic of faithfulness on attraction. These authors used computer software to form men's faces that looked more masculine or more feminine. They found that more masculine-looking men were perceived as more attractive than their more feminine-looking counterparts only when the men were described as being faithful to their girlfriends, but not when they were described as being unfaithful to their girlfriends. Similar results were obtained when the men were described as flirting with another woman while on a date with the participants.

Regardless of whether personality or physical attractiveness is more important when meeting a potential mate, the research reviewed above suggests that personality characteristics can strongly influence our impressions of a potential mate. Furthermore, there is also strong evidence that personality characteristics can enhance perceptions of physical attractiveness and our attraction to a potential partner.

Chapter summary

In this chapter we have reviewed research suggesting that we can form very accurate first impressions of target individuals even before actually meeting them in person (zero acquaintance). Increasing acquaintance can improve the accuracy with which we discern some personality traits, but not others. Women and more introverted individuals tend to be the most accurate person perceivers, but finding a person to be particularly attractive can help us to perceive that person more accurately. Research shows that although traits like intelligence, a good personality, and a good sense of humor are highly valued by individuals looking for a mate, traits that we think will be important in romantic partners are not always the traits that drive our decisions about those potential partners in real-life or experimental scenarios. We present our suggestions for future reading below.

Suggested reading

Bressler, E. R., & Balshine, S. (2006). The influence of humor on desirability. *Evolution and Human Behavior, 27*(1), 29–39. doi:10.1016/j.evolhumbehav.2005.06.002
    This article is interesting to read and contains some funny jokes (as well as some jokes that are not funny).
Eastwick, P. W., & Finkel, E. J. (2008). Sex differences in mate preferences revisited: Do people know what they initially desire in a romantic partner? *Journal of Personality and Social Psychology, 94*(2), 245–264. doi:10.1037/0022-3514.94.2.245
    This article is long, but I really like the fact that the authors critically examine the supposed importance of mate characteristics in real-life interactions.
Kurzban, R., & Weeden, J. (2005). HurryDate: Mate preferences in action. *Evolution and Human Behavior, 26*(3), 227–244. doi:10.1016/j.evolhumbehav.2004.08.012
    This article is rich with information about real-life mate preferences.
Li, N. P., Bailey, J., Kenrick, D. T., & Linsenmeier, J. W. (2002). The necessities and luxuries of mate preferences: Testing the tradeoffs. *Journal of Personality and Social Psychology, 82*(6), 947–955. doi:10.1037/0022-3514.82.6.947
    This article employs a different method for measuring mate preferences, the allocation of "mate dollars." It is really interesting to see how changing the way you measure a dependent variable can change your results.
Levesque, M. J., & Kenny, D. A. (1993). Accuracy of behavioral predictions at zero acquaintance: A social relations analysis. *Journal of Personality and Social Psychology, 65*(6), 1178–1187. doi:10.1037/0022-3514.65.6.1178
    This article employs some very sophisticated statistical analyses, but it is interesting to read about the accuracy of first impressions of personality and behavior.

Evolutionary Theory

4

Evolutionary theory

According to evolutionary theory, reproduction – passing along one's genes and ensuring the survival of one's offspring – is of primary importance for all species. Many of the mate preferences discussed in the previous chapters are compatible with evolutionary theory. For example, the preference for an attractive mate, a mate with a pleasing personality, and even our ability to form quick and accurate impressions are all consistent with the predictions of evolutionary theory. An attractive mate might enhance the possibility of bearing offspring and the possibility of the offspring surviving, or even the possibility that any resulting offspring would be more competitive as mates when they reach maturity. A pleasing personality might enhance the likelihood that a mate would be a good long-term partner as well as a good parent. The ability to form quick and accurate impressions may prevent us from pursuing relationships with unsuitable partners. In this chapter we review evolutionary theory as well as its predictions for mating strategies and desirable mate characteristics. We also highlight research addressing changes in women's mate choices across their menstrual cycles and whether men can detect women's fertility. Finally, we discuss gender differences in sexual jealousy and how suspected or real infidelity can lead to mate guarding and intimate-partner violence.

Evolutionary psychology

Evolutionary psychology is essentially the study of the Darwinian principles of natural and sexual selection applied to humans. Evolutionary psychologists such as myself (Cousins) believe that humans have been shaped over eons to fit our environment. This process shaped not only our physical features, but also our psychological features. Just like our bodies, our minds evolved to solve problems faced by our ancestors. The driving forces of evolution are natural and sexual selection.

In natural selection, traits that give an advantage to an individual allow those who bear the advantageous traits to out-reproduce individuals who do not carry the traits. For example, when I ask students what animal they think represents "survival of the fittest," they often mention lions. When I ask my students to explain, they often tell me: because lions are strong and fierce, they exemplify what it means to be "fit." While being strong and fierce may lead to passing on more genes, this is not always the case. It could be the healthiest, the smartest, the quickest, or the best looking individuals (female lions love a dark-colored mane) that out-reproduce their competitors. The most important task that an individual can perform, according to evolutionary theory, is to pass on one's genes – being "fit" in an evolutionary sense means having more surviving offspring than other individuals. So in my view, the species that exemplifies "survival of the fittest" is the lowly cockroach because it flourishes in virtually every part of the globe. I like to think that natural selection acts like a sieve (which you might use to sift the shells from the sand at the beach). What does this mean? It means that the beneficial traits remain and are passed on and the traits which are not beneficial get filtered out and are no longer a part of the population of traits. The remaining traits serve a specific adaptive purpose. As an aside, the term "survival of the fittest" was coined by Herbert Spencer, not Charles Darwin, and the term is generally not used by biologists because of the confusion I describe in this paragraph. Just remember that natural selection is the major driving force of evolution and that higher gene representation (e.g., leaving more descendants) is paramount.

Sexual selection includes two processes: one in which members of the same sex compete for access to mates (intrasexual selection), and another form of sexual selection which involves members of one sex preferring members of the other sex based on characteristics which indicate genetic quality. For instance, male frigate birds have a special throat sack which they can inflate. Usually this sack is empty and shriveled looking, but during the mating season, males blow it up to impress female frigate birds. Female frigate birds are choosy; they like a big, red sack. The bigger and redder it is, the sexier they find it. These males are preferred by females over males that do not seem able to inflate their sacks. Hormonal analysis of frigate birds shows that testosterone is higher in males that have fully inflated sacks (Chastel et al., 2005). Thus, females may prefer male frigate birds with the best genetic quality by choosing those with the biggest and reddest throat sacks. In this way the frigate birds exhibit both forms of sexual selection, with males competing with one another for access to females as well as the females preferring a trait in the other sex which indicates genetic quality. Both types of sexual selection influence human mating strategies as well.

Mating strategies

A media moment: An American reality television show called *Sister Wives* showcases a polygynous family. Kody, the husband, has four wives and the series chronicles the trials and tribulations of daily life for Kody and his family as he scurries between wives and struggles to balance time with his 17 children. Would you want to be a wife in a plural marriage? A husband with multiple wives? A large number of cultures allow polygynous marriages, in which a man can marry more than one woman. Do you think that polygynous marriages are evolutionarily advantageous? What about polyandrous marriages, in which a woman can marry more than one man?

Marriage is a common mating system across cultures. In most Western cultures, such as in the United Kingdom and Australia, monogamous marriage is the norm. However, around the globe, approximately 80 percent of cultures allow polygynous marriages (in which one man has multiple wives). Although this is a common marriage system across cultures, most men within those cultures marry monogamously. Why? Only men with high status can afford to have more than one wife (Schmitt, 2005). A handful of cultures are polyandrous, but this mating system is exceedingly rare in humans and is becoming ever rarer. Less than 1 percent of cultures are polyandrous. Polyandry emerges in places where making a living from the land is difficult. In harsh conditions where land cannot be divided and still support a family, women may marry multiple men, often brothers.

Sex differences in mating strategies

Below are two personal ads (adapted by the author from real personal ads). Can you guess which ad was posted by a woman and which one was posted by a man? (LTR stands for long-term relationship.)

> I have just ended a serious LTR and I am not into the local dating scene. I have a great career, a nice home, and a large boat. I'm hoping to meet someone special who loves traveling. Although I can afford to travel anywhere, I prefer to spend time at home. I would like to bring a very attractive individual here to enjoy a few days of sailing or just relaxing on the beach. I will pay for everything. You must have a great smile and a sexy figure. I am fit, funny, and successful. If you are interested please send a recent picture.

> I am a witty, passionate, adventurer. I am 5'8", blond, good body, well-read and well-informed. I love to travel and have traveled for work, but I would rather travel with someone special. I am independent but would like to share life's ups and downs with someone. I find confidence and a good career sexy. I am looking for a LTR, so please be respectful in your responses.

If you guessed that the first personal ad was placed by a man you were correct. Which clues led you to your conclusion?

Both men and women prefer kind and honest partners and put these traits toward the top of their lists of preferred qualities in a potential mate (Buss & Barnes, 1986; see Chapter 3 for a more extended discussion of preferences for non-physical traits). However, for other characteristics, men's and women's preferences differ. Evidence indicates that around the globe, men are more interested than women in short-term sexual relationships and having many sex partners. Men tend to compete more for access to mates and are less choosy than women about the qualities of a potential partner. So what is it that women want? With no constraints, women want it all: tall, good looking, sexy, kind, funny, intelligent, wealthy, and powerful. Across 37 cultures Buss (1989) found that women seek mates who have resources or the potential to acquire them (Note: In Spain this difference was not significant, but it was in the expected direction; this was the only country that did not show a statistically significant difference). Women rate resources as being a much more important quality than men do, although the degree of preference for resources does vary across cultures. South American and African women place more emphasis on a partner's resources than do women from Western Europe, including the United Kingdom. Men, on the other hand, rate physical attractiveness as being more important than do women. This is not true just in Western cultures, either. It is true in places as diverse as Nigeria, Japan, Venezuela, New Zealand, and Canada, among others (Buss, 1989).

Now that we have established that sex differences exist, why are some traits more important for men than for women (and vice versa)? Parental investment theory handily explains these findings. According to this theory, sex differences in the minimum level of parental investment drive sex differences in mate choice. The sex that is more investing in offspring is choosier about selecting a mate, and the sex that is less investing in offspring competes more for access to mates (Trivers, 1972). Think about this sex difference for a moment: Which sex necessarily has to invest more time in order to produce an offspring? Men or women? Women have a higher minimum investment, with the absolute minimum investment in offspring being nine months. For men, the minimum level of investment may be as short as a couple of minutes.

In addition to the time it takes for women to gestate, during the course of an average pregnancy, women must allot more than 30,000 calories to her growing fetus in addition to the calories she needs for her own normal bodily maintenance activities. While extra calories are easy to come by in our modern society (with 24-hour grocery stores and freezers that can store months' worth of food for a family), during the course of human evolution, those calories may have been much more difficult to obtain. This heavy load on women meant they had to be choosy about mating. If they were going to invest so much time and energy in an offspring, they needed to choose the best man with whom to mate. Keep in mind that most women continue their heavy investment in their children beyond the minimum, doing much of the child care as well as breast feeding their children, frequently for two or more years. In fact, one researcher assessed age at weaning in 30 hunter-gatherer groups and found that the average

age at weaning is 30.9 months, which means that women spend on average about 2.5 years breastfeeding one child (Kelly, 1995). Breastfeeding probably posed an additional nutritional burden of well over 100,000 calories.

These energetic costs borne only by women resulted in their being much choosier in a mate than are men, and much less interested in short-term, mainly sexual relationships, such as one-night stands. Women needed an investing partner, one willing and able to provide for them as well as for any offspring (over eons, that mainly meant men who could provide meat through hunting). Women across a variety of cultures rarely hunt for food, and they provide for their families mainly by foraging, although women may sometimes collect insects, fish, or small mammals. Women in hunter-gatherer societies vary in the percent of calories they contribute to their families' diets, but among the Ache (a hunter-gatherer tribe from Paraguay), women contributed about 13 percent of the calories (Hill & Hurtado, 1996) while !Kung women (from the Kalahari Desert in Africa) contributed much more to their families' daily calories, frequently contributing 60–80 percent of the calories (Lee, 2003). Even when women provided a large percentage of the total calories, men were important in supplying calories and nutrients unique to animal products.

One reason women rarely hunt is that it entails risk that they simply could not take because of their importance in raising young offspring (Campbell, 2005). In addition, hunting would be a difficult endeavor for a woman of reproductive age, who may have to carry one or more children plus hunting gear. Women simply could not move fast enough to hunt as effectively as men. I frequently show my students a picture of a !Kung San woman from southern Africa carrying an infant in a sling, an older child on her shoulders and all the gear she needs to forage for the day. The image is striking in the degree of difficulty foraging entails with such small children; hunting would be nearly impossible. !Kung San women frequently travel eight or ten miles searching for plant-based foods (Draper, 1975).

It is clear why women prefer men with resources, now we need to address why men prefer young and attractive women. It is a given that men do not become pregnant, so they are not obligated to invest in their offspring the way women must in order to become parents. This frees men to mate with many women (and possibly to impregnate all of them). If they can swing it (pun intended), it pays men to have as many short-term matings with fertile women as possible. This is the way in which men can increase their reproductive success. Of course, most men cannot attract that many mates (and some are lucky just to get one mate). For those men who were able to attract many women, their reproductive success hinged on mating with as many fertile women as possible. There are two constraints here: The first is that women are only fertile for a short window of time each month (we address this issue further below) and the second is that once women reach menopause, they are no longer capable of having children. This evolutionary pressure eventually led men to prefer traits in their partners which indicate fertility.

Youth is a good indicator of fertility, since things like wrinkles, gray hair, and sagging skin are associated with older, menopausal women. Other indicators of fertility are associated with health. For example, acne in women is frequently related to a condition called polycystic ovary syndrome, which is known to reduce women's fertility (Mayoclinic.com). Other skin conditions may make a person less attractive and indicate a diseased state. It was important to men to locate fertile women, so preferring youth and markers of physical attractiveness makes sense in light of what they indicate about the health and fertility status of women (see Chapter 1 for a discussion of physical attractiveness).

Although men, more than women, are interested in short-term relationships, while women, more than men, are interested in long-term relationships, both short-term and long-term relationships are important for both sexes. Buss and Schmitt (1993) elucidate the importance of both types of relationships in a paper about "sexual strategies theory." According to this theory, men may seek long-term relationships under specific circumstances, such as a way to form alliances with another family or to overcome the fact that women's fertility status is "concealed" (more on this later in the chapter). When seeking long-term mates, men's preferences shift to favor women with higher reproductive value. Women may seek short-term relationships as a way to increase genetic quality of their potential offspring (see the section below on women's shifts in desire across the menstrual cycle). Evolutionary theory can explain the variety of choices people make about the type of mate they desire – and how long they want to keep that mate.

Assessing personal ads and speed dating through an evolutionary lens

Much of the research on mate choice involves asking people to make ratings of what they consider to be important in a mate. While this is an approach that readily yields results, there is always a degree of uncertainty about whether people place the same degree of importance on those same characteristics when making real decisions about a potential mate (see Chapter 3). For this reason, researchers face a quandary: How do they assess these same choices in a real context? In the past couple of decades, researchers have assessed a variety of real dating contexts, including personal ads, online-dating websites, and speed dating.

One of the first evolutionary approaches to assess real-world mate choice involved a study of newspaper personal ads. Personal ads are great for studying mate choice because researchers can assess the content of ads posted by real people and determine which characteristics individuals seek in a mate, the type of relationship they are seeking, as well as what are some of the characteristics the individual includes to describe his or her own qualities. In his study of personal ads, Wiederman (1993) found that men sought physically attractive partners (such as in the man's personal ad presented above). This preference included an interest in a pretty face as well as a good body. Women, meanwhile, sought partners who were financially successful or had traits that might lead to financial success; they also sought honesty in a mate. With regard to the traits people used to describe themselves, men and woman also differed. Men described themselves in terms of their financial success and their honesty, while women described their physical attributes (as in the woman's personal ad displayed above), including a good body. This study is important in supporting the ideas of evolutionary psychologists using a sample of individuals who were actually seeking a mate. One of the downsides of this study is that Wiederman was unable to assess which ads were most successful. Evolutionary psychologists expect that men offering financial resources and women offering physical attractiveness will be most valued in the mating market and most able to secure the type of mate they seek. (Chapter 1 explores some other interesting research using personal ads to assess mate preferences for height and physical attractiveness.) More recent research using speed dating overcomes this limitation and assesses not only what people sought in a mate but the actual dating outcomes.

Speed-dating events are held in many locations around the world, and researchers have become involved in some or even created their own events in order to assess real-world mate choice. At a typical speed-date event, individuals get about five minutes to speak with another individual. After the five minutes elapse, each individual makes a rating of their "date," stating whether they are willing to keep in touch. Typically, individuals have 10–15 dates at a speed-dating event. (See Chapter 3 for a further discussion of speed dating.)

Eastwick and Finkel (2008) set up a speed-dating event at their university. Before the event, they had participants self-report the importance of various characteristics in a potential mate. (This portion of the research is similar to the traditional research on mate choice.) Then, they had individuals participate in a speed-dating event. At the end of the event, the researchers were able to assess actual mate choice by assessing which individuals said "yes" to contact in the future. As discussed in Chapter 3, the self-report results replicated the findings of many other researchers: men seek physical attractiveness and women seek resources – or traits that indicate the ability to acquire resources – in a potential mate. Although the self-report part of the study supported evolutionary predictions, actual mate choice at the speed-dating event was not predicted by the self-reported partner preferences, as would be expected if people possessed and acted on an evolved psychology. Ratings of physical attractiveness significantly predicted both men's and women's reports that they wanted more contact with the date in the future. Again, an evolutionary hypothesis would not predict such a result. This result puts a stick in the wheel of an evolutionary explanation. Or does it? Is it possible that we do not possess evolved desires that predict mate choice, as is seen in every other species?

Since Eastwick and Finkel's (2008) study seems to indicate that evolved preferences do not play a role in actual mate choice during speed-dating events, Li et al. (2013) decided to test the mate-preference priority model, which is the idea that while many traits are important to both men and women, individuals benefit from "screening out" mates who lack essential criteria – those criteria most tied to reproductive success. The process of screening for these essential traits must happen very early in the mate-selection process, before people invest time and resources in a relationship that will likely fail. According to this model, men and women share many similarities in preferences for an ideal partner and for short-term, sexual relationships, but for actual long-term relationships, men and women diverge in which traits they emphasize as being "necessities." Women must possess a minimum level of physical attractiveness; men must exceed a minimum level of resources and status (which is related to resource acquisition). Where men and women differ in mate choice is best seen when there are individuals who *lack* essential traits. Only when these individuals are included do sex differences emerge. Li et al. (2013) set up a number of situations, including online messaging and speed dating, in which the status and physical attractiveness of a potential partner reflected low, medium, and high levels of those traits as seen in the general population. This last bit is important because using just college students or professionals means that, in many cases, the minimum levels of status and attractiveness considered necessary are present. When the researchers included individuals who possessed low levels of physical attractiveness and status, sex differences emerged: men placed more emphasis on physical attractiveness, and women placed greater emphasis on status. Only by making the research more reflective of the variability seen in the population can we establish that men and women do indeed differ in their mate preferences in ways predicted by evolutionary psychology.

Mate choice tradeoffs

So far we have talked about relatively straightforward preferences for features of an attractive mate. Certain characteristics are preferred consistently by one sex more than the other, at least when researchers average across different individuals within one sex or the other. However, most of these studies assessed single preferences and did not force people to choose one trait over another or to manipulate important qualities in the participants. In the real world, people face tradeoffs in the "mating market." The way mate choice works in the real world can be compared to economics: there is a finite pool of potential mates who vary on a number of important qualities (just like you have a finite amount of money and sometimes might have to decide whether to buy new shoes or to pay your telephone bill). Additionally, one's own qualities influence mate choice. People tend to match their mates on many characteristics; this is called assortative mating. Tall people tend to mate with other tall individuals. Intelligent individuals tend to mate with other intelligent individuals. However, men with more money may have access to women who are highly attractive (even in comparison to a man's own attractiveness). Some researchers have tried to manipulate characteristics of individuals in a mating market to observe the effect on mate choice.

What the research says

Yong and Li (2012), attempted to manipulate resource availability to investigate its effect on mating standards. To do this, they had a sample of 153 students, both men and women, exposed to one of three conditions. In the control condition, participants were exposed to 52 blank strips of paper, the approximate size of paper money. A second group was exposed to a small amount of money, 52 Singaporean $2 bills. A third group was exposed to a large amount of money, 52 Singaporean $50 bills. Consistent with the predictions of evolutionary theory women, overall, had higher expectations for a mate than men did, and these standards did not differ with the conditions women were exposed to. In other words, women in the control group, the small money group, and the large money group all had similar requirements for a mate. For men, the findings differed depending upon the resource condition. Men had the highest mating standards when they were exposed to the condition in which there was a large amount of money. When the researchers teased out men's preferences by condition, they found that men's standards for physical attractiveness in a potential mate were higher when they were exposed to the larger amount of money compared to when they were exposed to either the control or the small amount of money. Their other standards did not change across the different conditions. This study is important because it shows that while sex differences exist in mate choice, mating strategies may shift in response to environmental stimuli. Specifically here, men's mating strategy shifted in response to money. The bottom line: if you are a man and have money, seek out the most attractive mate possible. If you do not have money, your standards should remain lower – because any mate is better than none at all.

Think critically

In what other ways could researchers test the idea that men's and women's mating strategies alter depending on environmental changes? Are there manipulations that could be made which might alter women's mating preferences but not men's?

Changing desires across the menstrual cycle

If you are a woman, think about your last menstrual cycle. Did you know when you were ovulating? Even though most women do not know when they are about to ovulate, women do, in fact, display different behaviors and attitudes when they are fertile.

As reviewed earlier, research in evolutionary psychology strongly supports the idea that women prefer signs of men's dominance and earning power (or potential earning power) when seeking a mate, especially a long-term mate. The real world is much more complex, however. In the 1990s an interesting line of research emerged assessing how women's mate choices change across the menstrual cycle. Researchers, influenced by evolutionary biology and the knowledge that many female animals show signs of estrous (a distinct period of time when the female is fertile and interested in mating), started to assess whether humans also showed shifts in their preference for a mate in fertile and non-fertile periods of a single menstrual cycle.

Perrett et al. (1998) were initially interested in whether women preferred men with more masculine faces. These researchers manipulated images of men, making one image more masculine than the original face and making another image that was more feminine than the original face. They found that overall women preferred both Caucasian and Japanese men with *feminized* faces (as opposed to average or masculinized faces). To the researchers, this result was surprising. First, anecdotal evidence suggested that women like masculine faces. Secondly, theoretically women were expected to like masculine faces because they were a cue of high testosterone levels and good genetic quality. I saw this paper presented at the Human Behavior and Evolution Society Conference in 1998. My graduate advisor at the time (Steve Gangestad) spoke with the researchers at length and suggested that they take into account whether the women were fertile at the time of the ratings. He thought that fertile women would prefer masculinized male faces. And he was right. These same researchers went back to Scotland and Japan to collect more data and analyze it, this time taking into account women's fertility status. When they accounted for fertility status, their research showed that women preferred more masculine faces when they were fertile compared to the rest of their menstrual cycle, but only when women rated the faces as being attractive for a short-term relationship. Women always preferred the more feminized faces for long-term relationships (Penton-Voak et al., 1999). (See Chapter 1 for further discussion of related research.)

Around the same time, Gangestad was becoming interested in differences in women's preferences across the menstrual cycle. Gangestad wanted to know if women preferred men with good genetic quality (Gangestad et al., 1994), but how could these researchers assess the genetic quality of an individual during that person's lifetime. Research by biologists showed that females of a variety of species preferred physically symmetrical males (e.g., Møller, 1992). These males were considered to possess good genetic quality, or "good genes," and we know from some of these studies that symmetrical males have more offspring (the direct measure of genetic quality) than do less symmetrical males (e.g., Swaddle, 1996). Researchers could measure the symmetry of bilateral traits (traits that appear on both sides of the body, such as eyes) and therefore they could assess, indirectly, the genetic quality of different people. As discussed in Chapter 1, in a perfect world, certain traits appear on both sides of our bodies and should be completely symmetrical; our left and right sides should be exactly the same. During development, a variety of circumstances can affect the development of those bilateral traits. Individuals who can withstand developmental disruptions – such as exposure to toxins, illness, or not having enough food – and still be symmetrical have good genetic quality. Thornhill and Gangestad (1999) began to wonder if the same process occurred in people and whether women's preference for genetic quality increased when they were fertile.

What the research says

Thornhill and Gangestad (1999) decided to test the idea that women preferred symmetry when they were fertile. Male and female participants were asked to wear a t-shirt for two nights. They were given a "blank" t-shirt to wear to bed at night. This t-shirt was unscented. In addition, the men in the study could not smoke, wear cologne or other scented products, and could not eat spicy food. (This last requirement must have been the most difficult because the research took place in New Mexico, where the state question is "Red or Green?" meaning do you prefer to eat red chiles or green chiles, both of which are quite spicy.) The men brought their t-shirts into the lab and placed them in plastic bags. Then women were brought into the lab and asked to smell each t-shirt and rate the t-shirt on two dimensions: how sexy does it smell (unsexy to sexy) and how pleasant does the t-shirt smell (unpleasant to pleasant). Men did the same thing for t-shirts worn by women. In addition to rating the t-shirts, normally ovulating women (those not on any form of hormonal contraceptive and premenopausal) were asked a few questions about their menstrual cycle to assess their fertility status. What Thornhill and Gangestad found was that men had no preference for the scent of symmetrical women over women who were less symmetrical. For women's rating of men, the story differed: high-fertility women preferred the scent of symmetrical men. However, low-fertility women actually disliked the scent of these same men. So, what smelled most attractive varied depending on women's menstrual cycles. How did the researchers explain these findings? Women may use a mixed mating strategy: mate with a kind and understanding long-term mate and seek out a man with high genetic quality for an extra pair copulation (a short-term sexual relationship). In this way, the long-term mate is a nice guy who sticks around to help raise any offspring, but the woman can also benefit by having offspring fathered by a man with high genetic quality.

The biggest strength of this research is that no other perspective outside of evolutionary psychology predicted, nor could explain, these findings. One of the limitations of this research is that the researchers did not directly test women's fertility status through blood tests or ovulation-prediction kits. However, this is only a drawback in that the results should be stronger without the "noise" of women who were not actually in the fertile window or who were anovulatory but seemed like they were high fertility. (See Chapter 1 for more discussion of the importance of scent in identifying a mate.)

Think critically

Why do you think that women, but not men, preferred the scent of symmetrical mates? What other traits do you think might be preferred by high-fertility women but not low-fertility women? Why?

Since this research was first published, a long line of research has shown that when women are fertile they behave and feel differently on dimensions related to mate choice. Women prefer to wear more provocative clothing when they are fertile (as assessed by a drawing of what they would wear to a social event), possibly as a way to out-compete other women for access to men (intrasexual competition, see Durante et al., 2008). A woman's gait is also more provocative when she is fertile; when raters saw fertile women walking, they rated the walking as sexier than women who were not fertile (Guéguen, 2012). Women even avoid their fathers when they are fertile, which may be a way to decrease the chance of inbreeding – or more likely – to avoid their father's control over their choice of a mate (Lieberman et al., 2011).

Can men spot fertile women?

Men, can you detect when your girlfriend/spouse is about to ovulate? Most likely you are shaking your head and answering "no" right now. However, researchers began to question whether men could detect subtle signs of fertility status in women. Other male animals can clearly detect fertility in mates, so why not humans?

There is an interesting and growing body of literature to support the idea that men do, in fact, detect cues of women's fertility status. What this literature indicates is that women's fertility status is not as concealed as researchers used to think. Men show preferences for women who are near ovulation and they may mate guard fertile partners more than partners in the non-fertile phase of the menstrual cycle (Gangestad et al., 2002). In research on women's movement, including gait and dancing, men rated high-fertility women's movements as more attractive (Fink et al., 2012) and sexier (Guéguen, 2012). Men even have an endocrine response to fertile women. After male subjects smelled t-shirts worn by high- and low-fertility women, researchers measured their testosterone levels. The findings were that, compared to men who rated the t-shirts of low-fertility women, men who smelled t-shirts worn by high-fertility women had higher testosterone levels (Miller & Maner, 2010). Researchers believe these results could indicate that men who smell a fertile woman will be more likely to behave in ways that enhance their chances of mating with her. Potentially, men with higher testosterone may act more dominant and be more competitive toward other men. Right now it is unclear whether this change in testosterone gives them a competitive edge against other men or whether it makes them more attractive to women.

What the research says

Geoffrey Miller et al. (2007) assessed lap dancers' earnings across the menstrual cycle. These dancers perform topless (but wear bottoms) and during lap dances the patron sits in a chair and the dancer sits on the man's lap. These dances tend to be very intimate and the dancers typically receive tips from their patrons. In the current study, lap dancers were recruited through emails sent to industry contacts, advertisements in newspapers, and flyers posted near clubs. Researchers asked 18 lap dancers to record their earnings, mood, hours worked, and menstrual cycle information every night for 60 days. Seven participants were using hormonal contraceptives and 11 were not using any form of hormonal contraceptive. This is important because it is well documented that use of hormonal contraceptives affects women's attitudes and behaviors. The researchers then broke down each woman's cycle into three phases: days 1–5 were the menstrual phase, when women have their period, days 9–15 were the fertile phase and days 18–28 were the luteal phase. In this way, there are two non-fertile phases (menstrual and luteal), and the researchers could assess whether menstruation had a negative effect on wages and whether this phase differed from the luteal phase. Miller and his colleagues also assessed whether the hours that were worked differed across the three phases of the menstrual cycle (they did not). This is important to assess, because if women worked more hours when they were fertile, they may have made more money because of the number of additional hours worked.

As the authors predicted, women who were normally ovulating (i.e., not on any form of hormonal contraceptive) earned the same amount of money as women who were on hormonal contraceptives, but only during the menstrual and luteal phases of their cycles. During the fertile phase, women who were normally ovulating made significantly more money during lap dances than women who used hormonal contraceptives. Pill (hormonal contraceptive) users did not show a mid-cycle peak in the amount of money they earned. The amount of money women earned during the fertile phase when using hormonal contraceptives was U.S. $193 per shift while normally ovulating women made U.S. $276 per shift.

What makes this research incredibly interesting is the fact that men are somehow picking up on women's fertility status. To those of us studying these issues, this is fascinating because women's fertility status had been considered to be "concealed," unlike the very obvious estrous seen in other animals (e.g., female cats howl and female chimps display sexual swellings which very obviously indicate their fertility status). What this difference in earning across the cycle indicates is that men pick up on cues of women's fertility status and that they prefer (via a monetary tip) women who are most fertile (i.e., the ones in the fertile phase who are not on hormonal contraceptives). Women may "leak" cues of fertility status through the intimacy of the lap dance; they may smell better, have a smaller waist to hip ratio or have more symmetrical breasts. Some of the limitations of this study are that women self-reported their earnings. This could be problematic if women in different phases of their cycle systematically over- or under-report their earnings. In addition, the researchers did not determine which things changed the monetary tips a woman received. These limitations indicate that more research is necessary to fully understand this phenomenon.

Think critically

What are some other limitations of Miller et al.'s (2007) methodology? What are the cues that men might use to detect whether a lap dancer is fertile?

Sexual jealousy

A personal moment: In college a friend of mine, Shelly, started dating a new guy. He was very good looking and my friend worried that he would cheat on her. In an attempt to figure out if he was interested in someone else, my friend started stalking him, walking by his classroom to make sure he was in class where he told her he was headed (he was telling the truth) and trying to figure out if he was talking to other women. Of course, this level of jealousy was detrimental to her relationship, which did not last long. So, if jealousy can prematurely ruin a relationship, is there any benefit to feeling jealous?

What the research says

In a now classic study, Buss et al. (1992) asked participants which situation would be more distressing: if their partner formed a "deep emotional attachment" to someone else or if their partner enjoyed "passionate sexual intercourse" with someone else (p. 252).

If you were a participant in their research, what would you answer? What do you think someone of the other sex would answer? What Buss et al. (1992) found has been a source of interest for researchers and non-researchers alike. Men were more upset by the thought of their partner having sex with someone else (60 percent of them) and women were more upset thinking about their partner falling in love with someone else (83 percent of them). Participants who reported more jealousy in response to questions about sexual versus emotional infidelity also showed signs of increased physiological distress in the same pattern. Men showed significantly more electrodermal activity and electromyographic activity in their corrugator supercilii muscle (in other words, they furrowed their brows more) during the sexual infidelity scenario, supporting the notion that they had greater physiological distress when thinking about sexual infidelity. Women showed the opposite pattern: they had greater physiological responses to the emotional infidelity scenario.

Think critically

Buss et al. (1992) showed that men and women have emotional and physical responses to jealousy, and that what is most upsetting is different for men and women. Other people have noted that emotions often come with physiological responses. What type of physical reaction do you have when you are afraid? Is it different than when you are happy? What hypothesis could you make about the underlying function of different emotions such as disgust, fear, and love?

The reasoning for Buss et al.'s (1992) findings is as follows: because ancestral men were not able to be completely assured of their paternity (because they cannot bear children themselves), they had to find ways to keep their partners from becoming impregnated by another man. Raising someone else's child would have been a waste of a man's precious time and resources. To really understand why this is a problem we should think about a time when people often lived on the edge of hunger. People had to hunt and gather all the food they needed; there was no grocery store to go to when food ran out and no refrigerator to preserve food for long periods of time. Raising someone else's child diverted scarce resources away from a man's own offspring and negatively impacted his reproductive success. That is, a guy who raised another man's child had fewer surviving and reproducing biologically related children. If jealousy can preempt a partner's potential infidelity, at least some of the time – or if jealousy can prompt an individual to leave an unfaithful partner – then the benefits of jealousy outweigh the costs of jealousy (for example, an angry partner).

A media moment: One of the songs I like to listen to when I am driving is a song by The Killers called "Mr. Brightside" (The lyrics can be found here: http://www.metrolyrics. com/mr-brightside-lyrics-the-killers.html). This song addresses both the emotional and physical response to sexual infidelity, and every time I hear it I think about Buss et al.'s (1992) research on jealousy (I admit to being a bit geeky about research). The song addresses the emotional response that occurs when the songwriter suspects his girl-friend of cheating on him. The songwriter, Brandon Flowers, wrote this song after finding out that his girlfriend did in fact cheat on him. This song reached number 10 on both the US Billboard Top 100 chart and the UK Singles. The song also won accolades in the music industry. In the United States, *Rolling Stone* magazine listed it as one of the top 100 songs of the decade and in the United Kingdom Absolute Radio did the same. I think the song resonates with people because many of us have experienced these very emotions brought about by an actual or suspected infidelity.

We have spent a lot of time discussing the underlying reason why men feel jealous about sexual infidelity, but why are women jealous? It makes sense that men try to protect their paternity because (barring locking up their part-ners) men can never be certain that they are the true biological father of any offspring; but what about women? We all know that women are also jealous in romantic relationships, but they are always certain any offspring are theirs and not another woman's child. And, like my friend, Shelly, a woman risks losing a good guy if she is too jealous. So what is the point of jealousy in women?

Again think about a time when people had to hunt and gather all the food they needed to consume. If a woman's partner strayed and diverted at least some resources to his dalliance partner, then the woman risked losing precious resources to her rival (such as that nice hunk of water buffalo meat). Funneling resources to another woman may increase the *man's* reproductive success, but it would certainly lower that of his wife. This prompts the question: Why are women more upset by circumstances in which their partners are clearly falling in love with their rivals? A man who solely has sex with another woman may not channel any resources to her, but if he "falls for" her then he will be more likely to share his water buffalo meat with her. So, women were more likely to lose access to precious resources if their partners fell in love with other women (rather than just having sex with them). In women, jealousy over a partner's emotional infidelity – or the possibility of it – helped to protect her and her children from having resources diverted to another woman. When male invest-ment is necessary in order to raise offspring, as in humans, the costs to females of lost resources from a mate can be high (i.e., the death of her children is an extreme but possible outcome).

Cross-cultural differences in jealousy

These sex differences in jealousy are robust across cultures (Buunk et al., 1996; Burchell & Ward, 2011). In a study comparing sex differences in the United States, Germany, and the Netherlands, researchers found that in all three cultures men were more distressed when thinking about their partner having sex with someone else than they were by the thought of her falling in love with someone else. Buunk et al.'s (1996) results from the United States replicated Buss et al.'s results (1992): about 60 percent of men stated that thinking of their partner enjoying passionate sex with another man was more upsetting than their partner forming a deep emotional attachment to another man. The number dips to about 25 percent in Germany. Men from the Netherlands fall between these figures and about 50 percent of them stated that sexual infidelity would be more distressing than emotional infidelity. The results for women across the three cultures were more consistent: 18 percent of American women, 16 percent of German women, and 28 percent of Dutch women felt that sexual infidelity was more upsetting than emotional infidelity (Buunk et al., 1996).

Overall, this study suggests that men and women in all three cultures differed in the same ways; men, more than women, found that sexual infidelity was more upsetting than emotional infidelity. However, the three cultures differed in the *magnitude* of this sex difference in attitude toward sexual infidelity. Women's bias toward finding emotional infidelity more upsetting than sexual infidelity is consistent across cultures, whereas men's views on which is more upsetting vary more from culture to culture. The difference between German and American men in the percent of men indicating that sexual jealousy is more upsetting than emotional jealousy was 33 percent. That is, a third fewer German men reported that sexual infidelity was more distressing than emotional infidelity when compared with their American counterparts (Buunk et al., 1996).

Does this difference across cultures mean that evolution has not contributed to sex differences in response to sexual and emotional infidelity? The short answer is "no." The longer answer is that adaptations, those traits that evolved to solve specific problems in past environments, are often expressed differently in different environments. This is referred to as being a *facultative trait* or one that is contingent on environmental circumstances. It might be easier to understand facultative traits by understanding how a callus is formed. We are genetically programmed to form calluses, but only in response to repeated friction between our skin and another object. The friction between our skin and another object is the environmental input. At birth, babies' feet are smooth and soft. When my children were infants I loved to rub the soles of their feet and feel how soft they were. Now that my twins are six and run barefoot all day long (I can barely get them to wear shoes when there is snow on the ground), they have substantial calluses on their feet and the skin there is tough and no longer soft. It took six years of playing outdoors with no shoes to develop those calluses. If my children never had any object rub against their skin repeatedly, their feet would be soft and callus-free. Adaptations respond to environmental stimuli and, thus, we should expect jealousy to be triggered by contexts that are specific to one's environment. Therefore we should not be surprised to see differences in the magnitude of sex differences in various environments. Keep in mind that men, in all three cultures, were more upset than women by sexual infidelity compared to emotional infidelity.

There are many potential explanations for why the magnitude of the sex differences in response to infidelity ranges so widely among cultures. One particularly interesting one is that the attitudes toward extramarital affairs differ among these cultures. Americans tend to view extramarital affairs negatively (75 percent), while Dutch individuals are much less likely to disapprove of extramarital affairs (45 percent; Buunk & van Driel, 1989). Views of sex are, in general, more liberal in Germany and the Netherlands than the United States, and sex roles in Germany and the Netherlands are more egalitarian (Hofstede, 1980; Pongrácz, 2006; Widmer, Treas, & Newcomb, 1998). Even in countries with more liberal sexual attitudes and egalitarian sex roles, compared to women, men are more upset by sexual infidelity than by emotional infidelity, but the magnitude of the sex difference varies across cultures and is much smaller in those countries with more liberal sexual attitudes.

In an Australian study, researchers replicated Buss et al.'s (1992) main findings that men find sexual infidelity more distressing than emotional infidelity while women find emotional infidelity more distressing than sexual infidelity (Burchell & Ward, 2011). This study is interesting because the researchers directly tested which factors might prompt an individual to report that sexual jealousy is more upsetting than emotional infidelity. This is important because we know that there is variability, both across cultures and within the sexes, in reports of what is more upsetting. Burchell and Ward (2011) found that for men, three factors emerged and were important in their report of being more upset by sexual infidelity: having an avoidant attachment style (see Chapter 7 for a discussion of attachment styles), having a partner who cheated on them in the past, and having a high sex drive. For women, being in a relationship predicted *lower* sexual jealousy and having a high sex drive predicted *higher* sexual jealousy.

A personal moment: Why was my college friend, Shelly, so worried that her new beau was going to cheat? Shelly was a student at an American university and, thus, American sexual mores may have shaped the interactions between her and her boyfriend. The fact that sex differences in one's distress over sexual versus emotional infidelity are quite large in the United States, possibly due to the more conservative sexual attitudes and less egalitarian sex roles, means that we might expect her to feel that emotional infidelity is more upsetting, and that her boyfriend probably found sexual infidelity more upsetting. Shelly knew her boyfriend might have the opportunity to cheat because he was a really good looking guy (this is the environmental input) and because he was a good catch, she was motivated to keep him as a boyfriend. Unbeknownst to Shelly, her jealousy adaptation was at play in shaping her response to her attractive boyfriend.

Rival characteristics which trigger jealousy

So far we have discussed how men, more than women, report more jealousy regarding a sexual infidelity, while women, compared to men, report more jealousy at the idea of their partner falling in love with another woman. But do specific characteristics of a rival elicit more jealousy? Are men or women more jealous if a potential rival is physically attractive? More dominant?

What the research says

Massar et al. (2009) assessed how being primed to think about certain qualities of a rival affected jealousy ratings for men and women. These researchers used subliminal primes, in this case presenting participants with rival characteristics (such as the words *beautiful, attractive, power, success*), which were shown so quickly that people were not aware of what they saw. Participants were next asked to visualize a situation in which they saw their girlfriend or boyfriend flirting with a stranger. The participants then indicated how jealous they felt. Massar et al. (2009) did not find sex differences in overall levels of jealousy. However, they did find that how jealous individuals said they were, depended both on characteristics of the individual and the rival.

For all participants, mate value was assessed through self-reported answers to questions about such things as how often they received compliments from the opposite sex. Women with low mate value were more jealous than women with high mate value, but high mate value women reported more jealousy toward attractive rivals compared to dominant rivals. What does this tell us? Not surprisingly, low mate value women become jealous about *any* rival. They are more at risk of being replaced by a rival, so being jealous of every rival makes sense. High mate value women need only pay attention to rivals who are a threat to them – those who are physically attractive.

While women's jealousy depended on their own mate value, men's jealousy did not change with their mate value. What did affect men's jealousy was their relationship satisfaction. Men who were very satisfied with their romantic relationships reported more jealousy when presented with a rival in comparison to men who were less satisfied with their relationships. In particular, highly satisfied men were especially jealous when presented with a dominant rival in comparison to men who were not satisfied with their relationships. Committed men, under most circumstances, forego the pursuit of short-term mating (i.e., pursuing many sex partners) and therefore they place greater emphasis on maintaining their relationships. For this reason, a dominant rival, who is more likely to be attractive to the man's partner, elicits more jealousy. These men become jealous under the circumstances most likely to make their partners stray. For men who are less satisfied with their relationships, they may still be pursuing short-term matings and therefore are less jealous. (Who has time for jealousy when pursuing multiple sex partners?) For women, relationship satisfaction was not related to jealousy.

Why do women care about physically attractive rivals while men care about dominance? Males are interested in mating with attractive women and women are interested in mating with dominant men, so men and women pay attention to different cues in a rival. These feelings can be readily elicited and with information that people are not even aware of, as in the subliminal cues used by these researchers.

Think critically

This research takes place in the confines of a lab. Do you think that the same results would occur in "real life"? What are the pros and cons of doing experimental research on topics such as jealousy?

Other research also indicates that people negatively evaluate attractive rivals. Maner et al.(2009) showed that both men and women "preferentially encoded and remembered" attractive rivals (compared to less attractive rivals, p. 83). In addition, attractive rivals were negatively evaluated. Usually people feel positively toward attractive individuals, but when it comes to a potential rival, men and women both feel negatively toward an attractive rival. These findings indicate that people are attuned to the threat of rivals and may be prepared to act in ways that keep those rivals away from their mates. We will return to this point later in this chapter.

Sexual orientation and jealousy over rivals

All of the jealousy research discussed previously has assessed heterosexual individuals. Research on heterosexual individuals alone cannot determine how the jealousy adaptation works. Two possibilities both support an evolutionary analysis of how the jealousy adaptation works. The first possibility is that the mechanism is sex-specific. If the adaptation is sex-specific, men and women respond to *different* characteristics of a *rival*. According to this idea, men and women are attuned to specific traits, such as dominance or attractiveness, and which traits they are attuned to depends on whether they are male or female and has nothing to do with sexual orientation. So, if the sex-specific mechanism is supported, then *both heterosexual and gay men are expected to become jealous over the same types of rivals* (Buunk & Dijkstra, 2001).

The second possibility is that the adaptive mechanism is a more general, partner-oriented mechanism (Buunk & Dijkstra, 2001). The partner-oriented mechanism assumes that *individuals become upset over rival characteristics which their mate finds attractive*. For instance, if a woman's partner becomes sexually interested in a highly attractive woman, then highly attractive rivals will elicit more jealous responses. With the partner-oriented mechanism, *the sex of the individual does not matter as much the partners' interest in certain qualities*, such as attractiveness.

What the research says

Buunk and Dijkstra (2001) collected data from 39 lesbians and 35 gay men, all of whom were recruited from Danish gay bars and from organizations in Groningen, the Netherlands. The researchers conducted an experiment by manipulating the attractiveness of a photograph of a supposed rival (high attractiveness versus low attractiveness) as well as by manipulating the dominance of a rival through a description of the rival (high versus low dominance). In the high-dominance description, the rival is described as knowing what she/he wants, taking the initiative and being influential over others – all characteristics associated with highly dominant individuals. In the low-dominance manipulation, the rival is described as being a subordinate at work, being guided by a mentor, not knowing what she/he wants, being compliant and letting others take the initiative – all characteristics of subordinate individuals.

What the researchers found was that gay men were more jealous over a rival who was described as being dominant, while lesbians were more jealous over a rival who was described as being attractive. *In gay men and lesbians, what this amounts to is a mismatch between the characteristics that elicit the most jealousy and those characteristics that are the most threatening to their relationship due to their partner's preferences for those traits.* In heterosexual individuals, "jealousy functions optimally in guarding the mate" (p. 403) but this is not so in gay men and lesbians. The researchers concluded that this indicates strong support of the sex-specific mechanism (the first option) for eliciting jealousy over rivals.

This research is important because it shows how the jealousy adaptation works. In this case, it works in the same way for women, regardless of sexual orientation. This means that lesbians become jealous of traits that are not as desired by their partners – so, in a way, they are jealous about the wrong characteristics. The same thing occurs in gay men – they are not concerned about the traits of a potential rival that are highly attractive to their mates. In heterosexual individuals, the adaptation works better; men and women become jealous over traits that are desirable to their partners.

Think critically

Buunk and Dijkstra (2001) show that comparing heterosexual individuals to gay men and lesbians can elucidate the way in which an adaptation works; it gives us insight into the underlying structure of the adaptation. Are there any other areas in which comparing gay and straight individuals may show how adaptations are structured? Should we expect that gay men and lesbians will show similar patterns as heterosexual individuals in all areas?

Mate guarding

There are phone apps for everything. This includes apps aimed at stalking another individual. Frequently marketed to jealous boyfriends, some stalking apps allow the user to record all phone calls and text messages, as well as to record audio and video if the phone is not in use. If the GPS is enabled, the app user can also detect the person's location. In other words, for a small fee, the user can bug a room, learn a person's whereabouts, and check out their private messages, all remotely. Why would people go to these lengths to figure out what their partners are up to?

Again, it all comes back to men's paternity uncertainty. Our male ancestors had to find ways to keep their partners faithful. Investing in an unfaithful partner – and another guy's child – reduced a man's reproductive success. Evolution found a solution: make men jealous about potential sexual infidelity. Women also perform some mate guarding, most likely to keep a mate from diverting resources toward a rival. In both men and women, jealousy should function to reduce infidelity. That burning desire to keep your mate to yourself inclines people to act in ways that may keep a partner from straying: checking up on her, following her, keeping track of her whereabouts, these are the types of behaviors that may follow feelings of jealousy. These behaviors are called *mate guarding*. Jealousy motivates individuals to perform various mate guarding behaviors.

More specifically, mate guarding is a way to keep access to a mate, to prevent rivals from poaching a mate, and to prevent a mate from deciding to leave the relationship (Buss, 2002). Mate guarding is a behavioral outcome of jealousy and is a means to discourage a mate from cheating. In some bird species males literally follow their female partners around during breeding season. In some insects, males stay attached to females after sex as a way to keep male rivals away. Male bedbugs have a "hypodermic" penis that can be inserted anywhere on the females' abdomen. His sperm then travel to her blood which then transports the sperm to her reproductive system. Females have counter-adaptations to this threat of unwanted paternity and have evolved a second genital system which allows them to selectively prevent fertilization (Carayon, 1966, as cited in Eberhard, 1990). People also mate guard, sometimes in ways that are similar to birds, for example, staying close to a partner when they are out together, deterring rivals from approaching a mate through vigilance and signaling that the partner is "taken." Modern technology also aids in mate guarding and means that people have some unique strategies for mate guarding a partner – bugs cannot text to check up on a mate or "Facebook stalk" their mates (but then again some bugs have hypodermic penises which humans, thankfully, do not possess).

Some mating strategies may put men and women in conflict with each other. For instance, think back to my friend Shelly. Her jealous, mate guarding behavior put her in conflict with her boyfriend. While it may have benefited Shelly to keep track of her boyfriend and any potential rivals, it was not in his best interest to be treated that way. When males and females are in conflict regarding mating tactics, males may develop adaptations to try to "one up" females, which put selection pressure on females to develop counter-adaptations. A good example to illustrate this is the example of the male bedbugs illustrated above. Male bedbugs have a hypodermic penis which means they do not need to have females' consent to mate. Females have countered with a second genital system that allows them to selectively use sperm to fertilize their eggs. When males and females are in conflict in this way we refer to it as *sexually antagonistic co-evolution*.

Humans may also face a conflict over what is best for men and women. One arena for this conflict is mate guarding. Mate guarding has costs for the individual being guarded; it reduces mate choice, especially when individuals are interested in being unfaithful. Our research shows that women are more resistant to mate guarding when they have cheated on a partner (Cousins et al., 2009). In addition, women resist mate guarding by men with lower levels of prenatal testosterone exposure, particularly when women reported having cheated. There are probably costs to resisting mate guarding by some types of men. Men exposed to more prenatal testosterone are more physically aggressive toward their partners. Women clearly realize this and modify their resistance to mate guarding when conditions indicate that there is a risk of being assaulted by a partner (Cousins et al., 2009).

What other factors predict resistance to mate guarding? Our research indicates that women resist mate guarding attempts by their partners when they report that their partners mate guard more frequently. Women who state that both they and their partners are more controlling are also more resistant to mate guarding. In addition, women with less intimacy and investment in their relationships also show higher levels of resistance to mate guarding (Cousins & Fugère, unpublished). Women who seek independence but are also in controlling relationships and those who are not as "into" their relationships are the very women who resist their partner's mate guarding attempts.

A media moment: If your jealousy and mate guarding fail to keep your mate from showing interest in someone else and you think your partner has cheated, there is always the *Check Mate 5 Minute Infidelity Test Kit* (getcheckmate.com). It allows the user to test for the presence of semen on clothing. The premise (at least for jealous boyfriends) is that if one's girlfriend cheated, there will be semen on her underwear. If a guy tests his girlfriend's underwear and it tests positive for semen when he did not have sex with her, he can be assured that she had sex with someone else. Users of the website report feeling relief (after a negative result) or being reassured at finally having answers when their partners' undergarments do test positive.

Mate guarding and intimate-partner violence

Another area of romantic relationships that can be informed by evolutionary theory is the study of intimate-partner violence, including both dating and domestic violence. There is a substantial body of research indicating that jealousy and control of a partner's sexuality are primary causes of many cases of intimate-partner violence (Daly & Wilson, 1988; DeKeseredy & Schwartz, 1998; Lloyd & Emory, 2000). Evolutionary psychologists have argued that intimate-partner violence is an extreme version of mate guarding wherein an individual (often a man) uses violence to punish a mate who has been unfaithful or may be unfaithful in the future. In research on motives for homicide, Daly et al. (1982) found that the accusation of being unfaithful or a rival showing interest in one's mate were among the leading motives. The underlying motivation is jealousy over an actual or suspected infidelity.

What the research says

In my own research, I (Cousins) have found support for the notion that men, but not women, use physical aggression when they believe their partners are sexually interested in someone else. My colleague Steven Gangestad and I collected data from 116 undergraduate dating couples. Each couple completed a series of questionnaires about their relationship. In order to decrease participant reactivity, each individual completed his or her questionnaire alone, in a small office. One of the advantages of having couples come into the lab is that we could assess each individual's beliefs and behaviors as well as their perceptions of their partner's behaviors and beliefs. We felt that sometimes the *perception* of a partner's behavior might be more important than their partner's actual behavior (Cousins & Gangestad, 2007).

We assessed two models of how sexual interest in a partner outside the relationship related to mate retention tactics and violence. The first model assessed men's use of physical aggression and the second model assessed women's use of physical aggression toward their partners. We predicted that when women self-reported an interest in other men, their partners picked up on this and subsequently acted in a more proprietary manner. We then predicted that proprietary men, but not attentive men, were more likely to be physically aggressive toward their partners. We predicted that there would be no link between proprietariness and intimate-partner violence in women because we believed that violence was not a mate retention tactic used by women.

What we found was that men did, indeed, pick up on cues that their partner was showing interest in other men. Men who perceived that their partner was interested in other men were more proprietary but not more attentive. Proprietary men were more likely to be physically aggressive toward their female partners. We then did a separate analysis assessing the relative impact of women's self-reported interest in other men and men's report of whether they believed their partner was interested in other men. We found that men's violence toward their partners was predicted by their perception of their female partner's interest in other men as well as their partner's rating of her commitment to the relationship. However, women's actual infidelity, their self-report of their interest in other men and their self-report of alternatives to their current partner were not significant predictors of male physical aggression. What this tells us is that men's perception of their partners' interest in others is a more important determinant of male intimate-partner violence than women's actual interest in others.

We then performed the same analyses assessing whether women picked up on cues of their partner's self-reported interest in others and the impact of this on women's proprietary and violent behavior toward their partners. As we anticipated, we did not find the same results. Women did pick up on their partners' cues of interest in women outside their relationship, and women who perceived that their partners were interested in other women were more proprietary. However, proprietariness did not predict women's intimate-partner violence. Again, we tried to predict women's use of intimate-partner violence from men's self-reported interest in other women, women's perception of their partners' interest in other women, men's self-reported number of infidelities in the current relationship, men's report of their dating alternatives, and their commitment to the relationship. Unlike men, none of these predicted women's use of intimate-partner violence.

How do we explain these sex differences in what causes intimate-partner violence? The evidence indicates that men, but not women, use physical aggression as part of a mate retention strategy to keep their partners from cheating or to punish them if they stray. It is clear that both men and women can pick up on actual cues of interest in others, but that it is the *perceived* threat to a relationship that is the most important predictor of intimate-partner violence, at least for men. Nothing we assessed predicted women's intimate-partner violence. We were not surprised by these results. Evolutionary theory predicts that men and women may use different mate retention strategies. As we discussed above, women should – and do – use mate retention strategies to keep a mate interested in a relationship. Loss of a mate was an important problem for women to solve. However, the best strategies for women, on average, differ from those of men. Because women were important in the survival of their offspring, women tend to take fewer risks than men. Using violence is always a risky strategy and may cause physical harm, so women tend to use other tactics instead of physical violence (for a more detailed analysis of women's use of aggression, see Campbell, 2005). Men, on the other hand, experience greater payoffs through the use of physical aggression in romantic relationships, as well as more broadly in their interactions with other men.

Thinking critically

In what ways do women use aggression (hint: not necessarily physical aggression)? Are the ways in which women are aggressive less harmful than the ways in which men are aggressive?

A media moment: *Sleeping with the Enemy* is a movie about a woman, Laura, who escapes an abusive husband, Martin, at her own risk, knowing that he will pursue and kill her if he finds her. In the movie, Martin becomes violent when he thinks Laura is flirting with a neighbor. Martin beats Laura, although she never flirted with the neighbor. This movie shows the link between jealousy and intimate-partner violence. Do you think that killing a partner because of an infidelity – or suspected infidelity – has benefits for the killer? What is the point of killing an unfaithful partner if the reason for intimate-partner violence is to keep a partner faithful?

Chapter summary

In this chapter we covered some basics of evolutionary psychology, especially as they relate to attraction and mating. We discussed how men tend to prefer attractiveness in a partner because of its association with health, youth, and fertility, as well as how women tend to prefer status or wealth in a mate, as well as indications of good genetic quality (usually measured by assessing symmetry). These traits may not be shown in some studies using speed dating and other methods, especially when the sample is not reflective of the population. We also highlighted changes in women's mate choices across the menstrual cycle to optimize the likelihood of a partner possessing good genes. Men appear to be able to detect women's fertility status; they prefer the scent of ovulating women and mate guard them more when they are fertile. Sexual jealousy research indicates that men feel more jealous over sexual infidelity while women are more jealous about emotional infidelity – and that these sex differences are upheld across cultures. What makes heterosexual individuals jealous is tied to characteristics their partner is interested in, but this is not the case for gay men and lesbians. Finally, we discussed how mate guarding stems from jealousy and is a way people try to keep a partner from cheating. Suspected infidelity, proprietary behavior, and intimate-partner violence are linked in men, but not in women. We present our suggestions for further reading below.

Suggested reading

Campbell, A. (2005). Aggression. In D. M. Buss (Ed.), *The handbook of evolutionary psychology*. Hoboken, NJ: John Wiley & Sons Inc.
This is a review chapter about aggression. One of the things that is great about this chapter is the detailed explanation of why sex differences in aggression exist and how they are related to mating strategies.
Cousins, A. J., Fugère, M. A., & Franklin, M. (2009). Digit ratio (2D:4D), mate guarding, and physical aggression in dating couples. *Personality and Individual Differences, 46,* 709–713. doi:10.1016/j.paid.2009.01.029
This article shows the importance of both male and female strategies in mate guarding and resistance to mate guarding.
Li, N. P., Yong, J. C., Tov, W., Sng, O., Fletcher, G. J. O., Valentine, K. A., Jiang, Y. F., & Balliet, D. (2013). Mate preferences do predict attraction and choices in the early stages of mate selection. *Journal of Personality and Social Psychology, 105,* 757–776. doi: 10.1037/a0033777
There are two strong points about this article. The first is that it tests some competing hypotheses about mate choice, and the second is that they use a variety of techniques to do so, including experimental and non-experimental paradigms.
Massar, K., Buunk, A. P., & Dechesne, M. (2009). Jealousy in the blink of an eye: Jealous reactions following subliminal exposure to rival characteristics. *European Journal of Social Psychology, 39*(5), 768–779. doi:10.1002/ejsp.579
This article shows how experiments can be done to elicit jealousy. In this case the experimental manipulation was below conscious awareness and still had an effect.
Penton-Voak, I. S., Perrett, D. I., Castles, D. L., Kobayashi, T. T., Burt, D. M., Murray, L. K., & Minamisawa, R. R. (1999). Menstrual cycle alters face preference. *Nature, 399*(6738), 741–742. doi:10.1038/21557
This was the first work that suggested that women's choice for masculine features changes across the menstrual cycle. It is also cross-cultural and shows that this is true in both the U.K. and Japan.

Initiating and Enhancing Attraction

Think back to a time when you first felt attracted to someone. How did you encounter that person? Did you observe her from across the room? Did a friend introduce you? What inspired your feelings of attraction toward that individual? And what heightened your initial feelings of attraction? In this chapter we examine fundamental precursors to attraction as well as factors that can enhance attraction.

Fundamental precursors to attraction

How did you meet your most recent romantic partner? Did you live near one another? Did you work together? Did you attend the same school? Did you have mutual friends? Some of the most common precursors to attraction include close physical proximity, familiarity, similarity, and reciprocal liking. We tend to like others more when they are close to us, familiar to us, similar to us, and when they like us.

Physical proximity

People in close physical proximity often become attracted to one another as friends or as potential romantic partners. Merely increasing one's physical proximity to another individual may be enough to increase liking for that individual (Slane & Leak, 1978, see Chapter 6 for further discussion of this research). Consider research described by Festinger et al. in 1950, which investigated the friendships of married students living in apartments at Massachusetts Institute of Technology (MIT). The authors found that the students were most likely to be friends with others living in apartments close to theirs. Similarly, Byrne (1961b) found that students sitting next to one another in class for 14 weeks had stronger relationships than those who sat next to one another for only 7 weeks or 3.5 weeks. In a more recent exploration of proximity effects,

Back et al. (2008) found that German students who were randomly assigned to sit near one another during an introductory psychology class liked one another more one year later versus students who did not sit as close to one another during class.

A personal moment: I am sure you can apply the research on liking and physical proximity to situations in your own life, as I have. For example, my best friends from college lived in the dorm rooms right next to mine during our freshman year, two good friends from Glee Club sat next to me during rehearsals, and my husband and I became close friends with our next door neighbor, Art, when we bought our first home. When we discuss proximity research in my Social Psychology classes, many of my students report becoming friends with those students who sit next to them throughout the semester. Although I have not yet had students admit to becoming romantically involved because of physical proximity in my classes, I have suspicions about two of my students who sat next to each other in one of my Attraction seminars. (I hope they will let me know if they start dating.)

When people are in close proximity, they become more familiar with one another, thus potentially facilitating liking through the mere exposure effect (Reis et al., 2011; we address the mere exposure effect below). However, proximity does not always lead to liking. Ebbesen et al. (1976) analyzed the proximity of both liked and disliked individuals to married women living in a condominium complex in California. These researchers found that both liked and disliked individuals lived closer to the participants than would be expected on the basis of chance. In fact, in this project, proximity was more important in the development of negative rather than positive relationships. The authors interpreted the liking and disliking results differently. Ebbesen et al. posited that liking relationships develop with those who live nearby due to increased familiarity through seeing each other and interacting frequently. Conversely, the authors proposed that disliking relationships develop with those who live nearby due to "environment-spoiling actions" (p. 517) such as neighbors being too noisy or disposing of their trash inappropriately. Nonetheless, this research suggests that proximity does not always lead to liking and may sometimes lead to disliking.

Mere exposure theory

As stated above, increased familiarity may lead to liking. In 1968, Zajonc proposed a simple theory to explain liking, called mere exposure theory. In this theory, Zajonc posits that the more we encounter a stimulus, the more we like it. (As stated earlier, mere exposure theory can be used to explain the proximity effects described above; we encounter individuals who are in close physical proximity to us more often and thus like them more than individuals whom we encounter less frequently.) In his article, Zajonc reviews a series of studies showing that we like those stimuli which we encounter more frequently. Of course, in the case of people, we not only like those whom we encounter more frequently, but we also *choose* to encounter more frequently those people whom we like, which may intensify the mere exposure effect.

What the research says

In his seminal research testing mere exposure theory, Zajonc (1968) showed that, in many languages, positive words (e.g., comfortable) occur more frequently than their negative counterparts (e.g., uncomfortable). Likewise, when asking participants which word in a word pair they preferred, participants overwhelmingly chose the positive word (e.g., encourage) over the negative word (e.g., discourage). In an experimental test of the same phenomenon, researchers asked participants to read aloud a list of nonsense words. The researchers varied the frequency with which the nonsense words appeared on the list. Thus, some nonsense words were never read aloud and some were read up to 25 times. The participants were then asked to rate the nonsense words on a scale ranging from 0 (bad) to 6 (good). Zajonc found that even words with no meaning were rated more positively the more often they were encountered. Finally, Zajonc attempted to manipulate interpersonal attitudes by differentially exposing participants to photographs of unknown target persons. Zajonc asked university students to participate in the study, which purportedly was to test one's memory for photographs. Yearbook photographs of unfamiliar men were presented to the participants with varying frequency. Then, the participants were asked to rate how much they thought they might like the person shown in each photo. Similar to the results for words described above, Zajonc found that the targets in photographs presented more frequently were rated more positively than the targets whose photographs were presented less frequently.

Think critically

In Zajonc's (1968) research, he showed that participants rated targets more positively when they saw their photographs presented more often. Do you think he would find the same results if the participants were asked to interact with one another with varying frequency? What if you had a negative interaction with another person? Would increasing the frequency of your interaction improve your rating of him?

Moreland and Beach (1992) extended Zajonc's research in a study investigating the mere exposure effect on attraction to a fellow student in a more naturalistic setting. Four female graduate students (who were rated in a pretest as similarly attractive) were randomly assigned to attend a large lecture-style class for either 0, 5, 10, or 15 classes during one semester. Then, at the end of the semester, the students in the class were asked to evaluate photographs of the four graduate students in terms of attractiveness, perceived intelligence, warmth, and desire to work together on projects with them. Despite the fact that most students did not remember seeing any of the women before, and that the graduate students were asked not to interact with the students in the class, the graduate student who attended class the most often was perceived as the most attractive. The students' responses also indicated that they would enjoy spending time with her as well as working on a project together, more so than the graduate students who attended less often.

In a recent illustration of increased familiarity facilitating increased liking, Reis et al. (2011) showed enhanced liking among students who met either in person or online. These researchers explored the impact of the number of interactions and total interaction time on liking for a same-sex stranger. Unacquainted undergraduates from the United States interacted with one another in person or through online chats. When the students met in person, they were asked to read and respond to two or six questions with their partners (the responses were restricted to 30 seconds each in order to control overall interaction time). When the students met online, they were asked to chat for approximately 15 minutes either one, two, four, six, or eight times. Through both studies, the authors found that more frequent interactions (i.e., eight interactions versus fewer interactions) as well as more interaction time (i.e., answering six questions versus two questions) led to increased liking. The authors posited that certain factors – such as increased knowledge about a partner (as well as a partner knowing more about you), more comfort with a partner, and the responsiveness of a partner – might facilitate increased liking through more frequent social interactions. One limitation identified by Reis et al. was that because the research was conducted in the United States, the findings might not apply to more collectivistic cultures in which friendships may develop more slowly and cautiously.

A personal moment: You have probably "fallen victim" to the mere exposure effect in your own life, perhaps without even realizing it. Have you ever found that you liked a song on the radio the more often you heard it played? Or have you noticed that you liked a sports team's new uniforms the more often they wore them? As a graduate student I would get together each Wednesday with my friends Lizzy and Brian at their home to watch a favorite television show together. At the beginning of the season of our favorite show, we all watched a commercial for a soft drink and declared that we disliked the new advertising jingle. At the end of the season, we all danced and sang along each time the jingle aired.

You may be thinking, "Wow, this mere exposure idea sounds great! So let me just hang around that cute guy at the gym, and then, eventually, we will start dating." There are some things to keep in mind when trying to exploit the mere exposure effect for your own benefit: First, there appears to be a ceiling effect. This means that after a relatively small number of exposures, you do not see increases in liking with additional exposures to a stimulus. A meta-analysis by

Bornstein (1989) showed that research with a smaller number of exposures (anywhere from 1 to 99) yielded small or moderate increases in liking, whereas those with more than 100 exposures yielded only small increases in liking. Second, the exposures should be very short. In fact, according to Bornstein, exposures of less than one second yielded the strongest increases in liking, while those longer than one second and longer than one minute were less effective. Third, it may be better if your potential partner does not realize that he is seeing you repeatedly. When participants recognized that they had seen a stimulus over and over again, it decreased the strength of the mere exposure effect.

In another interesting exception to mere exposure theory, research performed by Little et al. (2013) suggests that women may prefer familiarity in an opposite-sex partner more than men do.

What the research says

Little et al. (2013) conducted an online research project involving four separate studies with samples of heterosexual individuals primarily from the United Kingdom and North America. In the first study, the researchers showed men and women photographs of male and female faces (the targets presented in the photographs were also White). Each photograph was shown two times and rated for attractiveness after each presentation. In results that supported the mere exposure effect, both men and women rated the male faces as more attractive after the second exposure. However, only women rated the female faces as more attractive after the second exposure, men actually rated the female faces as *less* attractive after the second exposure. In the second study, the authors demonstrated that after a second exposure to the female faces the men rated the faces as less attractive as a short-term partner (for example, as a one night stand). In the third study, the authors found that both men and women rated faces of the other sex as more trustworthy after the second exposure, but men rated women as significantly *less* sexy after the second exposure. Finally, in the fourth study, the authors revealed that women found men's faces more attractive if the faces were viewed as more similar to their current partners' faces, while men viewed women's faces as *less* attractive if the faces were viewed as more similar to their current partners' faces. Taken as a whole, the authors interpreted these results to show that men are more likely to prefer novelty and women are more likely to prefer familiarity in an opposite-sex partner. The authors believe that these preferences might be linked to the potential evolutionary benefits to men for mating with multiple partners and to women for mating with a trustworthy long-term partner (see Chapter 4).

Think critically

In Little et al.'s (2013) research project, the participants rated the attractiveness of five male and five female faces, followed by the same male and female faces presented along with ten previously unseen faces. With a relatively small number of faces to judge, do you think the participants realized they were rating the same faces again? How might that influence the results? If the participants did realize that they were seeing the same faces again, why might men and women rate the targets differently after the second exposure?

Similarity

When I begin my Social Psychology classes, I ask the students a variety of questions, which we address throughout the semester. I am sure you have heard the old sayings "birds of a feather flock together" and "opposites attract." I ask my students: Which one rings true for you? This question always provokes a lot of discussion. Some students are certain that "birds of a feather flock together" because someone's sister and her new husband both like to ski, enjoy eating sushi, and want to travel to Ireland someday, while some students are positive that "opposites attract" because their moms prefer neutral colors and their dads prefer bold colors, or their dads spend all day knitting while their moms are out riding Harley Davidson motorcycles. Whatever your personal experiences may be, the overwhelming majority of research shows that those who are attracted to one another (romantic couples, friends, etc.) also tend to be similar to one another in a variety of ways. Similarity is an important determinant of liking.

Similarity of attitudes

One of the most important ways we tend to be similar to our loved ones is in holding similar attitudes. Think about some of your important relationships – with your parents, siblings, friends, romantic partners. On what types of issues do you share similar attitudes? On what types of issues do you differ? Intuitively, a recent meta-analysis by Montoya and Horton (2013) reveals that similarity on important attitudes is a more significant determinant of liking than similarity on less-important attitudes. In one of the first studies to investigate similarity and liking, Byrne (1961a) found that college students liked their counterparts better if they shared similar attitudes to their own. Furthermore, this effect was intensified if their counterparts particularly shared their important attitudes.

What the research says

Byrne (1961a) asked college students from the United States to complete questionnaires assessing their attitudes toward a variety of topics (for example religion and movies). Further, the students were asked to indicate which attitudes were the most and least important to them. The researcher then took the questionnaires completed by the participants and designed fictitious questionnaire responses to reflect attitudes that were either similar to or different from the attitudes initially expressed by the participants. Also, two other versions of the questionnaires were developed to reflect similarity on either the most important or least important issues. The students were then told to review a questionnaire purportedly completed by another student in another class, and they were asked to rate that student based on his/her responses to the questionnaire. Not surprisingly, the students liked their fictional counterparts better if their partner's attitudinal responses were similar to their own. Additionally, when the responses on the items the participants judged to be important matched their own, the participants liked their partners more.

Think critically

Byrne (1961a) found this relationship between similarity and liking by using fictionally created opinion surveys; the participant and his or her supposed counterpart never met in person. What if the counterpart's opinions seemed to be different on the questionnaire, but the individual appeared likable in person? Do you think the relationship between similarity and liking would disappear after a positive in-person interaction even if the counterpart initially expressed different attitudes from yours?

There is some evidence that attitude similarity and liking are associated across cultures. Byrne (1971) replicated his results linking similarity with attraction in samples from Texas, Hawaii, India, Japan, and Mexico. These students completed attitude inventories and then received one of two experimentally manipulated inventories to evaluate. The researchers examined the degree of similarity between each participant's responses and his or her fictional counterpart's responses. Byrne found that in all cultures, as the degree of similarity between the participant and the fictional counterpart increased, predicted liking for the counterpart increased as well. Cross-cultural research by Gebauer et al. (2012) suggests that similarity remains important across cultures, but it may be more important in countries whose residents are less influenced by physical attractiveness.

Although similar attitudes may play a role in the initiation of a relationship, similar attitudes may be more important to the *maintenance* of a relationship. Prior research reveals increased similarity among couples in long-term relationships. For example, Byrne and Blaylock (1963) found that husbands and wives were similar to one another in their political attitudes. Interestingly, these authors also found that husbands and wives perceived more similarity in their political attitudes than actually existed, so actual similarity may not be as important as perceived similarity. Correspondingly, Keller and Young (1996) found that married couples were more similar to one another on psychological traits such as imagination and intelligence than dating couples. In contrast, dissimilarity may pose a risk to long-term relationships. For example, Clarkwest (2007) found that African-American married couples tended to be less similar to one another (on factors such as income, education, attitudes towards women's employment, and attitudes toward infidelity) than their non-African-American counterparts, and that this dissimilarity resulted in an increased risk of divorce.

Similarity of attitudes may be so important to maintaining relationships that when we perceive dissimilarity between our own attitudes and those of a loved one, we may try to change our attitudes to match theirs or try to change their attitudes to match ours. Davis and Rusbult (2001) found that dating couples who were made aware of differences in their attitudes, tended to change their attitudes to match their partners' sentiments. Dating partners tended to defer to their companions on issues that were less important to them and to try to change their companions' attitudes on issues that were more important to them.

A personal moment: One day I was driving around town with my two sons when a Bruce Springsteen song came on the radio. ("The Boss" is my favorite musician.) Because my older son also likes Bruce, I pointed out that he sang the song. My younger son (he is three years old) replied, "I don't like Bruce Springsteen," to which I immediately responded: "Don't ever say that again." Of course I will continue to love my youngest son whether or not he develops a liking for Bruce Springsteen's music, but my attitude toward Bruce Springsteen is too important to me to change my attitudes to match his. Therefore, at that moment I began secretly plotting ways to increase his liking for Bruce, including surreptitiously exposing him to Springsteen's music. Maybe I can change his attitudes through mere exposure? This anecdote provides an illustration of the importance of similar attitudes, especially important attitudes, in close relationships.

Similarity of personality

Similarity of attitudes may be more fundamental to successful romantic relationships than similarity of personality. (In fact, when students assume that opposites attract, they may be thinking about personality characteristics rather than attitudinal similarity.) Research by Luo and Klohnen (2005) suggests that married couples tend to resemble one another more in their attitudes than in their personality characteristics. These authors invited newly married couples from the Midwestern United States to participate in a research project involving marital assessment. The adults in this sample were primarily Caucasian and were required to be less than 50 years old in order to participate in this project. They completed a variety of assessments measuring attitudes, values, personality characteristics, attachment styles, religiosity, and marital satisfaction. The researchers found that "real couples were significantly more similar to one another on values, religiosity, and political attitudes than randomly paired couples" (p. 312). Similarity of attachment styles was also related to marital satisfaction (see Chapter 7 for a discussion of attachment styles). However, even though the couples tended to be less similar in their personalities than in their attitudes, similarity of personalities was positively related to marital satisfaction. Interestingly, these researchers also found "profile-based similarity to be a consistently stronger predictor of satisfaction than difference-score-based similarity" (p. 320). This finding means that it does not matter as much how different you and your spouse are in absolute levels of a personality trait like extroversion, but rather whether your overall pattern *across* personality traits roughly matches your partner's overall pattern. For example, regardless of whether you are more extroverted than your spouse, if both of you are relatively more extroverted and more agreeable, and relatively less conscientious and less neurotic, you may experience a more satisfying romantic relationship.

The authors note that because this research was conducted with newlyweds, future research will be necessary to assess couples in non-marital relationships or in longer marriages.

Why do we like others whose personalities are similar to ours? Because of our generally positive evaluations of ourselves, those who remind us of ourselves might also be evaluated positively (Tenney et al., 2009). Alternatively, those who have personalities more similar to our own might be perceived as more familiar and therefore be easier to understand and easier to like (Tenney et al., 2009).

Although personality may be one of the first things you consider when trying to discern whether you are similar to a romantic partner, relatively few studies have assessed similarity of personality among romantic partners, and those that have assessed this relationship have yielded mixed results (Barelds & Barelds-Dijkstra, 2007), perhaps due to the way similarity of personality was measured (i.e., as an absolute difference between partners on individual traits rather than similarity on an overall personality profile, Luo & Klohnen, 2005). In an attempt to further investigate this relationship, Barelds and Barelds-Dijkstra recruited married or cohabitating adults from a Dutch telephone directory to participate in their research. The average relationship length for these couples was 25 years. These researchers found that the effects of similar personalities varied with the type of relationship initiation. For example, adults who reported being friends before becoming romantic partners and who differed in their levels of extroversion also rated their relationships as poorer than those with more similar levels of extroversion. Furthermore, adults who reported falling in love at first sight and who differed in their levels of conscientiousness similarly reported reduced relationship quality. Although these researchers measured differences on individual traits and not differences on the patterns across traits, Barelds and Barelds-Dijkstra found that dissimilarity on personality traits was related to less satisfying romantic relationships.

As discussed in Chapter 3, during a speed-dating event with undergraduate students, Luo and Zhang (2009) found no evidence that similarity was associated with liking. Luo and Zhang investigated similarity on both physical characteristics and personality characteristics. These authors state that in experimental research such as Byrne's (1961a) when extraneous variables are controlled and similarity is manipulated, similarity may have a greater effect on liking than in a more realistic setting in which a number of factors vary simultaneously. Also, Luo and Zhang's research explored preferences for partners only known for a few minutes. Keller et al. (1996) suggest that it takes more time to perceive similarity on psychological variables than it does to perceive similarity on physical variables.

Similar perceptions of the self

Although the phenomenon of self-verification is not usually mentioned in similarity research, the preference for a partner who verifies our opinions of ourselves (in other words a partner who sees us similarly to the way we see ourselves), may be a special case of the preference for similarity. Therefore, we not only prefer others whose attitudes match our own, but we prefer partners whose perceptions of *us* match our own (e.g., Swann, 1987). This phenomenon is called self-verification, and we will discuss this concept in more detail in Chapter 7. The research in this area generally shows that we prefer romantic partners to see us as we see ourselves (e.g., Katz & Beach, 2000). This preference is so strong that we even prefer our partners to see us as we see ourselves when we see ourselves negatively (Swann, 1987).

Similarity in physical attractiveness

It may be surprising to some to learn that we tend to pursue relationships with those who match our own levels of physical attractiveness. For example, married couples tend to be similar to one another in levels of physical attractiveness (both when rating themselves and when rated by others), even more so than are dating couples (Feingold, 1988). Feingold suggests that couples who are more similar in their levels of physical attractiveness may be more likely to stay together than those who are less similar in physical attractiveness.

Feingold's interpretation is consistent with some current research regarding online dating. Shaw et al. (2011) found that although users of an online dating service tended to contact potential dates who were more attractive than themselves, they were more likely to receive favorable replies to their overtures from potential dates who matched their own levels of physical attractiveness. Likewise, Thao et al. (2010) found that adolescents from the Netherlands who perceived themselves as attractive to members of the other sex more strongly desired to date an attractive target rather than a less-attractive target.

Similarly, Todd et al. (2007) found in a study of speed-dating preferences among German men and women that, although men tended to choose as potential dates any woman whom they perceived to be physically attractive, women tended to choose as potential dates men whose level of physical attractiveness matched their own. Montoya (2008) suggests an interesting interpretation for matching in physical attractiveness. He states that although individuals continue to be attracted to those who are objectively good-looking, unattractive individuals perceive a greater likelihood of having a relationship with those whose levels of attractiveness match their own. Therefore, less attractive individuals seem to consider a broader range of others as physically attractive, essentially extending their lower boundaries of what they consider to be physically attractive.

You may recall that we discussed the link between physical attractiveness and facial symmetry in Chapter 1. Heterosexual dating couples even seem to match one another in symmetry, such that more symmetrical men tend to date more symmetrical women (Burriss et al., 2011). This similarity in symmetry may be one factor which drives the similarity in physical attractiveness findings discussed above.

Intriguingly, it is also possible that we seek mates who not only match our own levels of physical attractiveness, but who actually look like us. Fraley and

Marks (2010) performed a fascinating study showing that participants liked composite photographs better if their own photograph was morphed with a photograph of a stranger of the other sex (versus a control condition in which another participant's photograph was morphed with that stranger of the other sex). Importantly, the participants did not know that their own photographs were being merged with the other photographs, and the authors stressed that when participants realized that the composites were designed to resemble themselves, they found the composite photographs less appealing. Complementary results were obtained by Little et al. (2003) who found that men self-reported that their female partner's hair color and eye color were similar to their own.

A media moment: Interestingly, in Little et al.'s (2003) research, the association between one's opposite-sex parent's physical characteristics and one's partner's physical characteristics was stronger than the association between self and partner physical characteristics. Consistent with this finding, Fraley and Marks (2010) also found that participants rated target photographs as more sexually attractive if they had been subliminally primed with a photograph of their opposite-sex parent. I guess there is some evidence to support the song my dad used to sing to me and my brothers when we were children. The song goes "I want a girl, just like the girl that married dear old dad" (Dillon & Von Tilzer, 1911).

Although we may try to choose partners who match our own levels of physical attractiveness or who look similar to us, it is also possible that long-term couples actually become more similar in physical appearance over time. Zajonc et al. (1987) showed participants facial photographs of male and female members of couples around the time of their weddings and around the time of their 25th anniversaries. Although participants could not reliably match couples at the time of their weddings, they could match couples at the time of their 25th anniversaries. Zajonc et al. explained this effect by suggesting that over the years of living together, partners empathize with one another and thus mimic one another's facial expressions. Over time their facial structures change in similar ways so that after a few decades, their faces look more similar to each other.

Similar names

Even more surprising than our preference for a mate similar to us in physical attractiveness is our preference for a mate with a similar name. We are more likely to marry those whose names are similar to ours (such as my friends John and Jen who have been married for 20 years, or my relatives Mary and Malcolm, who have been married for ten years; Jones et al., 2004). We also like random others better if their names begin with the same letter as ours (such as my super-awesome girlfriends Renee and Rebecca, who met as college roommates) or if they share our birthdays (such as my friends Antonio and Claire who share the same birthday and have been married for seven years). The researchers suggest that we have these preferences because of positive associations with the letters in our names and the numbers in our birthdays (Jones et al., 2004).

Similarity debates

There are some interesting debates regarding the relationship between similarity and liking (see Kassin et al., 2011 for a good summary of these debates). One debate centers around the causal relationship between similarity and liking. Does similarity lead to liking or liking lead to similarity? The other debate concerns whether similarity leads to liking or whether dissimilarity leads to disliking.

Directionality

When two variables are correlated with each other, such as similarity and liking, it is sometimes unclear which variable causes which, or whether both variables influence one another. This situation is sometimes referred to as a *directionality problem* (Beins, 2013). In purely correlational research assessing similarity and liking, it is possible that similarity causes liking, that liking causes similarity, or that both variables influence one another. In Byrne's (1961a) experimental research discussed above, involving the attitudes of college students, it is obvious that similarity led to liking (and not that liking led to similarity) because the students never actually met the hypothetical target person and thus did not have the opportunity to become more similar to each other. However, in Byrne and Blaylock's (1963) correlational research involving married couples' political attitudes, it is possible that similarity led to liking or that liking led to similarity. For example, my husband and I share similar political attitudes, but I am not sure whether we shared those attitudes before we met, or whether our attitudes became more similar as a result of discussing our attitudes frequently and consuming similar news sources. As Kassin et al. (2011) suggest, it is probable that both of these processes operate in relationships, so that those who are similar to each other in important ways are more likely to like one another and then once they like one another, they are more likely to become similar to each other as well.

A media moment: In the 2007 comedy *Knocked Up* (directed by Apatow), Seth Rogan's character, Ben, is laid-back and irresponsible. Katherine Heigl's character, Alison, has a high-powered television career and has just been promoted. The two seem at first to have nothing in common; but upon learning that they are expecting a baby, they start spending time together and engaging in shared activities. As they get to know one another better, they become more similar as well. Ben enjoys playing with Alison's sister's kids; Alison helps Ben work on his website. Eventually Ben gets a job and begins reading baby books, becoming more similar to Alison in some important ways. Also, as Ben becomes more responsible, Alison becomes more relaxed. Although the movie portrays Ben and Alison as opposites at first, they may also have been similar to one another even before they met. For example, family members are important to both of them. Ben is very close with his dad and Alison is very close with her sister. Furthermore, they are similar in age and ethnic background (see Luo & Klohnen, 2005), and they went to the same bar on the same evening. Then, through their attraction and shared responsibility for their child they may also, over time, become more similar to each other.

Dissimilarity

Another debate concerning similarity research involves a discussion of whether similarity leads to liking or dissimilarity leads to disliking (see Rosenbaum, 1986). Rosenbaum critiques correlational research showing a positive relationship between similarity and liking and contends that similarity does not produce liking, but rather that *dissimilarity* produces disliking. In support of Rosenbaum's hypothesis, Montoya and Horton (2013) performed a meta-analysis of research assessing similarity and liking and concluded that dissimilarity has a larger effect on attraction than similarity. Dissimilarity may have a larger effect because dissimilar attitudes attract more attention (similar to the negativity bias discussed in Chapter 2, see Jia & Singh, 2009).

An investigation by Norton et al. (2007) suggests that *perceptions* of dissimilarity can lead to disliking. The participants were assigned to receive different numbers of randomly chosen traits (e.g., "ambitious…boring…dependable…industrious…opinionated…polite…stubborn…and talkative" p. 99). Participants rated whether those traits were also self-descriptors and rated their liking for the hypothetical target person. These authors found that participants who received more trait descriptors for their target also liked the target less than those who received fewer trait descriptors. Interestingly, these authors also found that participants who viewed the first trait presented as dissimilar to themselves rated the target as less similar overall than those who viewed the first trait as similar to themselves. Norton et al. interpreted these results to show that early perceptions of dissimilarity influenced perceptions of subsequent traits as dissimilar as well (recall Asch's 1946 research concerning first impressions, as discussed in Chapter 2). Norton et al.'s research thus suggests that perceptions of dissimilarity lead to disliking, but also that once a target is perceived as dissimilar, subsequent evaluations of that target may be viewed through the lens of dissimilarity.

As Kassin et al. (2011) review, both similarity-liking and dissimilarity-disliking processes are likely to operate. Indeed, Byrne et al. (1986) acknowledge that both similarity and dissimilarity may impact attraction. Byrne et al. suggest that we may first distinguish potential friends or romantic partners on the basis of whether they are similar or dissimilar to us, and then choose our friends or romantic partners from those who are similar.

Reciprocity

Have you ever noticed reciprocity in your liking and disliking relationships? We tend to like others who like us and to dislike others who dislike us. In their review of research addressing the relationship between similarity and liking, Montoya and Horton (2013) also suggest a reciprocity interpretation for the positive relationship between these two variables. These authors suggest that "people anticipate that those with similar attitudes will like them, and those with dissimilar attitudes will dislike them. In effect, people like similar others because they expect those others to like them" (p. 78). The expectation that a target person will like us can be a strong determinant of our liking for that person in return.

When I discuss reciprocity with my students, I like to introduce it as the "sixth-grade" approach to attraction. Can you remember being in sixth grade and having one of your friends tell you that one of your classmates liked you? How did you respond? Typically, when we find out that someone likes us, we are more likely to like him as well. In a cross-cultural examination of factors associated with liking, Riela et al. (2010) found that, among both American and Chinese students, reciprocity was mentioned most often in the respondents' own accounts of what led them to like their most recent partner, with Chinese participants even more likely to mention reciprocal liking than their American counterparts.

Kenny (1994) describes this reciprocal liking between two individuals as "dyadic reciprocity" (p. 101). As Kenny reviews, dyadic reciprocity tends to increase with acquaintance, so that as individuals get to know each other better, their liking for one another also becomes more reciprocal. Reciprocal liking can help to ensure that we do not waste valuable resources on targets who are not interested in us (Greitmeyer, 2010).

A media moment: In one episode of the NBC series *Seinfeld*, Elaine is stretching at the gym while trying to attract the attention of an attractive man across the room. Meanwhile, the man next to her says, "Jimmy is pretty sweet on you....you are just Jimmy's type." Thinking that he is referring to the man she has her eye on, Elaine replies that she would like to get to know Jimmy. Eventually Elaine finds out that the man next to her was actually referring to himself in the third person. Consistent with Greitemeyer's (2010) suggestion that reciprocal liking can help to ensure that we do not waste valuable resources on targets who are not interested in us, Elaine agrees to date Jimmy, not only because he likes her, but also because the other man she was initially interested in is gay.

Reciprocity may be a more important determinant of liking when a potential partner is particularly physically attractive (Greitmeyer, 2010). Greitmeyer presented participants from Austria with photographs of potential partners who were physically attractive, moderately attractive, and unattractive. He found that participants feared rejection more when their potential partner was attractive, thus making it more important to know that the partner liked the participant. Furthermore, in addition to liking being reciprocal, disliking may be reciprocal as well. Greitemeyer showed that when participants learned that their partners did not like them, they were less attracted to those partners.

Reciprocal liking for another may be the strongest when we remain uncertain about just how much another person likes us (Whitchurch, Wilson, & Gilbert, 2011). These researchers asked undergraduate women from the United States to review the Facebook profiles of four men who had purportedly reviewed their profiles and liked them. The researchers manipulated how much the men supposedly liked the women's profiles. In one condition the women were told that they were viewing the profiles of the men who liked them the most; in another condition they were told that they were viewing the profiles of the men who liked them neither the most nor the least but about average; and in the final condition the women were told that they were being kept blind to the men's ratings, but that these men either liked them the most or about average. Consistent with previous research regarding the effects of reciprocity, the women liked the men more when they thought the men liked them best, rather than when they thought the men liked them about average. However, in the condition in which the women were unsure of the level of the men's liking, they rated the men most favorably. The researchers postulated that uncertainty led the women to think about those men the most, which then enhanced their liking for them. Although there was a level of uncertainty in this research, the effects still support the idea of reciprocity; the women liked men who were reported to like them. Future research should determine whether uncertainty still enhances liking when there is a possibility that the other *dislikes* you.

In order for reciprocity to influence liking, a potential partner's preferences may need to be explicitly stated. Although Back et al. (2011) found that speed-dating participants expected their dating preferences to be reciprocal (they thought that those with whom they desired future dates would also desire future dates with them), actual preferences were not reciprocal. Luo and Zhang (2009) also failed to find evidence for reciprocity among speed-dating partners during the event. However, after the speed-dating event concluded, and after learning their partners' feedback, Luo and Zhang's participants felt more favorably toward those who had chosen them as potential dates.

Reciprocal liking may not only increase attraction, but it may also be involved in the process of falling in love. Aron et al. (1989) collected qualitative responses from students and non-students regarding their accounts of falling in love. These authors found that the experience of falling in love was often preceded by discovering that another liked them. In this research, the effect of reciprocity was mentioned so often that the authors suggested that "people are just waiting for an attractive person to do something they can interpret as liking them" (p. 251). Interestingly, references to similarity of a potential partner to the self as well as physical proximity were also mentioned as precursors to falling in love (see Chapter 8 for more research regarding love).

Eye contact

One indicator of reciprocal liking is eye contact. Mutual eye contact may evidence liking or loving between acquainted individuals and can even enhance liking and loving feelings between unacquainted partners (Kellerman et al., 1989; see Chapter 6 for more information about this research). In an observational study, men who glanced around the room more (presumably making eye contact with women in the room) were more likely to subsequently initiate a conversation with a woman versus men who looked around less often (Renninger et al., 2004).

When we make eye contact with others, we prefer the direct gaze of a happy face, particularly when the face is of the other sex (Conway et al., 2008; Jones et al., 2006). This preference for eye contact from the other sex may serve to guide mating efforts. For example, Jones et al. suggest that we prefer "the most attractive individuals who are likely to reciprocate one's own social effort" which will in turn help "to maximize the potential benefits of one's choices about whom to attempt to engage in social interaction, and potentially in partnership" (p. 591). Further emphasizing the relevance of eye contact to mating decisions, Mason et al. (2005) found that female faces displaying a gaze shift toward the participant increased liking by both men and women (versus a gaze shift away from the participant), but increased perceptions of physical attractiveness only in men.

In a fascinating study investigating perceptions of the attractiveness of faces, eye contact, and brain activity, Kampe et al. (2001) found that attractive faces showing direct eye contact increased activity in the ventral striatum, while attractive faces with an averted gaze decreased activity in the same area. The authors suggest that increased activity in this region of the brain stimulates dopamine reward systems. The authors interpreted these results as evidence of "automatic evaluation of the likely reward" (p. 589) of interaction with a partner.

Although eye contact may be an important precursor to, or indicator of, attraction, the frequency or duration of eye contact may vary with culture. Senju et al. (2013) found that participants from the United Kingdom were more likely to maintain eye contact even when an avatar looked away, while participants from Japan were likely to shift their gaze to follow the direction of the avatar's gaze. These authors suggest that Western cultures tend to value eye contact while Eastern cultures value both eye contact as well as averted gaze.

Factors that can enhance attraction

Once we perceive a prospective mate as physically attractive, a variety of factors can enhance his or her attractiveness. As we review below: physiological arousal can enhance attraction to good-looking individuals, wearing the color red enhances both men's and women's attractiveness, and everyone gets better looking later in the evening.

Physiological arousal

Think back to a great first date you had in the past. What did you do on this date? Did you watch an exciting movie? Rollerblade on the boardwalk? Take surfing lessons together? Go dancing? If you had an exciting first date, some of the excitement from your activity may have influenced the attraction you felt toward your partner. Increased physiological arousal increases the desirability of attractive individuals (Foster et al., 1998).

A personal moment: I love discussing the research on physiological arousal because it reminds me of my first date with my husband, Dave. Because Dave lived in California when we met, and I was attending graduate school in Connecticut, the next time we arranged to meet, we planned to go to the Grand Canyon. So our first official date was to the Grand Canyon. When I tell my students about our first date, they are usually incredulous. One student even quipped "Where was your second date? Paris?" I am sorry to say that my husband and I have not yet been to Paris together. But we did, or at least I did, experience a great deal of physiological arousal at the time of our first date. Think about how you feel after you exercise, your heart is racing, your pulse is quickened, your breathing is faster, and so forth. Now imagine standing on the rim of the Grand Canyon and looking at the breathtaking scenery. Your heart might race and you might feel those same symptoms of physiological arousal. (I think I was experiencing extra physiological arousal because I also had the irrational feeling that I would somehow fall into the Grand Canyon while standing on its rim.) The really interesting thing about physiological arousal and attraction is that sometimes we transfer physiological arousal from one stimulus to an attractive partner. Maybe this is why I found Dave so attractive?

What the research says

Dutton and Aron (1974) performed an ingenious field experiment testing the transfer of physiological arousal to an attractive opposite-sex individual. Specifically, they were interested in whether feelings of anxiety could intensify attraction. The researchers asked an attractive female research assistant to stop men who were crossing a bridge without a female companion and ask them to fill out a survey (the survey was supposedly on the impact of scenic imagery on creative writing). Men ranging in age from 18–35 participated while crossing two different bridges in Vancouver, Canada. One bridge was a suspension bridge, very high above the ground, that swung and swayed. The other bridge was very low to the ground and very stable. The researchers hypothesized that the men who crossed the high bridge would feel a lot of physiological arousal (or in this case, anxiety) due to crossing the bridge and that some of that arousal might be attributed to the attractive woman administering the survey. Upon completing the survey, the research assistant offered to explain the research in more detail if the men wished to call her for an explanation. Dutton and Aron found that the men who crossed the high bridge felt more attracted to the female confederate and also were more likely to call her. The authors attributed these results to a transfer of those heightened feelings of physiological arousal from crossing the high bridge to the female research assistant. Men who were already feeling physiologically aroused were more likely to feel attracted to the research assistant than were men who crossed the low, stable bridge.

Think critically

In Dutton and Aron's (1974) research, men chose whether to cross the high or low bridge; they were not randomly assigned to cross one bridge or the other. What type of problem does this cause in interpreting the results of this research? What type of men might be more likely to choose to cross a high, swinging suspension bridge? What type of men might be more likely to choose to cross the stable bridge?

In Dutton and Aron's (1974) project exploring physiological arousal and attraction, if different types of men chose to cross the two different bridges, personality type and physiological arousal levels might be confounded with one another. That is, if only "daring" men chose to cross the high bridge, while only "conservative" men chose to cross the low bridge, it would be impossible to determine whether different personality types or different levels of physiological arousal influenced the men's decision, later, to call the attractive woman. Therefore, Dutton and Aron employed a variety of controls to ensure that their results could not be explained by this confound. First, in the original study, a male interviewer also stopped men on both the low and high bridge. There were no differences in tendency to call for results when the male research assistant interviewed men on each bridge. Further, Dutton and Aron followed their field experiment with two other studies. In one study the female research assistant stopped men ten minutes after they had crossed the bridge or while on the bridge. Once again, they found that men who filled out the questionnaire while crossing the bridge (versus ten minutes later) were more likely to call the attractive research assistant. Further, in a laboratory experiment, the researchers experimentally manipulated anxiety (by an anticipated electric shock). Those men who were expecting a painful electric shock were more attracted to a female confederate. So it seems that increased physiological arousal can increase the perceived attractiveness of an attractive woman.

Similarly, Meston and Frohlich (2003) also showed that heightened physiological arousal increased the perceived attractiveness of a target person. These authors performed research showing that roller-coaster riders at an amusement park were more attracted to a target person after they had ridden the roller coaster than when waiting in line before riding the roller coaster. (They were shown a photograph of a person of the other sex who was previously rated as average in attractiveness.) However, in the same study, the authors found that attraction for one's own romantic partner was not increased by the thrill of riding the roller coaster. Meston and Frohlich believed that attraction toward one's own partner may not have been increased because the attraction ratings for one's own partner were already so high (typically a 6 or 7 on a 7-point scale).

Based upon the research reviewed above, it seems the events that increase physiological arousal can also increase attraction to a good-looking person. Interestingly, these effects even seem to occur when we realize that the physiological arousal stemmed from a source other than a prospective romantic partner (see Foster et al., 1998). Furthermore, research by Ma-Kellams et al. (2012) suggests that Asian participants may be more vulnerable to these effects than their European–American counterparts. These authors found an increased tendency for Asian participants to attribute physiological arousal to an attractive confederate of the researchers following a virtual walk over a deep chasm. But before rushing out to participate in a dangerous or exciting activity, consider this qualification: arousal can also increase feelings of revulsion for an unattractive target.

What the research says

White et al. (1981) asked male undergraduate students from the United States to participate in a study purportedly assessing attitude similarity and attraction. In order to assess their attitudes towards a variety of stimuli, the researchers asked the men to listen to music, complete puzzles, and exercise. The men were randomly assigned to jog in place for 2 minutes or for 15 seconds (ostensibly to activate their attitudes about exercise). Then the men watched a video of a potential partner and rated their first impressions of her. The men were randomly assigned to watch a video of a woman who was presented in an attractive (hair done nicely, makeup on, nice clothing) or in an unattractive manner (unattractive makeup, head covered with a scarf, sloppy clothing). The authors found that the woman was liked more when she was presented as attractive and the men had jogged for two minutes. But, the woman was liked less when she was presented as unattractive and the men had jogged for two minutes. The authors interpreted these results to suggest that the arousal from the exercise intensified the men's feelings of attraction or revulsion toward the woman in the video.

Think critically

In White et al.'s (1981) research, one woman was made up to look either attractive or unattractive. Presumably, this woman knew whether she was being made to look attractive or unattractive. Could this knowledge have influenced her behavior on the video? Could her behavior (and not necessarily her perceived attractiveness) thus account for the results?

The research reviewed above on physiological arousal suggests that if you want to attract a mate, you should make yourself look as attractive as possible and then proceed to an exciting venue. I always advise my students to hang out at the gym if they are looking for a potential date. However, I do not advise my students to exercise at the gym. Rather, they should make themselves look as attractive as possible and then just hang around (or better yet, walk by and capitalize on excitation transfer and mere exposure at the same time) while their potential mates do the exercising and experience all the physiological arousal. Alternatively, I advise my students to go dancing, thus maximizing their attraction to their date as well as their date's attraction to them. Below, we review research on dancing which suggests that good dancing can also enhance feelings of attraction.

Dancing

In addition to dancing elevating physiological arousal and thus potentially enhancing our attraction to physically pleasing others, you may be surprised to learn that how a potential partner dances may allow us to evaluate some of his other characteristics as well. Intuitively, one might expect that good dancers would be perceived as more attractive than poor dancers (Weege et al., 2012); however, good dancing may also indicate that individuals possess other desirable characteristics, such as good genes, physical strength, or pleasant personalities.

Interestingly, much of the research on dancing has been conducted with German participants. For example, Weege et al. (2012) found that women spent more time watching and felt more attracted to good dancers than to bad dancers. (In this research, the women viewed avatars displaying the men's dance motions rather than real men dancing.) Furthermore, Hugill et al. (2009) found that men's dancing ability (as rated by women who judged avatars) was correlated with their physical strength (as measured by handgrip strength). Perhaps most surprisingly, Fink et al. (2012) found that men's dancing ability was linked to men's self-ratings on certain personality characteristics. Men who were judged as good dancers rated themselves higher on the traits of conscientiousness and agreeableness. The authors suggest that dancing may serve to convey information about health and fitness as well as personality characteristics, which may then inspire our mate choices.

Positing that dancing may be a courtship signal which could indicate "good genes," Brown et al. (2005) showed that in a sample of Jamaican men (who had been previously classified as very symmetrical or asymmetrical), women rated the symmetrical men as better dancers than asymmetrical men. Although symmetrical women were also rated as better dancers than their more asymmetrical counterparts, the relationship was much stronger for men than it was for women. As discussed in Chapter 1, symmetry may be a signal of good genes and, thus, a potential benefit to mating with a symmetrical partner.

While men's dancing may indicate the quality of their genes, women's dancing may indicate their fertility status. Most research on perceptions of women's dancing involves men's reactions to women across their menstrual cycles. For example, Miller et al. (2007) found that normally ovulating lap-dancers earned more tips during the most fertile portion of their cycle, while lap-dancers using hormonal contraceptives showed no such shift in tip earnings (see Chapter 4). Furthermore, Fink et al. (2012) found that men rated women's dancing as more attractive during the fertile portion of their menstrual cycle (relative to the non-fertile portion of their cycle).

The contrast effect

Stimuli (even prospective romantic partners) are not generally perceived in a vacuum. For example, when my friend Louise (see Chapter 1) scrolls through profile pictures, she does not consider each photo independently; she compares and contrasts men with one another. She might say, "This guy is much more attractive than the other men I've seen," or "this guy is much less attractive." Or, when she goes out with her friends, she might observe a group of men and discern which one of the group she finds to be most attractive. Other targets can impact how attractive a potential partner is perceived to be. The contrast effect can help to explain why some targets are rated as more or less attractive relative to other targets.

The contrast effect is one of my favorite topics to talk about in class because it is so easy to illustrate. If you have ever been to an establishment with both a pool and a hot tub, you will easily comprehend the contrast effect. Imagine you go to the pool with the intention of taking a swim. You dip your foot into the pool and test the temperature. It will likely feel a little chilly because at that point you are comparing it with the temperature of the air, which is likely a little warmer. But then imagine that you decide to soak in the hot tub first, and you get used to the steamy hot water. If you then return to the pool and you dip your foot back into the pool again, how would the pool water feel now? Because you are now contrasting the temperature of the pool with the warm feeling of the hot tub, the pool will feel much colder. A similar process can happen in judging the attractiveness of a potential partner. A target person may seem more or less attractive depending upon a comparison (or contrast) with another person.

What the research says

Kenrick and Gutierres (1980) performed some entertaining research with male dormitory residents from the United States in the late 1970s. The researchers asked two male college students to approach men who were watching the original *Charlie's Angels* series on television or men who were watching another show. The students asked the men to rate a photograph of a woman as a potential blind date for a friend. The authors found that men who were watching *Charlie's Angels* rated the photograph of the woman as less attractive than those men who were watching another show. The authors interpreted these results as showing the contrast effect, that a woman of average attractiveness looked less attractive when compared (even unconsciously) to the beautiful women in the *Charlie's Angels* series.

Think critically

In Kenrick and Gutierres' (1980) research, the research assistants approached men who were already watching one show or another. Do you think these results might differ if the men were randomly assigned to watch a television show? How might men choosing to watch *Charlie's Angels* differ from men who chose to watch a different show?

Once again, the contrast effect is a valuable thing to keep in mind when looking for a potential mate. I advise my students to go to their next social event and wait outside the door for someone unattractive to arrive. Then, I advise them to follow that person into the party. Hopefully, a potential partner will be watching the door and see the unattractive person walk in, followed by my student, thereby enhancing the attractiveness of the student. What is interesting about the contrast effect is that in order for the effect to occur, the stimuli must be presented successively, not simultaneously (Geiselman et al., 1984), so if you are hoping to capitalize on this effect, you cannot walk into the party *with* the unattractive person, you have to walk in *after* the unattractive person.

In "contrast" to the contrast effect, Geiselman et al. (1984) found evidence for what they call an "assimilation effect" (p. 409) for stimuli that are presented simultaneously. In a series of four studies, the researchers presented photographs of a "target" face along with other "context" faces (p. 409) to undergraduates from the United States. These authors found that a target face of average attractiveness was actually perceived as more attractive when presented simultaneously with context faces which were highly attractive. So hanging around with more attractive individuals on a regular basis may enhance our attractiveness as well. Conversely, when the target faces were presented right *after* the context faces, a contrast effect occurred, the target faces of average attractiveness were perceived as less attractive when following a highly attractive context face.

Perceivers may consciously or unconsciously compare targets to one another, in some cases enhancing the attractiveness of a particular target and in some cases diminishing the attractiveness of a particular target. However, both the contrast effect and the assimilation effect may be short-lived and may cease to impact perceptions once the comparison stimuli are no longer in view. The duration of these effects should be investigated in future research.

The color red

Another strategy individuals may want to use to appear most attractive to the opposite sex is to wear the color red. In a variety of experiments, Elliot and Niesta (2008) showed that undergraduate men from the United States viewed a photograph of a moderately attractive woman as more physically attractive when her photograph was presented with a red background (rather than a white, gray, or green background). Furthermore, a different photo of another moderately attractive woman was also rated as more physically attractive by men when the woman wore a red shirt rather than a blue shirt. This effect seems robust across cultures. In a separate study, Elliot et al. (2013) replicated this effect with a sample of adult men from a small country in western Africa.

In another study investigating women's perceptions of male targets, Elliot et al. (2010) showed that women found a photograph of an attractive man as more attractive when presented with a red background (rather than a white or gray background) and when he wore a red shirt (relative to a green, gray, or blue shirt). (The research involving women's perceptions of men was performed in the United States, Germany, China, and England.) Perceptions of men's sexual attractiveness and social status were enhanced by the color red, but perceptions of agreeableness or extroversion were unchanged based upon the color of the man's shirt.

Just as men and women perceive members of the opposite sex (but not the same sex; see: Elliot & Niesta, 2008; Elliot et al., 2010) as more attractive when they are wearing the color red, women are also more likely to choose to wear the color red if they are expecting to converse with an attractive rather than an unattractive man (or with a woman). The researchers gathered background information from women and created bogus descriptions of potential interaction partners who were either described as attractive or unattractive male partners, or "average" or attractive female partners. The researchers then told the women that they would need to choose a standard shirt to wear during the conversation "for the sake of experimental control" (p. 600) and were shown photographs of red and green shirts (or red and blue shirts) in a random order. Women were more likely to choose the red shirt when they were expecting to interact with an attractive man (rather than an unattractive man, or an average or attractive woman). The researchers interpreted these results as showing that women use the color red as a sign of their potential sexual interest in a male partner.

Using the color red in order to enhance attractiveness should be done with a few caveats in mind. First, as suggested above, if women use the color red to signal sexual interest, men may expect women wearing red to be appropriate partners for short-term rather than long-term relationships. Future research will be necessary to test this suggestion. Second, research by Schwarz and Singer (2013) suggests that the color red enhances perceptions of sexual attractiveness only for young women (in this research, the young women were perceived as approximately 23 years old), not for older female targets (perceived as approximately 48 years old). Future research should determine whether men's age impacts their attractiveness when wearing red as well.

Closing time

Another strategy one might want to use in order to appear most attractive is to arrive at the end of the evening. A number of researchers have shown evidence for what is deemed the "closing time" effect; both men and women appear better looking at the end of the evening. In 1979, Pennebaker et al. asked men and women at three different bars in the southern United States to rate the attractiveness of the members of the opposite sex at different times of the evening. In this research, members at one bar were approached at 9 p.m., members at a second bar were approached at 10:30 p.m., and members at a third bar were approached at 12 a.m. (30 minutes prior to closing time). The researchers found that both men and women rated members of the other sex as more attractive later in the evening relative to earlier in the evening. In their article, the authors acknowledged the limitations of their research design: because individuals at one bar may have actually been more attractive than individuals at another bar, and because the amount of alcohol consumed may have influenced the participants' ratings, the effects observed could not be exclusively attributed to the time of the evening.

In order to rectify some of the design limitations of Pennebaker et al.'s (1979) research, Johnco et al. (2010) conducted a repeated-measures study of the attractiveness of same-sex and opposite-sex individuals at a bar in Australia while controlling for blood-alcohol levels. The researchers measured both attraction to other individuals as well as blood-alcohol content throughout the evening. In this study, as in Pennebaker et al.'s research, participants rated the "average physical attractiveness of the opposite-sex participants and same-sex partici-pants" (p. 264) rather than making ratings of particular individuals. The results revealed that participants found members of the other sex as more attractive as the evening progressed while attraction to members of the same sex stayed the same. Although, as one might expect, alcohol consumption increased over time, the attractiveness effect remained even after controlling for blood-alcohol content. (Other research shows that level of intoxication and perceptions of the attractiveness of opposite-sex targets are positively related: see Lyvers et al., 2011.) Johnco et al. interpreted these results as consistent with mere expo-sure theory (discussed earlier in this chapter), stating that participants may have viewed members of the other sex more positively after repeated exposure to them throughout the night. The authors also speculate that same-sex indi-viduals were not rated as more attractive because attention throughout the evening might be directed toward members of the other sex.

Although not mentioned by Johnco et al. (2010), one limitation associated with their research on the closing time effect is that the participants' responses may have been impacted by demand characteristics. Demand characteristics are cues that might lead the participants to discern the purpose of the study and thus adjust their behaviors or responses (Beins, 2013). If a researcher approached you repeatedly throughout the night and asked you how attrac-tive you perceived the other bar patrons to be, might you expect that the research had to do with perceptions of attractiveness over time? If so, you might consciously or unconsciously adjust your responses due to the demand characteristics of the situation. So both the between groups design employed by Pennebaker et al. (1979) and the repeated-measures design employed by Johnco et al. have limitations associated with them. However, the replication of similar results across the two designs can strengthen our confidence in this effect. The closing time effect should be explored in future research designed to minimize demand characteristics (for example, providing participants with filler items to answer or randomly approaching patrons at the same bar at different points throughout the evening). The impact of demand characteristics on perceptions of attractiveness may also be relevant when rating one's own level of attractiveness. Current research reveals that people perceive *themselves* as more attractive after consuming alcohol or after consuming a non-alcoholic beverage which they believe to be alcohol (Bègue et al., 2013).

Chapter summary

In this chapter we reviewed research presenting several important bases for attraction (i.e., proximity, familiarity, similarity, reciprocity). We are more attracted to others who are physically close to us, whom we encounter frequently, who are similar to us, and who like us. We also reviewed factors that can enhance attraction to targets (i.e., physiological arousal, contrast effects, the color red, closing time). Furthermore, we reviewed some interesting research on the effects of dancing and eye contact on perceptions of attractiveness. Dancing, especially good dancing, may provide cues to other characteristics of a potential mate, such as good genes, strength, personality characteristics, or ovulatory status (in women). Eye contact may serve as an indicator of initial attraction or may serve to increase liking between individuals. We present our suggestions for future reading below.

Suggested reading

Davis, J. L., & Rusbult, C. E. (2001). Attitude alignment in close relationships. *Journal of Personality and Social Psychology, 81*(1), 65–84. doi:10.1037/0022-3514.81.1.65
    This research shows that the desire for attitudinal similarity within a romantic relationship is so strong that we may even change our own attitudes to match our partners' attitudes when we perceive a discrepancy.
Dutton, D., & Aron, A. (1974). Some evidence for heightened sexual attraction under conditions of high anxiety. *Journal of Personality and Social Psychology, 30*(4), 510–517. doi:10.1037/h0037031.
    This classic research is interesting to read because of the nature of field research as well as the need to eliminate other plausible causes in non-experimental research. The subject matter is also very interesting.

Elliot, A. J., & Niesta, D. (2008). Romantic red: Red enhances men's attraction to women. *Journal of Personality and Social Psychology, 95*(5), 1150–1164. doi:10.1037/0022-3514.95.5.1150

This series of experiments shows that the color red enhances women's attractiveness. These authors also do a very good job of eliminating other possible causes in their experimental research.

Fraley, R., & Marks, M. J. (2010). Westermarck, Freud, and the incest taboo: Does familial resemblance activate sexual attraction? *Personality and Social Psychology Bulletin, 36*(9), 1202-1212. doi:10.1177/0146167210377180

If you read this article, you will enjoy learning how the authors manipulated family resemblance. It may not be enjoyable to learn that family resemblance is related to increased sexual attraction.

Whitchurch, E. R., Wilson, T. D., & Gilbert, D. T. (2011). "He loves me, he loves me not ….": Uncertainty can increase romantic attraction. *Psychological Science, 22*(2), 172–175. doi:10.1177/0956797610393745

This article is short, but highlights the counter-intuitive possibility that uncertainty in liking may be more attractive than certainty.

Part II
Romantic Relationships

Assessing and Changing Attitudes toward Romantic Partners

6

For many years now, I have begun my Social Psychology course with a discussion of attitudes. An attitude can be defined as "a positive, negative, or mixed reaction to a person, object, or idea" (Kassin et al., 2011, p. 206). Attitudes are often conceptualized as *feelings*, so this topic lends itself well to relationship examples. If you have your eye on a potential romantic partner, how do you feel about that individual? Do you have a positive attitude toward her? If you currently have a romantic partner, consider how you feel about that individual. Do you feel positively? Is your relationship likely to continue? If you have an *ex*-romantic partner, consider how you feel toward that individual. Do you have a positive or negative attitude toward your ex? And has your attitude changed since your break-up? In this chapter we feature new ways to measure attitudes toward romantic partners, and we present theories which help to explain why our attitudes toward our partners may change.

Implicit attitudes toward romantic partners

A relatively new and intriguing method of assessing attitudes toward romantic partners involves assessing implicit attitudes or "spontaneous affective reactions" (Eastwick et al., 2011a, p. 994). Researchers have used these methods to investigate participants' implicit reactions to both hypothetical and real-life romantic partners. These studies have revealed some interesting results. For example, in a project exploring implicit attitudes toward physical attractiveness in an ideal romantic partner, Eastwick et al. (2011a) found that men and women were equally likely to associate physical attractiveness with an ideal romantic partner (see Chapter 1 for a discussion of the importance of physical attractiveness to both sexes). Furthermore, Zayas and Shoda (2005) found that favorable implicit attitudes toward a current romantic partner were positively correlated with a secure attachment style (see Chapter 7 for more information about attachment styles). Conversely, Imhoff and Banse (2011) found that favorable implicit attitudes toward an ex-partner were associated with more distress after a break-up (especially for participants who had not initiated a new romantic relationship). Before we describe this research in more detail, we should first explain what implicit attitudes are, how they are assessed, and how they differ from explicit attitudes.

Background information on implicit and explicit attitudes

In Eastwick et al.'s (2011a) article, the authors define implicit attitudes as "spontaneous affective reactions" (p. 994). Therefore, implicit attitudes can be thought of as our "gut" reactions to a particular stimulus, whether positive or negative. According to Greenwald and Banaji (1995) implicit attitudes are automatically activated, without effort on the part of the participant. For example, when my older son, Roy, was a baby he used to tote a Curious George doll with him wherever he went. When my younger son, Russell, was a baby his choice was Rudolph the Red-Nosed Reindeer. Over time I began to associate George with my son Roy and Rudolph with my son Russell. So if I were to encounter one of those characters now – perhaps I might see Curious George on television – that stimulus might automatically elicit a positive implicit attitude or "spontaneous affective reaction" even if I did not consciously associate Curious George with my son.

Greenwald and Banaji (1995) also describe implicit attitudes as being: unattainable through introspection; inaccessible to conscious thought or self-report; not deliberative; and outside of the control of the participant. In these ways, implicit attitudes are different from explicit attitudes, which are attitudes that you can think about and control the expression of. For example, if I asked whether you preferred red jelly beans to black jelly beans, you could think about your prior experiences eating jelly beans, deliberate about which tasted better, and express your preferences. You could even control your explicit responses. Imagine that you really preferred red jelly beans, but you knew that I also preferred red jelly beans and there was only one red jelly bean left. You could control your explicit responses by graciously stating that you preferred black jelly beans, thus allowing me to eat the last red jelly bean.

Implicit attitudes, on the other hand, are not controllable; they happen automatically, whether we intend to experience them or not. In fact, research by Cunningham et al. (2003) illustrates that stimuli are sometimes spontaneously evaluated even when participants are performing another type of task. In Cunningham et al.'s research, some participants were asked to judge stimulus persons as good or bad, and some participants were asked to judge stimulus persons as associated with the past or present. All participants performed this task while an fMRI measured their brain activity. The results showed that regardless of whether the participants were asked to judge good/bad or past/present, the researchers found activation in the amygdala, the area of the brain associated with emotion. These results suggest that participants were automatically evaluating the stimulus persons as good or bad even when they were not explicitly asked to do so (Cunningham et al., 2003).

Furthermore, because implicit attitudes are not controllable (Greenwald & Banaji, 1995), they are not vulnerable to distortion due to concerns over social desirability. For example, it may be socially desirable to express positive explicit attitudes toward one's romantic partner (LeBel & Campbell, 2009; Morry et al., 2010; Murray et al., 1996a). Murray et al. found that married and dating couples from Canada expressed more positive explicit attitudes toward their partners than the partners expressed about themselves. Furthermore, Murray et al. also found that married and dating partners tended to rate their counterparts more favorably than a "typical" partner. Similarly, Morry et al. found that married couples from Canada rated their partners higher than themselves on positive traits. However, even though people may tend to express positive *explicit* attitudes about their companions, individuals may differ in the degree to which they experience positive *implicit* attitudes toward their partners.

Assessing implicit attitudes toward potential partners

Because we cannot consciously think about our implicit attitudes, they must be measured by different methods than we use to assess explicit attitudes (i.e., self-report measures). As reviewed by Nosek et al. (2011) there are currently more than 20 different tasks that have been developed in order to assess implicit attitudes. The most commonly used methods for assessing implicit attitudes involve reaction-time tasks predicated on the fact that two concepts which are strongly implicitly linked to each other in memory ought to be quickly associated with each other (Nosek et al., 2011). Below we review research using a variety of different ways to evaluate implicit attitudes toward hypothetical and actual romantic partners.

What the research says

In Eastwick et al.'s (2011) exploration of implicit attitudes toward ideal romantic partners, participants were asked to perform a reaction-time task called a GNAT (Go/No-go Association Task, see Nosek & Banaji, 2001). The participants were primarily White and Asian-American undergraduate students from the United States. In order to complete the task, the participants read and classified words that appeared in the center of a computer screen. On some trials, the participants were told to press the space bar ("go") if the word was a synonym for physical attractiveness (i.e., "nice body, good looking, sexy," etc.) or a synonym for an ideal partner (i.e., "wonderful partner, desired partner, perfect partner," etc., p. 996). For these trials participants were also instructed *not* to press the space bar ("no go") for distractor words (i.e., words that were not synonyms for physical attractiveness, such as "understanding, supportive, considerate," etc.) or for words that were synonyms for a non-ideal partner (i.e., "terrible partner, undesired partner, imperfect partner," etc., p. 997). On other trials, the pattern for responding was altered; participants were asked to press the space bar for words that indicated a synonym for physical attractiveness or a synonym for a non-ideal partner. The researchers recorded participants' reaction times when physical attractiveness was paired with "ideal partner" and compared those to reaction times when physical attractiveness was paired with "non-ideal partner." As predicted, the authors found that reaction times were faster when "physical attractiveness...was paired with the concept of an ideal partner rather than a non-ideal partner" (p. 997). Importantly, there was no sex difference in implicit attitudes toward the physical attractiveness of an ideal partner. Men did not more strongly associate physical attractiveness with an ideal partner than did women.

Think critically

In Eastwick et al.'s (2011) research, they found that men and women did not differ in their implicit attitudes toward a physically attractive ideal partner. However, the concept of physical attractiveness was presented verbally (i.e., nice body, good looking, etc.). Do you think the results of this research might differ if photographs of physically attractive or unattractive potential partners were presented rather than verbal descriptors?

In Eastwick et al.'s (2011) research described above, the participants also related their explicit attitudes regarding ideal partners. Participants rated how much terms like "nice body, good looking, sexy" (p. 997) would describe their ideal romantic partner. Interestingly, although men and women differed in their explicit attitudes (with men expressing a stronger desire for physical attractiveness in an ideal partner), men and women did not differ in their implicit attitudes (the tendency to more quickly associate physical attractiveness with an ideal partner). Correspondingly, in another study discussed within the same article, the authors reported that the implicit preference for a physically attractive ideal partner was also related to a preference for a physically attractive real-life partner at a speed-dating event. Eastwick et al.'s research suggests that although we may not realize it, both men and women react more positively to physically attractive partners on a very basic level.

Assessing implicit attitudes toward current romantic partners

In Zayas and Shoda's (2005) research, participants completed a different type of task to measure implicit attitudes toward current romantic partners. These authors found that a positive implicit attitude toward one's current romantic partner was associated with a more secure attachment style.

What the research says

In Zayas and Shoda's (2005) research project, undergraduate students from the United States who were currently involved with romantic partners were invited to complete an Implicit Associations Test (IAT; see Greenwald et al., 1998). The IAT used in this project was similar to the GNAT described above in that it is also a reaction-time task presented via computer which measures implicit attitudes. The IAT task differs slightly from the

GNAT task, however. In the IAT task administered by Zayas and Shoda, participants were asked to generate a list of words that uniquely described their relationship partner (e.g., "first name, nickname, hair color, city of birth," p. 1014) as well as a list of words that would not describe their romantic partner. Additionally, this research employed lists of pleasant (e.g., "success, health, peace") and unpleasant (e.g., "bomb, rotten, disaster," p. 1014) words as stimuli. A word from one of the four word lists appeared in the center of the screen, and participants had to classify it using the response keys of "A" on the left side of the keyboard and "5" on the numerical keypad on the right side of the keyboard. For some trials, partner descriptions and pleasant words shared a response key (for example, the "A" key) and non-partner descriptions and unpleasant words shared the other response key, while for other trials the pattern was reversed. As predicted by the researchers, participants performed this task faster when the partner descriptions and positive words shared the response key. Furthermore, the more quickly participants responded when partner and positive words were paired, the more secure the participants rated their attachment style to that partner (see Chapter 7 for information about attachment styles).

Think critically

Zayas and Shoda (2005) found that positive implicit attitudes toward a current romantic partner were related to a more secure attachment style. Do you think participants' implicit attitudes cause a more secure attachment style? Or that a secure attachment style causes more positive implicit attitudes? Is there a third variable which could potentially cause both a more secure attachment style and a more positive implicit attitude? Which of these variables do you think would change if the partnership was dissolved?

In LeBel and Campbell's (2009) research these authors used an implicit task involving ratings of the participants' partners' initials to assess implicit attitudes toward current romantic partners. Romantically involved undergraduates from Canada rated how "esthetically pleasing" (p. 1292) they found each letter of the alphabet when presented in a random order. The authors found that participants preferred their partners' initials to other letters, indicating positive implicit attitudes toward their romantic partners. Furthermore, the positivity of the students' implicit attitudes was associated with greater relationship satisfaction as well as a reduced likelihood of breaking up over a four-month period.

Positive implicit attitudes toward current partners seem to be beneficial to our relationships. We are more likely to have a secure attachment style, greater relationship satisfaction, and a reduced likelihood of breaking up if we have positive implicit attitudes toward our companions. Do you expect that it would be more beneficial to have a positive or negative implicit attitude towards an ex-partner?

Assessing implicit attitudes toward ex-partners

Imhoff and Banse (2011) explored the relationship between implicit attitudes toward an ex-partner and the distress experienced after the break-up of a romantic relationship. These authors used an interesting method to gather their sample. Undergraduates from Germany were asked to identify someone they knew who had recently experienced a break-up. These authors also used an interesting method to measure implicit attitudes. Imhoff and Banse used yet another type of procedure (an Affect Misattribution Procedure; see the article for a description, which also involved a reaction-time task completed via computer) in order to assess participants' implicit attitudes toward their ex-partners. Imhoff and Banse not only found that positive implicit attitudes toward an ex-partner were associated with more distress after a break-up, but also that positive implicit attitudes toward an ex-partner were associated with a stronger wish to reunite with that ex-partner. More surprisingly, the authors also reported that negative implicit attitudes toward an ex-romantic partner were associated with greater well-being after a break-up. These effects held only for participants who had not initiated a romantic relationship with a new partner. Participants with new partners not only exhibited less positive implicit attitudes toward their ex-partners, they also reported less distress following the break-up.

The above research shows that our implicit attitudes are related to our romantic behaviors and desires in important ways and in different ways than our explicit attitudes may be manifested. Future research should continue to assess implicit attitudes toward relationship partners and how those attitudes differentially predict romantic attraction and relationship characteristics.

Changing attitudes toward romantic partners

As discussed in the first three chapters, although first impressions tend to be very accurate and attitudes toward romantic partners tend to be positive, unless your relationship with a partner is going to be very short, you are likely to change your attitudes toward your partner during the course of your relationship. Attitudes may become more positive, more negative, or may even fluctuate in both directions over time. Reeder (2000) investigated undergraduates' perceptions of their opposite-sex friends over time and found that participants reported less romantic and less sexual attraction to their friends over time. Sprecher (1999) studied the changes in love, satisfaction, and commitment reported by heterosexual romantic relationship partners. She found that couples who stayed together over the course of the four-year data collection believed that their love, satisfaction, and commitment toward their partners had increased over time. Conversely, couples who had experienced a break-up reported that their satisfaction and commitment (but not love) had declined prior to the break-up. Although Sprecher collected data once each year for four years, she speculated that more frequent data collection might reveal increases as well as decreases in romantic feelings over time.

Recent research by Larson et al. (2013) supports this speculation that attitudes toward partners fluctuate over time. According to Larson et al., women change their attitudes toward their current romantic partners over the course of their menstrual cycles. These authors report that women who perceived their partners as more sexually attractive rated them more positively during the most fertile part of their cycles while women who perceived their partners as less sexually attractive rated them more negatively during the most fertile part of their cycle. Furthermore, Laurenceau et al. (2005) explored the feelings of undergraduate men and women toward their current romantic partners over a ten-day period. These authors found that both men and women who felt greater intimacy with their partners also expressed more positive feelings toward one another. Conversely, men who reported more conflict also felt more anxiety in their relationships.

A media moment: In Jane Austen's novel *Pride and Prejudice*, Mr. Darcy first observes Elizabeth at a ball. His friend, Mr. Bingley, tries to persuade Darcy to dance and identifies Elizabeth as an attractive dancing partner. Mr. Darcy, however, expresses ambivalence toward Elizabeth, stating that "she is tolerable, but not handsome enough to tempt *me*" (Austen, 2001, p. 183). Later, Mr. Darcy's attitude towards Elizabeth begins to shift. When they next meet, he begins to perceive her face as beautiful, thinking that "it was rendered uncommonly intelligent by the beautiful expression of her dark eyes" (p. 188). Furthermore, although at first "he had detected with a critical eye more than one failure of perfect symmetry in her form, he was forced to acknowledge her figure to be light and pleasing" (p. 188). As the book progresses, Mr. Darcy's attitudes again become more favorable. He states of Elizabeth that "it is many months since I have considered her as one of the handsomest women of my acquaintances" (p. 303). If Mr. Darcy's attitudes begin as relatively ambivalent and become more favorable, Elizabeth's attitudes start as negative and become positive. At the same ball, Elizabeth and her family perceive Mr. Darcy as "the proudest, most disagreeable man in the world" (p. 183). After some months, Mr. Darcy proposes to Elizabeth, and when she refuses him, she states "from the first moment...of my acquaintance with you...your arrogance, your conceit, and your selfish disdain of the feelings of others...have built so immovable a dislike; and I had not known you a month before I felt that you were the last man in the world whom I could ever be prevailed on to marry" (p. 268). But within a few more months Elizabeth "gave him to understand that her sentiments had undergone so material a change...as to make her receive with gratitude and pleasure his present assurances" (p. 349). In return, Mr. Darcy expresses his love "as sensibly and as warmly as a man violently in love can be supposed to do" (p. 349). So what processes underlie the changes in attitudes we sometimes experience with our romantic partners?

Cognitive dissonance theory

Two of my favorite theories regarding attitude formation and change have always been cognitive dissonance theory (Festinger & Carlsmith, 1959) and self-perception theory (Bem, 1967). We will begin our discussion of these theories with cognitive dissonance theory. Cognitive dissonance theory is a complex theory, but once you wade through its complexities, you will enjoy applying this theory to your own life.

First dates

To apply cognitive dissonance theory to attitudes toward romantic partners, I will use my favorite professor's essay question: "Imagine that you are a fairly boring person. Somehow you manage to get someone to invite you out for dinner. According to cognitive dissonance theory, which would improve your chances of having a second date – getting your date to pay for a really expensive meal at a fancy French restaurant, or a cheap one at the local burger joint?" (Rakowitz, 1995, p. 204). I ask this question of my students each year at the start of class, before we have discussed any theory or research. The students are usually in consensus that you should choose a moderately priced restaurant, and they are usually split as to whether "the guy should pick up the check" or the couple should "split the bill." They are typically intrigued to learn that based upon cognitive dissonance theory, both of these answers are wrong.

One of the early experiments testing cognitive dissonance theory was conducted by Festinger and Carlsmith in 1959. These authors were interested in what happens to a person's attitudes when one performs a behavior which contradicts one's attitudes. Taking the restaurant example, imagine that your date finds you pretty boring. What will happen to her attitude toward you if she pays for an expensive dinner (a behavior which presumably contradicts the attitude that she finds you very boring)? Festinger and Carlsmith proposed that when our attitudes and our behaviors do not match, we experience cognitive dissonance. According to Festinger and Carlsmith, this inconsistency is uncomfortable, and we are motivated to reduce that discomfort. As the authors suggest, one way to reduce the discomfort is to change our attitudes to match our behavior.

What the research says

In Festinger and Carlsmith's (1959) seminal research, the researchers asked participants (who were all male undergraduates from the United States) to complete a very boring and repetitive task for an hour. Then, a confederate approached the each participant and asked him to fill in for another researcher who had not shown up for work. The confederate stated that all the participant had to do was to convince a waiting individual (actually another confederate, a woman) that the research was fun and exciting. Furthermore, the participant was informed that he would be paid for performing this duty. The participant was offered either $1 or $20 to fill in for the researcher. The participant then met the female confederate and told her that he thought the task was fun and that she should participate in the research project. Then the participant was sent to an interviewer and asked how he felt about the task. Consistent with cognitive dissonance theory, the participants who were paid just $1 to lie to the confederate reported enjoying the task more than the participants who were paid $20 (which in today's American dollars is about $160, a sizeable amount for research participation).

Festinger and Carlsmith explained these results through cognitive dissonance theory. The participants who agreed to lie to the confederate for $1 had attitudes and behaviors that did not match. They were probably thinking, "This is the most boring thing I've ever done," and "Why did I just tell this poor woman that the task was fun?" In order to reduce the cognitive dissonance (and make themselves feel better about what they had said), they changed their attitudes so that they actually reported enjoying the task more themselves. Those participants who were paid $20 to lie to the confederate did not experience cognitive dissonance. They were probably thinking, "This is the most boring thing I've ever done" and "Why did I just tell this poor woman that the task was fun? Because I was paid $20 to do so." (Do not forget how much money $20 was worth in 1959.)

Think critically

In Festinger and Carlsmith's (1959) research, participants were asked to lie to a stranger. Do you think that it would cause more or less dissonance if the participants had to lie to a good friend? How do you think you would reduce your feelings of cognitive dissonance if you told a good friend that a boring task was actually very interesting and fun?

Now that we have reviewed the background research on cognitive dissonance theory, we can consider how to apply this theory to dating and mating situations. First let us answer the question posed by my favorite professor: If you are a very boring person, you should go to a very expensive restaurant, and your date should pick up the check. What *should* happen is that your date will be thinking, "This person is so boring," and "Why did I just spend so much money to take this boring person out to dinner?" Given these inconsistent cognitions, your date should start to change her attitudes to fit her behavior, and your date will end up with a more positive attitude toward you.

Before all of the "boring" readers rush out to expensive restaurants with prospective romantic partners, let us consider a few caveats. First, the changes in attitudes reported in Festinger and Carlsmith's (1959) research were small (but statistically significant). Those who were paid $1 were not *enthusiastic* about the boring task, but their attitudes were significantly more positive than those who were paid $20. Therefore, even if your date changes her attitude slightly and views you as a little less boring, it may not be enough of a difference to elicit a second date. Second, no research has been conducted specifically on this topic of boring people and expensive restaurants, so this theory may not work in the context of this particular situation. (See Cooper's [1971] research, reviewed below for a study that comes close.) I have been asking students to try this tactic in real life and report back as to whether it works or not, but none ever have. Perhaps I do not have any "boring" students. Perhaps they are just afraid to try it, but really, it cannot hurt. Even if your date does not end up liking you, at least you will not have to pay for dinner.

There are a few other things to keep in mind when making cognitive dissonance theory work for you in this particular dating situation. First, you need to do just enough to elicit the offer to pay for dinner from your date (maybe just asking, "Will you pay for dinner?") in order to bring about the behavior and the attitude change. If your date justifies her behavior in another way ("Maybe he didn't bring his wallet"), her attitude will not necessarily change in the desired direction. Second, if your date has an external justification for the behavior (like the $20 offered to participants in Festinger and Carlsmith's original research), she will not change her attitude in the desired direction. So if you ask, "Will you pick up the check because I don't get paid until Thursday?" then your date may experience some dissonance, but will reduce that dissonance by focusing on this external justification ("I am only paying because he doesn't get paid until Thursday").

Consistent with research conducted by Cooper (1971), your date must know how boring you are prior to going out to dinner, and she must believe that she has freely chosen to pay for dinner and not believe that she was forced to pay. In Cooper's research, he varied whether participants knew their partners' negative characteristics ahead of time (partners were described as either timid or overconfident on a problem-solving task) as well as whether the participants were allowed to *choose* to work with that partner or were *forced* to work with that partner. Cooper found that participants who knew their partners had negative characteristics and chose to work with those partners anyway, liked their partners more than did participants who believed they had no choice but to work with undesirable partners. Interestingly, although the participants liked their undesirable partners more when they freely chose to work with them, they still did not enjoy working on the problem-solving task with them. Cooper's research suggests that although your date may like you more if she freely chooses to pay for your dinner in light of your boring demeanor, she may still find the whole experience of dinner distasteful.

Effort

Cognitive dissonance theory can also be used to explain why we like those things which we work hard to attain. Similar to the research reviewed above, if we can somehow induce our potential dates to work hard in order to obtain a date with us, they should like us better in the end.

A personal moment: A few years ago, my cousin Nick was interested in dating a co-worker named Jill. One day we were talking on the telephone and Nick told me that he and Jill were going to meet over the weekend to play tennis at her place (which was an hour away from his place). I advised him to change their meeting place to his condo complex instead of hers and I filled him in on the finer points of cognitive dissonance theory as it relates to effort. As explained by Aronson and Mills (1959), cognitive dissonance can arise from enduring an unpleasant experience in order to achieve something which is desired but almost inevitably involves some negative aspects as well. In this case, the hard work of driving a long distance in terrible traffic to play tennis might be not be dissonant with my cousin's positive characteristics (he is a good-looking, nice guy) but might be dissonant with my cousin's negative characteristics (for example, his atrocious spelling ability). Jill may be thinking, "Why did I drive all the way here to meet Nick when he is such a bad speller?" In order to reduce the dissonance, Aronson and Mills suggest that one might amplify the positive characteristics (maybe he is better-looking than Jill originally thought) and minimize the importance of the negative characteristics (who cares about spelling anyway?). Unfortunately for my cousin Nick, our scheme did nothing to interest his co-worker in dating him. Fortunately for my cousin, Nick, he is now married to a wonderful woman, and he did not have to use any dissonance tricks in their relationship.

What the research says

Aronson and Mills (1959) performed research testing the effect of the severity of initiation on group liking. They reasoned that if one were to travel a great distance to see a movie, one should like that movie better than if one could easily see that same movie at the local theater (p. 177). So, too, should one like a group more if one has to work hard in order to gain admittance to it. The researchers recruited female undergraduates from the United States to join group discussions on the psychology of sex. In one condition, the women had to read lurid words associated with sex (such as "fuck," "cock," and "screw," p. 178) out loud before joining the group discussion while, in another condition, the women read more mild terms (such as "prostitute," "virgin," and "petting," p. 178). Then all the women listened to the same pre-recorded group discussion (which, according to the researchers, was designed to be dull and boring and was about the sexual behavior of animals rather than humans). As expected, the researchers found that the women liked the discussion groups more when they had read the lurid words prior to joining the group.

Think critically

In Aronson and Mills' (1959) research, the authors found that women liked a boring discussion more if they had to work hard to gain admittance to the group. According to cognitive dissonance theory, one's initial attitudes toward the group must be negative and, thus, dissonant with the hard work it took to gain admittance. Do you think that the women would still report enjoying the group discussion more if they worked hard to gain admittance to an engaging and intriguing group discussion? Why or why not?

Torn between two lovers

Cognitive dissonance theory can also be used to explain the process that happens after we make a tough decision (Brehm, 1956), such as choosing between two attractive partners. Many researchers have studied what happens to our attitudes after we make a tough decision. They often find that we value the choice we have made more than the non-chosen alternative, even though the two options were initially judged relatively equally.

What the research says

Brehm (1956) asked undergraduate women from the United States to rate eight potential items as "payment" for participating in a research project. The women rated items such as radios, coffee-makers, toasters, and lamps. In order to create dissonance, the women were asked to choose as payment one of two items which they had initially rated nearly equally in attractiveness. After choosing one item, the women were then asked to rate the desirability of all of the items again. According to Brehm, the positive aspects of the non-chosen item should cause cognitive dissonance. Brehm found that after choosing their preferred item, the women tended to rate the chosen item as more desirable and the non-chosen item as less desirable in order to reduce the dissonance.

Think critically

Brehm (1956) found that women rated chosen items as more desirable and non-chosen items as less desirable following their decisions. Do you think the results of this research would change if the researchers made the choice for the participants? If the researchers randomly assigned the participants to receive one of two similarly rated items, do you think the women would experience cognitive dissonance? Do you think they would still devalue the item that they did not receive even though they did not choose one item over the other?

These re-valuing and devaluing processes are so fundamental that even monkeys seem to reduce dissonance in this fashion. Recent research shows that monkeys prefer the color of chosen M&M's to those of the non-chosen color, even though the two alternatives were at first equally liked (Egan et al., 2007). However, people of different cultures may revalue alternatives for different reasons. Kitayama et al. (2004) suggest that Japanese participants (who typically exhibit a more collectivistic orientation) may adjust their preferences due to the concern of being negatively evaluated by others. Conversely, the authors suggest that participants from the United States (who typically exhibit a more individualistic orientation) may adjust their preferences following a decision due to an internal concern for consistency.

A media moment: In the *Hunger Games* trilogy, the main character, Katniss, loves both her old friend, Gale, and her games' partner, Peeta. Throughout the second and third books in the series, Katniss struggles with her feelings for both of them. In the second book, *Catching Fire*, Katniss states, "Gale is mine. I am his. Anything else is unthinkable" (Collins, 2009, p. 154). But later in the same book Katniss kisses Peeta and thinks, "instead of satisfying me, the kisses have the opposite effect, of making my need greater" (p. 448). Presumably, Katniss has difficulty choosing which man she wants to be with for the long term and feels cognitive dissonance over both men's positive and negative qualities. (Spoiler Alert: If you do not want to know who Katniss chooses, do not read any further!) Consistent with Brehm's (1956) research, at the end of the third book,

Mockingjay, after Katniss chooses Peeta, she emphasizes the good things about Peeta and the bad things about Gale. She states: "[W]hat I need to survive is not Gale's fire, kindled with rage and hatred. I have plenty of fire myself. What I need is the dandelion in the spring. The bright yellow that means rebirth instead of destruction. The promise that life can go on, no matter how bad our losses. That it can be good again. And only Peeta can give me that" (Collins, 2010, p. 388).

Not only can emphasizing the positive aspects of a potential partner help to quell the cognitive dissonance associated with choosing between two partners, but emphasizing the positive aspects of a current partner can improve attitudes toward that partner. Fletcher et al. (2000) invited undergraduate students from New Zealand in new romantic relationships (less than one month) to participate in their research project, which assessed ideal partner characteristics and relationships. These authors found that participants who perceived their partners more positively on certain traits tended to value those traits more over time, possibly reflecting the increased importance of those traits due to cognitive dissonance reduction. For example, if your partner is generous, but not thoughtful, you might come to value generosity more than thoughtfulness.

When in a romantic relationship, in addition to viewing our current partners more positively, we may devalue potential alternative partners in order to avoid cognitive dissonance (Johnson & Rusbult, 1989). Johnson and Rusbult found that when presented with an attractive alternative partner, undergraduate students in committed romantic relationships actually reported that they found the alternative partner less attractive and experienced less desire to date that alternative partner than students in less committed relationships.

What the research says

Johnson and Rusbult (1989) recruited as participants undergraduate students from the United States who were currently in romantic relationships. The students were told that their university was considering creating a new computer dating service. The students were asked to evaluate their attitudes toward the new dating service as well as to evaluate a person who was described as an early subscriber to the dating service. The participants reviewed a photograph of the subscriber as well as some personality information. Although the personality information was held constant, the photographs were manipulated by the researchers to represent very attractive, moderately attractive, and unattractive men and women. The students provided ratings of the subscriber as well as ratings of their current dating partners. The researchers found that for individuals who were strongly committed to their relationship partners, the most attractive targets were "devalued" (p. 974) most severely. The highly attractive individuals were rated by strongly committed participants comparably to the ratings of participants who evaluated the unattractive and moderately attractive targets. The authors suggest that those who were strongly committed to their current relationship partners might have devalued the attractive targets because acknowledging their attraction to those targets might be inconsistent with their commitment to their current romantic relationships.The authors report that a committed partner's thoughts that: "'I am a loyal and committed partner' would be dissonant with the belief 'I am attracted to an alternative partner.' One means of decreasing such conflict is to reduce the perceived attractiveness of the alternative, by disparaging some personal quality of the alternative" (p. 968). These authors also found that, over time, alternative partners were evaluated even less favorably by those in committed relationships.

Think critically

Johnson and Rusbult's (1989) research involved undergraduate research participants who were currently in romantic relationships. How might the results differ if the authors investigated attitudes toward alternative partners in a sample of married adults? How might the results differ if the authors employed a sample of adults in non-monogamous relationships?

Breaking up

Consistent with the research discussed above, cognitive dissonance theory would predict that after a break-up, attitudes toward an ex-partner should become more negative. Schneider and Kenny (2000) found results consistent with these predictions. These researchers asked participants to evaluate both a friend who was a previous romantic partner and a opposite-sex friend who had never been a romantic partner. They found that participants reported more positive feelings toward the friend who was never a romantic partner and more negative feelings toward their exes. Although this research was not designed to test cognitive dissonance theory, the theory would predict that participants should adjust their attitudes toward their ex-partners (in a negative direction) in light of their behavior (breaking up), perhaps especially for the participants who were the initiators of the break-up.

Of course attitudes toward a romantic partner may become more negative prior to a break-up (e.g., Sprecher, 1999), and future research examining attitudes toward a partner before and after a break-up would be necessary to test a cognitive dissonance interpretation, yet several aspects of Schneider and Kenny's research facilitate the interpretation of the results through cognitive dissonance theory. First, in Schneider and Kenny's (2000) research, the participants were still friends with their ex-romantic partners. If their attitudes became too negative prior to the break-ups, one might expect that the participants would not want to retain those ex-partners as friends. Second, one might predict that participants may have more positive feelings toward a opposite-sex friend who has not yet been a romantic partner in the hopes that said friend might one day become a romantic partner (e.g., Reeder, 2000). However, Schneider and Kenny found that in this research project, participants reported a stronger desire for a romantic relationship with their exes than with their friends.

Research investigating ex-spouses' opinions is also consistent with the predictions of cognitive dissonance theory. Gray and Silver (1990) found that both members of divorced couples tended to view themselves positively and take less responsibility for their divorces, while simultaneously viewing their ex-partners negatively and maximizing their partners' accountability for the divorce. The fact that partners were contacted soon after filing for divorce supports a dissonance interpretation; blaming one's partner could be used to reduce the dissonance felt over both the lingering positive feelings toward a partner and the behavior of divorce.

Geher et al.'s (2005) research is also consistent with cognitive dissonance theory's predictions. In their first study, the researchers asked undergraduates from the United States who were currently in romantic relationships to rate the personalities and attachment styles of both their current and former partners from a "significant monogamous relationship" (p. 258). They found that participants tended to "idealize their current partners ... and devalue their former partners" (p. 266), rating their current romantic partners more favorably on almost all personality characteristics as well as on attachment styles. The authors interpreted these findings as consistent with other cognitive dissonance research showing that we devalue non-chosen alternatives (see Brehm, 1956; Jarcho et al., 2011; Sparks et al., 2012). In a second study investigating dissonance effects, undergraduate students involved in romantic relationships were asked to write essays about the positive characteristics of their former partners. Some participants were given the choice to write the essay or not, while others were told that they were "obligated" to write the essay (p. 272). Consistent with what cognitive dissonance theory would predict, participants who chose to write essays regarding the positive characteristics of their ex-partners had more positive attitudes toward their exes and also showed more "autonomic nervous system functioning" (p. 276) after the experimental manipulation (a potential indicator of the negative feelings associated with experiencing cognitive dissonance).

Cognitive dissonance theory does not preclude the idea that attitudes can influence behaviors (for example, one might think "my feelings for my partner have become more negative than positive; I plan to break up with him tomorrow"). Rather, the theory highlights the less intuitive possibility that behaviors can influence attitudes (for example, one might think, "Why did I write such positive things about my ex? I guess he's not so bad after all").

The resolution of cognitive dissonance after a break-up is one way in which individuals can begin to ameliorate their negative feelings about the dissolution. Another way to reduce negative feelings following a break-up is to become involved with a new partner. For example, Spielmann et al. (2009) found that individuals who were anxiously attached to their ex-partners experienced less desire for their exes after experimental manipulations designed to highlight the enhanced likelihood of finding a new partner. Furthermore, individuals who reported being in a new relationship following a break-up also reported less desire for their exes. Although these authors did not interpret their results in the context of cognitive dissonance theory, the theory applies to their results. Individuals may simultaneously be thinking: "I still love my ex-partner" and "I am dating a new partner." Although, initially, these two competing thoughts may cause dissonance, over time a person may adjust his thoughts to match his behaviors (e.g., "Maybe I don't love my ex that much after all").

Sexual infidelity

Cognitive dissonance theory can also be applied to other aspects of romantic relationships. For example, Anderson (2010) proposes that young men experience cognitive dissonance over the competing desires of having a long-term partner and the desire for sex with other women. Anderson interviewed 40 White, heterosexual, undergraduate men from England who were in romantic relationships of at least three months. The men were informed that the goal of the interviews was to identify some reasons why men cheat on their partners. Anderson interpreted the results of the interviews as consistent with cognitive dissonance theory. According to the author, undergraduate men see sex with an alternative partner as a temporary way to reduce the dissonance created by the desire for a loving, long-term relationship and the simultaneous desire to have uncommitted sex with other partners. Interestingly, Anderson also suggests that men blame their indiscretions on intoxication, an external justification that can also reduce the discomfort associated with two conflicting thoughts, such as "I love my partner," and "I just had sex with another woman." Anderson highlights an interesting double-standard, suggesting that although men view cheating as a venue to reduce the tension created by their competing desires, he reports that few men were "willing to permit their girlfriends to do the same" (p. 866, see Chapter 8 for more information on sexual double standards).

Abusive partners

Enander (2011) contends that cognitive dissonance processes may be involved both with staying in an abusive relationship and in leaving an abusive relationship. Enander interviewed 22 adult women from Sweden who had left abusive partners. Through the qualitative analysis of these interviews, the author suggests that, initially, focusing on the positive aspects of a partner may reduce the cognitive dissonance associated with an early instance of physical abuse. The author states: "[W]hen the abuser is still perceived as mainly good, informants seem to tackle being hurt…by focusing on his good aspects[,]…that is, they try to align their feelings with the conceptualization of being in a loving relationship with a basically good partner" (p. 37). In other words, the women will first try to reconcile their thoughts (e.g., "my partner hurt me") and behaviors (staying in the relationship) by focusing on the good aspects of their partners, similar to the research reviewed above. However, as the author states, after experiencing more violence, the women will also experience more cognitive dissonance. The author speculates that an "increased level of violence" or "fewer good periods" or "negative impact of the violence on the children" (p. 44) will lead to increasing dissonance (i.e., more negative feelings toward their abusive partners, while still staying in the relationship). Finally, Enander suggests that women who have left their abusive partners will focus on the negative aspects of that partner in order to reconcile their feelings after leaving. The author states that, after leaving abusive partners, women "struggle to not feel 'good' feelings for partners/ex-partners that they have decided are basically bad and not worth living with" (p. 44).

In sum, when our feelings and our behaviors do not seem to match one another, we may feel cognitive dissonance. The easiest way to reduce the dissonance is to modify our feelings to more closely match our behaviors. Thus, cognitive dissonance theory can explain why we come to like our present romantic partners more or why we like our ex-partners less.

Self-perception theory

Another theory that can explain how we form or change attitudes toward romantic partners is self-perception theory. In 1967, Bem proposed self-perception theory as an alternative to cognitive dissonance theory. According to self-perception theory, one does not need to feel "dissonance" in order to infer one's attitudes. Bem suggests that we can just observe our own behavior and deduce our own attitudes the same way we might observe another person's behavior and deduce his attitudes.

Have you ever examined your behavior in order to discern how you felt about something? Have you ever laughed out loud while watching a television show and then inferred that you must find that show funny? Or have you ever winced while watching someone fall off of a skateboard and concluded that you would not like to try skateboarding yourself? Or have you ever noticed the butterflies in your stomach after meeting someone new and assumed that you must be excited to meet her? If so, then you have already experienced what Bem (1967) describes as self-perception. Self-perception theory and cognitive dissonance theory make similar predictions about attitudes; only the processes one uses to arrive at those attitudes are discrepant. Festinger (1957) proposes that dissonance is a necessary precursor to attitude change, while Bem (1967) believes that the only necessary precursor to deducing one's attitudes is observing behavior.

Although there is a great deal of research assessing both of these theories and whether dissonance is necessary or not, it is not my intention to review that research here. I will present a very interesting compromise proposed by Fazio et al. in 1977. Fazio et al. suggest that if one has a strong attitude and if one's behavior is highly discrepant from that existing attitude, then dissonance will occur and attitude change will arise consistent with the predictions of cognitive dissonance theory. Conversely, Fazio suggests that if one has no strong attitude to begin with, then one can merely observe his behavior and infer his attitude, consistent with the predictions of self-perception theory. So the two theories make similar predictions about attitudes and, most importantly, the researchers would agree that you should go to an expensive restaurant and your date should pick up the check.

What the research says

In an interesting test of self-perception theory, Slane and Leak (1978) investigated whether nonverbal behaviors such as physical proximity and eye contact could influence liking for a confederate of the researchers. The confederate was assigned to read a speech and the participants (male and female college students from the United States) were asked to listen to the speech while remaining as still as possible. The participants were randomly assigned to either a "high-immediacy" condition, in which they sat close to the confederate and were asked to lean forward and make eye contact with the confederate while he/she read the speech, or assigned to a "low-immediacy" condition in which they sat farther back and were asked to lean away and not make eye contact with the confederate. Confirming the predictions of self-perception theory, the authors found that participants who sat closer to the confederate and made eye contact with him/her during the speech also liked the confederate significantly more than did those in the low-immediacy condition. Interestingly, the authors point out that the participants liked the confederate more in the high-immediacy condition even though they did not realize that their behaviors influenced their attitudes.

Think critically

In Slane and Leak's research, the participants were asked to vary their behaviors in the high-immediacy and low-immediacy conditions. In the high-immediacy condition participants sat closer, leaned forward, and made eye contact with the confederate. In the low-immediacy condition, the participants sat farther back, leaned away, and did not make eye contact. Do you think *all* of these variables must change together in order to change their liking for the confederate? Or should any one of these variables be sufficient on its own? Which variable do you think would have the strongest influence on liking for the confederate?

Self-perception theory can help to explain our initial romantic interest in a partner. In a similar study to the one described above, researchers Kellerman et al. (1989) asked undergraduate students from the United States to gaze at one another's eyes or hands or to count the number of times their partner blinked his/her eyes. These researchers found that students who gazed at each other's eyes reported stronger feelings of attraction to and interest in their partners. In a second study, undergraduates who gazed into one another's eyes reported stronger feelings of love for one another, especially if the participants reported that their feelings were generally influenced by their behavior. The authors interpreted these results as consistent with self-perception theory. Once again, our behaviors toward an individual may influence our attraction to that person.

Self-perception theory can also help to explain our attitudes in longer relationships. Adams and Sprenkle (1990) posit that self-perception theory can clarify why individuals stay in less than satisfying marital relationships. These authors suggest that individuals may assume that "they are highly committed to each other *because* they have stayed together for so long" (p. 139). The authors explain that although commitment certainly leads to more stable relationships, that more stable relationships could also lead to increased commitment. Both cognitive dissonance theory and self-perception theory predict that we use our behavior to help us infer or change our attitudes. Future research might investigate whether interventions using these theories could improve attitudes among partners who are seeking couples' therapy.

Psychological reactance and the boomerang effect

Cognitive dissonance theory and self-perception theory can both explain the processes through which we change our own attitudes, but what happens when someone else tries to change our attitudes?

A personal moment: Have you ever tried to tell one of your girlfriends that the guy she is dating is a total loser? Did she thank you for pointing that out and stop dating him immediately? Or, worse yet, has your mother ever tried to convince you to stop dating someone? How did that turn out? When I was in high school my friend Jayda's parents felt that her boyfriend was too old for her and forbade her to see him further. Now, Jayda's boyfriend was more than ten years older than she was and may well have been too old to date a teenager, but her parents' forbidding her to see him backfired. Jayda became defensive about her boyfriend and her relationship with him. She ended up "falling in love" with him, becoming pregnant, and marrying him. Eventually, she also divorced him. So, why does this happen? Why, when others try to influence us, do our attitudes "boomerang" in the opposite direction? One possibility is the concept of psychological reactance, which is defined by Kassin et al. (2011) as "the theory that people react against threats to their freedom by asserting themselves" (p. 233).

What the research says

Heller, Pallak, and Picek (1973) investigated this issue of trying to influence others' attitudes and their subsequent attitude change or psychological reactance. These authors recruited male and female undergraduates from the United States and asked participants to indicate their attitudes toward a number of different topics, including the construction of nuclear power plants near inhabited neighborhoods (a timely issue then and now). Most of the participants in this sample were moderately opposed to the construction. In one condition of this experiment, a confederate assigned to work with the participant (ostensibly as his or her partner) spontaneously interjects that not only is he in favor of the construction but that he is going to try to convince as many people as he can to support the construction. In this condition (versus a condition in which the confederate claims he is not interested in the topic or a condition in which he says nothing), participants demonstrated attitude change in the opposite direction of what the confederate advocated, becoming even more strongly opposed to the construction.

Further, in another condition, the researchers told the participants that they could write essays either in favor of or against the construction. But, subsequently, the confederate sent the participant a note stating that he had decided that the participant should advocate a particular position (the confederate always asked the participant to write an essay corresponding to the participant's initial attitude). Once again, the participants showed "negative" attitude change, or change in the opposite direction of that advocated by the confederate (versus a condition in which the confederate did not ask the participant to assume a particular opinion). What is really interesting about Heller et al.'s (1973) research is that just by trying to "assign" participants an opinion, the participants changed their attitudes, even if the attitude change was *inconsistent* with their initial opinions. It seems that just threatening our independence causes us to "boomerang" (p. 273) in the opposite direction and to change our attitudes accordingly.

Think critically

In Heller et al.'s research, when it is clear that the confederate is trying to influence the participants' attitudes, the participants show attitude change in the direction opposite to that advocated by the confederate. If more covert methods were employed by the confederate, might his attempts to change the participants' attitudes be more successful? How would you advise a friend to proceed if he wanted to change someone's attitudes toward a particular topic?

This boomerang effect can also influence our attitudes toward potential romantic partners. Wright et al. (1992) showed that the "advice" of a confederate can cause a "boomerang" effect for ratings of members of the other sex. In this research women were asked to rate the attractiveness of two men based on profiles containing both physical information (for example, height and weight) and personality information (for example, leisure interests and career plans). In three separate conditions a female confederate either made no comment, commented that she liked profile "A" and that he seemed cute, or commented that she thought there was no choice but to choose "A." The women rated "A" as most attractive when the confederate made no comment on his attractiveness, and the women rated "A" as least attractive when the confederate indicated that she thought the participant had "no choice" but to choose A. One thing to keep in mind about Wright et al.'s (1992) research is that the participants in this research did not know the confederate. It is possible that if a good friend of ours were to say that she liked "A" or even that there was no choice but to choose "A," we might have a different reaction than if we received this advice from a stranger. Future research should investigate the impact of friends' and/ or relatives' advice on attraction and romantic relationships.

> A media moment: In Jane Austen's novel *Pride and Prejudice*, Lizzie's Aunt Gardiner references psychological reactance when she warns Lizzy not to become too attached to a young officer named George Wickham. "You are too sensible a girl, Lizzy, to fall in love merely because you are warned against it" (Austen, 2001, p. 245). Although Lizzy does seem to feel an inclination for Wickham at first, she also seems to heed her aunt's advice by not becoming attached to him too quickly.

Forewarning and the Internet

As Finkel et al. (2012) review, when Internet dating sites first became available, they were treated with the general trepidation usually afforded a new way to meet a potential date. However, as time has progressed, and more and more people have met their partners on the Internet, more people trust that modality for initiating dating relationships, especially when one finds it difficult to meet potential partners through other venues (Finkel et al., 2012).

In contrast to the research reviewed above on psychological reactance, it seems that forewarning can induce more caution regarding attraction formed via the Internet. Research by Leon et al. (2003) suggests that warning college students about the potential use of deception on the Internet (i.e., the use of a photograph of another person rather than oneself or the inflation of salary information) resulted in less attraction to target persons of the other sex. Moreover, the students reported that they were less likely to want to chat online or date targets when they were forewarned about the potential for deception. These results may differ from the research on psychological reactance reviewed above because Leon et al.'s (2003) research involved a general warning about deception on the Internet and not a warning about a specific person. If one had already formed an attraction to someone met on the Internet and then one received the warning, it might not induce more caution or less attraction. Future research should address this issue specifically.

Chapter summary

In this chapter we reviewed research utilizing new methodologies to explore implicit attitudes toward potential and current romantic partners. This research shows that positive implicit attitudes toward current romantic partners may enhance romantic relationships, while negative implicit attitudes toward ex-partners may be beneficial after the dissolution of a relationship. We also reviewed research suggesting that attitudes toward romantic partners may fluctuate or change over time (both long-term and short-term). Two intriguing attitude change theories were also reviewed, suggesting that our own behavior may strongly influence our attitudes toward our romantic partners. Furthermore, we may react negatively when others try to change our attitudes toward romantic partners. We present our suggestions for future reading below.

Suggested reading

Brehm, J. (1956). Postdecision changes in the desirability of alternatives. *The Journal of Abnormal and Social Psychology*, 52(3), 384–389.doi:10.1037/h0041006.
This article is a classic in Social Psychology and describes the changes in our attitudes after choosing between two equally attractive alternatives.

Geher, G., Bloodworth, R., Mason, J., Stoaks, C., Downey, H. J., Renstrom, K. L., & Romero, J. F. (2005). Motivational underpinnings of romantic partner perceptions: Psychological and physiological evidence. *Journal of Social and Personal Relationships*, 22(2), 255–281. doi:10.1177/0265407505050953
This article offers the most complete application of cognitive dissonance theory to romantic relationships. I also like the use of physiological measures described in this research.

Johnson, D. J., & Rusbult, C. E. (1989). Resisting temptation: Devaluation of alternative partners as a means of maintaining commitment in close relationships. *Journal of Personality and Social Psychology*, 57(6), 967–980. doi:10.1037/0022-3514.57.6.967
This research is so interesting because it suggests that we actually modify our perceptions of attractive others if we are in very committed romantic relationships.

Slane, S., & Leak, G. (1978). Effects of self-perceived nonverbal immediacy behaviors on interpersonal attraction. *Journal of Psychology: Interdisciplinary and Applied*, 98(2), 241–248.Retrieved from PsycINFO database.
This article is easy to read and provides a good application of self-perception theory to attraction.

Sprecher, S. (1999). "I love you more today than yesterday": Romantic partners' perceptions of changes in love and related affect over time. *Journal of Personality and Social Psychology*, 76(1), 46–53. doi:10.1037/0022-3514.76.1.46
I recommend this article because of its unique longitudinal design.

Zayas, V., & Shoda, Y. (2005). Do automatic reactions elicited by thoughts of romantic partner, mother, and self relate to adult romantic attachment? *Personality and Social Psychology Bulletin*, 31(8), 1011–1025. doi:10.1177/0146167204274100
This is one of the easier articles to read involving implicit attitudes toward romantic partners. It also contains interesting information on attachment styles and implicit attitudes toward our mothers.

Romantic Relationships

7

What if you are "done" dating and have already chosen a mate? How do social psychological theory and research inform our understanding of romantic relationships? First, our approach to romantic relationships may be related to our attachment styles which initially developed through early relationships with our primary caregivers; more secure relationships may have been associated with evolutionary benefits. These early attachment styles can also influence our relationships with our romantic partners. Second, relationships with romantic partners may be beneficial to us, but when we cease to benefit from our romantic relationships, we are more likely to leave them. Third, some psychological processes may help improve our perceptions of the benefits of our romantic relationships. In this chapter we will review how our attachment styles influence our romantic relationships, the benefits to romantic relationships (as well as the costs), and two theories which elucidate when we will feel satisfied with our romantic relationships (as well as when we are more likely to leave them). Then we will discuss several social psychological processes that can improve our perceptions of our relationships, such as self-verification, self-fulfilling prophecy, and relationship-enhancing attributions.

Attachment styles

A personal moment: It is with sadness that I begin this section on attachment styles. A few summers ago, when visiting my best friend Michelle and her parents, I spoke about my desire to attain a sabbatical and to write a book on attraction and romantic relationships. Michelle's parents were always interested in my work, and so we talked about the topics I might include in the book. Little did I know how well they were listening until Michelle appeared at my home a few months later with a copy of John Bowlby's (1969) book, *Attachment and Loss*. Michelle's father had found it in his office while doing some spring cleaning and he hoped I could use Bowlby's book when writing my own. As I begin this section on attachment, Michelle's father has recently passed away. I wish

I had written this section earlier so that I could have shared it with him. I have really enjoyed reading Bowlby's book and especially the little notes Michelle's father made in the margins (some dated before Michelle and I were born!). Interestingly, I also found in the book some newspaper clippings about a therapist who treated attachment disorders and about a mother reflecting upon the behavior of her infant when she was kept away from him while he was hospitalized and upon their reunion. I would have loved to discuss these connections with Michelle's dad.

Bowlby theorized that attachment within all relationships stems from our initial attachment to our "principal attachment figure" (usually our mothers, p. 305). The author reviews research on both human and nonhuman infants and their reactions to their mothers' behaviors. He details how infants become attached to their caregivers and also how infants react when separated from those caregivers. Even as infants, we are motivated to maintain close physical proximity to our caregivers and will actively try to keep them nearby by any means we can (such as crying or clinging when newborns, or trying to seek and follow as we become able to crawl and move independently). Bowlby considered these attachment behaviors to be shaped by evolution. These behaviors are adaptive (making it more likely that the infants will survive) in that caregivers can be ready and available to keep their babies safe and secure. According to Bowlby, a responsive caregiver can inspire feelings of security and trust in children which can lead to positive feelings regarding both the self and others. Bowlby posited that the attachment styles we learn during infancy create a cognitive representation of a parent–child relationship that we use throughout our lives.

Of particular interest to attachment researchers are Bowlby's (1969) descriptions of how children react when their mothers depart and when they return. Based on Bowlby's theory, researchers proposed that children react in predictable ways when their caregivers leave and return, and that these different reactions can be classified into attachment styles (see Ainsworth et al., 1978). Hazan and Shaver (1987) extended the research involving children's attachment to their caregivers to apply to romantic relationships. These authors suggested that romantic love/attachment is "experienced somewhat differently by different people because of variations in their attachment histories" (p. 511).

What the research says

Hazan and Shaver (1987) published a "love quiz" (p. 513) in a local newspaper in the central United States and analyzed over 600 responses. The authors used one quiz item to assign respondents to one of three attachment styles (see p. 515 of the article for the wording of this quiz item). Most participants endorsed the first statement, which indicated that respondents were comfortable being in close relationships and felt that they could depend upon their partners. This statement corresponds to a "secure" (p. 514) attachment style. The authors found that those with secure attachment styles described their relationships as happy, trusting, and supportive. The authors also reported that secure relationships tended to last longer. The next most frequently endorsed statement was the second, which said respondents were not comfortable trusting others, and that partners typically wanted to be closer than the respondents were comfortable with. This statement corresponds to an "avoidant" (p. 514) attachment style. Those with avoidant attachment styles tended to fear intimacy and to experience a lot of jealousy in their relationships. The least-frequently endorsed statement was the third, which indicated that respondents wanted to be closer than their partners wanted to be and worried that their partners did not love them. This statement corresponds to an "anxious/ambivalent" (p. 514) attachment style. Those with anxious/ambivalent attachment styles tended to be obsessed with their relationships and to be prone to extremes of attraction and jealousy. Interestingly, the researchers also reported that the respondents' perceptions of their relationships with their parents were related to their adult attachment styles. For example, respondents who indicated that their relationship with their parents was affectionate and caring were more likely to have secure attachment styles in their romantic relationships.

Think critically

Hazan and Shaver (1987) only examined attachment styles for one member of the romantic relationship. Do you think that securely attached individuals were also more likely to have securely attached partners? Might that explain why their relationships tended to last longer? What about insecurely attached individuals? Do you think that individuals seek romantic partners with similar attachment styles?

Consistent with Hazan and Shaver's (1987) findings, research on attachment styles tends to support the notion that people with secure attachment styles experience stronger and longer relationships with less conflict and greater relationship satisfaction (Schmitt et al., 2004). The findings are less encouraging for individuals with insecure attachment styles. People with more anxious attachment styles (as well as independent observers) rate their relationships as lower in quality (Holland et al., 2012). Avoidant individuals tend to be less committed to their romantic relationships and are more likely to be unfaithful to their partners (DeWall et al., 2011). However, the news for insecurely attached individuals is not all bad. Spielmann et al. (2009) found that anxiously attached individuals who were induced to believe that they could easily find a new partner felt less attachment toward their exes. In a separate investigation, Spielmann et al. (2013) found that avoidant individuals believed that a break-up of a relationship would hurt less.

Although much research on attachment styles uses Hazan and Shaver's (1987) original three attachment styles, some researchers prefer a model of adult attachment styles with four potential styles. Bartholomew and Horowitz (1991) proposed four categories of attachment styles related to positive or negative views of the self and others. According to their model, individuals with a secure attachment style (similar to the secure style discussed above) have positive views of both the self and others; individuals with a dismissing attachment style have a positive self-view, but negative views of others (this style was not included in the three-category model); individuals with a preoccupied attachment style (similar to the anxious–ambivalent style discussed above) have a negative self-view but positive views of others; and individuals with a fearful attachment style (similar to the avoidant style discussed above) have negative views of both the self and others. Regardless of whether one uses the three or four categories of attachment styles, researchers tend to agree that the dimensions of anxiety and avoidance are important determinants of attachment styles and relationship behaviors.

Which type of attachment style do you think you possess? Which type of attachment style would you like to possess? A secure attachment style may appear to be the most desirable, and in fact, some research shows that secure styles are the most prevalent across many different cultures. However, in some cultures, insecure attachment styles are more normative (Schmitt et al., 2004). For example, Schmitt et al. found that in more collectivistic cultures, and especially in East Asian cultures, the preoccupied attachment style was more common than the secure style. In some Western European cultures, the dismissing style emerged more frequently. So the most normative (and even the most socially desirable) attachment styles may vary with cultural norms.

Furthermore, attachment styles may vary over time or with different relationship partners. Although for many people attachment styles remain stable over time and even across relationships, sometimes attachment styles do change (see Baldwin & Fehr, 1995; Kirkpatrick & Hazan, 1994). The secure attachment style appears to be the most resistant to change, showing stability over time (Kirkpatrick & Hazan, 1994). However, Baldwin and Fehr critique the notion of an attachment "style" and prefer to think of attachment as malleable and more like a "state of mind" (p. 259) rather than as an enduring trait. Some researchers even distinguish between "dispositional" attachment styles (general attachment styles across partners) and "relationship-specific" attachment styles (attachment style with one particular partner, e.g., Sprecher & Fehr, 2011).

Moreover, Kirkpatrick and Hazan (1994) suggest that changes in relationships can lead to attachment style changes. For example, these researchers found that participants whose attachment styles were initially secure were more likely to change attachment styles if they had experienced a break-up. Additionally, participants who were initially avoidant were more likely to change attachment styles if they had begun a new relationship. So one's attachment style is not necessarily predetermined by one's relationship with one's parents or by a previous romantic relationship. Perhaps relationships are less likely to be secure until we find the "right" partner. Perhaps relationships are less likely to be secure until we find a partner with a secure attachment style. Future research should explore these possibilities.

Just as attachment styles can influence our expectations and behaviors within a relationship, they can also influence our reactions to the dissolution of a relationship. Davis et al. (2003) explored reactions to a break-up among individuals with different attachment styles who responded to a survey posted on the Internet. The respondents were mostly in their teens and twenties and were primarily White. Regardless of attachment styles, respondents who reported greater emotional involvement in the relationship were more distressed by the break-up. Individuals with more self-reported attachment anxiety were angrier with their ex-partners and were more likely to use drugs and alcohol to cope with the break-up. Paradoxically, these individuals were simultaneously more likely to maintain strong feelings for their exes as well as being more likely to seek a new partner immediately. Individuals who self-reported more avoidance in their relationships were more likely to use self-reliant coping strategies while more secure individuals were more likely to employ the assistance of friends and family members to help them cope with the break-up.

Not only are our own attachment styles important, but the attachment styles of our partners can also impact our romantic relationships. Luo and Klohnen (2005) found that couples' similarity with regard to their attachment styles was a strong predictor of relationship satisfaction among newlyweds. Furthermore, Brassard et al. (2012) found that men with anxious attachment styles and women with avoidant attachment styles were less satisfied with their sex lives, and also that their partners reported more sexual dissatisfaction as well.

As you will see throughout this book, our attachment styles can influence the way we approach and perceive our relationships. For example, in Chapter 5 we reviewed research suggesting that similarity in attachment styles enhances marital satisfaction (Luo & Klohnen, 2005); and in Chapter 6 we reviewed research showing that individuals with more secure attachment styles had more positive implicit attitudes toward their romantic partners (Zayas & Shoda, 2005). Later in this chapter we will discuss the tendency of individuals to explain their partners' behavior differently, depending upon their attachment styles (Sümer & Cozzarelli, 2004). Our next topic involves the benefits of romantic relationships; research in this area shows that individuals with an avoidant attachment style may be less likely to perceive the potential benefits (such as intimacy with a partner) of a romantic relationship (Spielmann et al., 2013).

Benefits of romantic relationships

Aside from the obvious evolutionary benefits of having a romantic partner (for example, if you have a romantic counterpart you may be more readily able to conceive offspring or to facilitate their survival), a variety of research shows that if you have a romantic partner, you will likely be happier and healthier than those without romantic partners. Furthermore, if you are married to your mate, that can increase your positive outcomes as well. However, marrying before you are sure about your relationship with your spouse can have negative consequences.

Our personal relationships may enhance our experiences of positive events and ease our distress during negative events. For example, Burns and Machin (2013) found that having high quality interpersonal relationships with others buffered Australian participants from the effects of negative life events. Those participants who reported higher quality support networks showed increased well-being and decreased negative affect over a six month period. Similarly, Gere and Schimmack (2013) found that relationship quality was positively correlated with subjective well-being among Canadian dating couples. Moreover, Krantz and McCeney (2002) found that greater social and emotional support was linked to better health outcomes, especially for men.

Marital relationships may offer increased health and happiness benefits, even more so than other types of romantic relationships. In a cross-cultural survey involving participants from 42 different societies, Diener et al. (2000) found that married individuals tended to express more life satisfaction than cohabitating partners; this effect was intensified in more collectivistic cultures. Furthermore, married respondents expressed more positive and fewer negative emotions than their divorced or separated counterparts. Likewise, Stavrova et al. (2012) replicated this "cohabitation gap" (p. 1063), showing that married people from 30 different cultures were happier than their cohabitating counterparts. However, Stavrova et al. also showed that in cultures with more egalitarian gender roles the advantage in happiness for married women was substantially reduced.

The inability to marry may be particularly destructive to the mental health of gay men and lesbians. Hatzenbuehler et al. (2010) found that lesbian, gay, and bisexual individuals living in US states with state constitutional amendments banning same-sex marriage were more likely than their counterparts living in states without such amendments (and their heterosexual counterparts living in states with amendments) to develop mood disorders and anxiety disorders. Roisman et al. (2008) found that gay men and lesbians, whether married or not, tended to view their romantic relationships just as positively as did heterosexual men and women. Furthermore, both gay and straight individuals in more committed relationships exhibited improved interaction quality with their partners (as judged by independent observers) versus their less-committed counterparts.

Of course one should not rush to get married just to improve one's health and happiness. Those who marry their partners, even though they have doubts about their relationships, experience less marital satisfaction and a higher likelihood of marital distress and divorce (Lavner et al., 2012).

Increased health and happiness as well as other benefits to romantic relationships have led some to theorize that we develop and maintain romantic relationships due to the potential rewards associated with them. Two theories which address the rewards and costs of romantic relationships are social exchange theory and equity theory. Below, we consider each theory in turn and then consider research which addresses both theories.

Social exchange theory

Social exchange theory was originally proposed by Thibaut and Kelley in 1959. In a revised version of their original book, *The Social Psychology of Groups*

(1986), the authors review their theory. According to Thibaut and Kelley, people in interdependent relationships encounter rewards and costs as consequences of being in the relationship. In order for the relationship to endure, the rewards should outweigh the costs. For example, Thibaut and Kelley state that it may be rewarding to have a partner who has a good sense of humor or a partner who is dependable. Conversely, it may be "costly" to have a partner who has a terrible sense of humor or a partner who is not dependable. Can you think of other benefits or costs to being in a romantic relationship? Love, sex, and companionship are often cited as potential benefits to a romantic relationship, while time, conflict, and money are often cited as potential costs. In your romantic relationship, do the benefits seem to outweigh the costs? Do you expect your relationship to endure?

Other factors that can influence our evaluation of the rewards and costs of a relationship were also reviewed by Thibaut and Kelley (1986). Thibaut and Kelley extended social exchange theory to include a discussion of one's "comparison level" and "comparison level for alternatives" (p. vi). Your comparison level is basically equivalent to your "standards" or what you expect from a relationship. Thus, someone with very low standards (someone who expects to benefit very little from relationships) is described as having a low CL (comparison level) and someone with very high standards is described as having a high CL. A partner with a low CL might be satisfied with a relationship with fewer rewards and more costs, while a partner with a high CL might only be satisfied with a relationship with more rewards and fewer costs. Research by Montoya (2008) suggests that attractive individuals may have higher comparison levels than their less attractive counterparts. He found that undergraduate students from the United States who were rated as more physically attractive tended to rate other targets as less attractive and expected to be less satisfied with potential relationships with those targets.

> Media moment: Jerry Seinfeld's character (Jerry) on the television series *Seinfeld* must have had a high comparison level. No matter which woman he chose to date, there was always a problem with her that he could not overcome. For example, one girlfriend had "man hands," one was too similar to him, one pushed him to eat too much meat, one laughed like Elmer Fudd, and one girlfriend's breasts were so perfect, he assumed they were fake. If Jerry had a lower CL, he might have had a romantic relationship lasting longer than one episode (although that may not have been as funny as his series of imperfect relationships).

Thibaut and Kelley (1986) also include the comparison level for alternatives (CL_{alt}) as part of their theory. The CL_{alt} refers to the benefits one might receive outside the relationship. For example, if you have a partner who is not meeting your relationship needs (not living up to your expected CL), you might consider your alternatives such as pursuing another relationship or being without a partner for a while. According to Thibault and Kelley, if your alternatives (CL_{alt}) seem more rewarding than your present relationship, you may leave the relationship you are in for one of those more rewarding alternatives.

In support of the idea that people leave their relationships when the alternatives seem better than their current relationships, in a cross-national study of factors associated with divorce, Barber (2003) found that it was more common in nations in which women were more economically independent and in which the proportion of men to women was higher. These data suggest that women are more likely to get divorced if they have alternative options that are more appealing (perhaps being alone is a more favorable option as long as she can support herself, or perhaps finding an alternative mate will be easier if there are a multitude of other potential male partners). In sum, according to social exchange theory, relationships that are rewarding will endure, while relationships that are too costly (relative to other alternatives) will be curtailed.

Equity theory

Equity theory was originally proposed by Adams in 1965. In some ways Adams's theory echoes social exchange theory; Adams also suggests that costs and benefits are important, but he proposes a more complicated relationship among rewards, costs, and investment in a relationship. In Adams's original article, he proposed that the ratio of each partner's rewards minus costs, divided by one's overall investment in the relationship will determine whether the relationship is satisfying and whether it will endure. Equity theory sounds complicated, but the gist of it is that the benefits of a relationship do not necessarily have to outweigh the costs in order for a relationship to be equitable. If both partners' ratios of benefits to costs are similar, the relationship is still predicted to endure. Thus, it is possible that both partners are gaining more rewards and fewer costs (or incurring more costs and fewer rewards), but as long as the situation for both partners is similar, the relationship is still equitable. Furthermore, the addition of investment to this model also suggests that we are less likely to leave relationships in which we have a more substantial investment (such as shared resources or children).

A relationship can be perceived as inequitable if one partner incurs more costs and reaps fewer rewards relative to the other partner in the relationship. In this case, one partner is called "underbenefitted" (Sprecher, 2001, p. 599) because she contributes more to the relationship, but benefits less from it. A relationship can also be inequitable when one partner incurs fewer costs and reaps more rewards in the relationship relative to her partner. In this case, the partner is called "overbenefitted" (Sprecher, 2001, p. 599) because she contributes less to the relationship, but benefits more from it relative to her partner. As you might expect, those who are underbenefitted are more likely to be dissatisfied with the relationship than those who are overbenefitted. Interestingly, Sprecher reports that those whose relationships are most equitable feel more positively about their relationships, even more so than those who are overbenefitted.

A personal moment: One of my friends, Tim, recently told me that his wife, Alicia, had gone back to work after taking a few years off to care for their children. When their children were both enrolled in school full-time, Alicia had at first resisted going back to work because of the demands of dropping off and picking up the children and shuttling them to their various after-school activities. However, after striking a deal with her employer to work only during the hours the children attended school, Alicia went back to work on a part-time basis. Tim told me that he was so happy that she had gone back to work. He said that when she was not working he perceived that Alicia was lunching with her friends and getting pedicures while he was working hard. Once Alicia went back to work, Tim started doing more of the housework himself and started feeling less like the underbenefitted spouse.

Research incorporating social exchange theory and equity theory

Research involving social exchange theory and equity theory generally shows support for both theories. Relationships that are perceived to be more rewarding are also viewed as more satisfying. Relationships that are perceived as more equitable are likewise viewed more favorably.

What the research says

In an article incorporating both social exchange theory and equity theory, Sprecher (2001) reviewed and tested both theories. Sprecher invited 101 dating couples from the US to participate in a longitudinal-relationships study. She asked the participants to respond to surveys while they were university students (their average age was 20), six months later, and then annually for the next three years. Approximately 40 of the couples remained together throughout the length of the study. In the surveys, Sprecher assessed the perceived rewards (such as love and affection, money and material goods, sex) received as a consequence of the relationship. Further, she also assessed whether each partner perceived that he/she was benefitting more from the relationship, perceived the relationship as equitable, or perceived that he/she was benefitting less from the relationship. Sprecher also asked about the participants' potential alternatives to their current relationships. The questionnaires included questions regarding whether it would be better to be unattached or whether it would be easy or difficult to find another partner. Finally, the participants were also asked to indicate how satisfied they were with their current relationships and how committed they were to those relationships.

As predicted by equity theory, Sprecher (2001) found that those participants who felt underbenefitted were less satisfied with, and less committed to, their current relationships. As predicted by social exchange theory, Sprecher found that those participants who felt more rewarded by their current partners were more satisfied with, and more committed to, their current relationships. Interestingly, in Sprecher's research project, rewarding relationships were more strongly related to satisfaction and commitment for women than for men. Further, those who were satisfied with and committed to their relationships had low CL_{alts} (they perceived fewer benefits from alternative relationship partners or from being single).

Because the participants in Sprecher's (2001) research were all relatively young and were in dating and not in marital relationships, Sprecher cautions against generalizing the results to more long-term relationships or even to older couples. She also suggests that there may be a "honeymoon period" during which perceptions of inequality do not impact satisfaction or commitment. Further, she states that if relationships become less satisfying for any reason, then partners may become more aware of inequity or costs in their relationships.

Think critically

Sprecher (2001) found that participants who felt underbenefitted were less satisfied with and felt less committed to their current relationships in a sample of young adults from the United States. Might you expect different results from participants of other cultural backgrounds? For example, would participants from more collectivistic cultures be less likely to view themselves as underbenefitted and thus also be more satisfied with their romantic relationships?

Recent research conducted by Joel et al. (2013) supports both social exchange theory and equity theory. This research reveals that asking an individual to track or to remember a partner's contributions to a relationship not only leads to more positive feelings toward the relationship, but also can lead to the individual increasing his own contributions to, and commitment to, that relationship. However, cross-cultural research exploring relationship-maintenance behaviors as well as perceptions of equity among college students in dating relationships from China, the Czech Republic, Japan, South Korea, Spain, and the United States shows that members of different cultures do not respond in the same ways to equitable and inequitable relationships (Yum & Canary, 2009). Although students from the United States, Spain, and Japan tended to try to maintain their romantic relationships most when those relationships were equitable, students from China and the Czech Republic showed no change in relationship-maintenance based on their equity status, and students from South Korea reported the strongest relationship-maintenance behaviors when they were overbenefitted. Similarly, Van Yperen and Buunk (1991) found that American students were most satisfied with their relationships when they were perceived as equitable, but Dutch students were more satisfied as their benefits increased, regardless of whether they felt equity or overbenefitted.

Van Yperen and Buunk (1991) interpreted their findings as consistent with differences in relationship orientation. According to these authors, the Dutch sample was more likely to have a communal orientation while the American sample was more likely to display an exchange orientation. Clark and Mills (1979) define a communal orientation as one in which partners respond to each other's needs over time, while they define an exchange orientation as one in which partners respond to a benefit by providing a benefit in return, sometimes referred to as a "tit-for-tat" relationship. If Americans are keeping a close eye on their rewards and costs, they may be less satisfied with an underbenefitting or overbenefitting relationship. However, if Dutch participants are more easygoing with regard to their accounting of benefits, they may just feel good about their relationships when they receive more benefits from them.

Perceptions of equity seem to be more important for women than for men. As reviewed above, Sprecher (2001) found that rewarding relationships were more strongly related to satisfaction and commitment for women than for men. Ledbetter et al. (2013) found that an equitable relationship was more predictive of relationship-maintenance behaviors among women than men. Furthermore, Caldwell and Peplau (1984) suggested that women in lesbian relationships are also distressed by the perception of inequity. Lesbians who perceived inequity in the relative power of the relationship partners reported less closeness and more relationship problems than lesbians in equitable power relationships. However, Utne et al. (1984) found no differences in the importance of equity among men and women.

Not only can perceptions of inequity lead to distress, but feelings of distress in a relationship may lead to perceptions of inequity as well, causing a cycle of negative feelings and perceptions (Grote & Clark, 2001). Grote and Clark also suggest the possibility that once a relationship becomes distressed, one may unwittingly seek confirmation of our feelings that we are underbenefitted in the relationship. However, Grote and Clark also note that perceptions of inequity might happen quite naturally because one is always present when making contributions to the relationship (for example, "I am always there when I wash the dishes") but one may not always witness her partner's contributions ("I am not always there when my husband washes the dishes"). It is not necessary for *actual* inequities to exist, but merely the *perception* of unfairness can lead to distress (Grote & Clark 2001). Although we may feel underbenefitted, we are less likely to leave our relationships when we are strongly invested in those relationships. For example, married individuals may be regarded as more invested in their relationships than are cohabiting individuals. Research by Yabiku and Gager (2009) shows that married couples are less likely to separate than their cohabiting counterparts, even when their sex life is unsatisfying.

In Adams's (1965) article reviewing equity theory, the author suggests a variety of ways in which one can address the perceived inequities in a relationship, ranging from changing what one puts into the relationship to trying to change what one gets out of the relationship. Another way that Adams suggests to address perceived inequities in a relationship is for one partner to change her perception of her inputs and outcomes. This method of addressing inequity seems particularly efficient since you do not have to change any of your behaviors, only your thoughts. (Sounds a little like cognitive dissonance theory, does it not? See Chapter 6 for a review.)

A media moment: In the autobiographical illustrated novel, *The Complete Persepolis*, by Marjane Satrapi (2007), the author reflects on a relationship that has recently ended. What she formerly perceived as benefits in the relationship, she came to see as costs. For example, when first breaking up with her boyfriend, Satrapi mourns the loss of the benefits of their relationship: "I had just lost my one emotional support, the only person who cared for me" (p. 233). But later, she decides that most of the benefits she perceived in their relationship were actually costs. She thinks, "How could I have been so blind? What relationship? What love? What support? What an asshole!!!" (p. 236). Satrapi's novel illustrates one of the ways we can address perceived inequity in a relationship: by changing our perceptions.

Another way to enhance the benefits you perceive in your relationship is to perceive your partner in a more positive light. In the next section, we will discuss how we see ourselves as well as how our partners see us.

Self-enhancement versus self-verification

Seeing our partners positively may be one way in which we can improve our perceptions of our romantic relationships. However, we need to be aware of how our counterparts view themselves as well. As we will review in this section, most people prefer to be viewed by others as they view themselves, especially in long-term romantic relationships (Kwang & Swann, 2010; Swann et al., 1994).

Most people see themselves positively most of the time (Brehm et al., 2005; Kwang & Swann, 2010; Morry et al., 2010; Sedikides & Gregg, 2008; Swann, 1987). Some research shows that this tendency to see ourselves positively (sometimes called self-enhancement) may be an automatic reaction (at least in participants from Western societies). For example, as reviewed by Sedikides and Gregg (2008) individuals who are busy thinking about other things also quickly ascribe positive traits to themselves. Similarly, research by Hixon and Swann (1993) reveals that participants with limited time to review feedback on themselves choose the more *positive* feedback as more accurate. However, when participants are given more time to review their evaluations, they tend to choose the feedback that more *accurately* describes themselves, whether they view themselves positively or negatively.

Interestingly, Heine and Renshaw (2002) found that while American students were more likely to self-enhance (they viewed themselves more positively than a group of their well-known peers viewed them), Japanese students were less likely to self-enhance (reporting a more negative view of themselves than their peers did). Furthermore, Heine and Renshaw found that individuals who were more individualistic were more likely to self-enhance while individuals who were less individualistic (including Americans who were less individualistic) were less likely to self-enhance, suggesting an interdependence orientation interpretation rather than strictly a cultural interpretation of these results. An interdependence interpretation was also offered by Kitayama et al. (1997). These authors stated that "historical and collective processes by which cultur-ally shared ideas of the self as independent or as interdependent are transformed into corresponding psychological tendencies" (p. 1263) to either self-enhance or self-criticize, with those from individualistic cultures more likely to self-enhance and those from collectivistic cultures more likely to self-criticize.

Although intuitively one might expect that we want others to see us posi-tively (consistent with self-enhancement motives) rather than as we really are (consistent with self-verification motives), research examining both motives suggests the contrary. As Swann (1987) reviews, most of the time, people prefer to self-verify rather than self-enhance. This means that we want others to see us as we really see ourselves, whether that self-perception is positive, negative, or a mix of both. Swann (1987) as well as Kwang and Swann (2010) suggest that sometimes it is difficult to tell whether others are self-verifying or self-enhancing because people generally see themselves positively overall.

In Swann's (1987) article, he reviews dozens of studies on the self, including self-verification and self-enhancement research. For example, Swann reviews research he conducted in which he examined roommate relationships and which suggests a preference for self-verification. Swann conducted this research (with co-author Pelham, as cited by Swann, 1987) showing that college students who were paired with roommates who saw them as they saw themselves (whether positively or negatively) planned to continue rooming together. Conversely, students paired with roommates who saw them differently from the way they viewed themselves (even if their roommates viewed them more positively than they viewed themselves) planned to change roommates. Swann suggests that we choose partners (for friendships, romantic relationships, or roommates) who see us as we see ourselves, which helps to sustain the self-verification process.

In Swann's (1987) review of the literature related to self-enhancement and self-verification, he does allow that people do sometimes self-enhance, if they can avoid the potential negative consequences of failing to live up to that enhanced self-image. Sedikides and Gregg (2008) echo this sentiment, stating that people will temper their self-enhancement if they know that they will be called upon to justify their positive evaluations of themselves. For example, I tell my students that they may or may not self-enhance when they are on job interviews, depending upon whether and when they will be expected to exhibit their skills. Imagine an interviewer asks if you know how to use a statistical program that you have not used in a long time. In this case you may self-enhance, responding that yes, you know how to use the program, because you will have time to re-familiarize yourself with the program before you actually start the job. Conversely, if an interviewer asks you if you know how to speak another language, you will probably want to self-verify, because a few weeks' worth of practicing may not be enough to avoid the embarrassment associated with trying to converse in a language you do not know. Kwang and Swann (2010) contend that the risk of rejection can also influence when one will self-enhance or self-verify. According to these authors, when the risk of rejection by a partner is higher, people are more motivated to self-enhance, but when the risk of rejection by a partner is lower, people are more motivated to self-verify.

Especially when considering the opinion of a romantic partner, the ideal situation may be to have a partner who sees you both positively and accurately. Research by Kenny and Acitelli (2001) suggests that it is not only possible but very likely that partners in dating and married relationships are simultaneously accurate and positively biased in their perceptions of each other. Additionally, research by Katz and Beach (2000) suggests that we like others most when they see us both positively (consistent with self-enhancement) and accurately (consistent with self-verification).

What the research says

Katz and Beach (2000) invited US undergraduate students who were not in romantic relationships to participate in a study involving attraction to potential romantic partners. The participants (who were mostly Caucasian) were asked to write descriptions of themselves that would be evaluated by other participants. Instead of other participants evaluating the self-descriptions, however, the researchers constructed feedback to be both self-enhancing and self-verifying, self-enhancing only, self-verifying only, or neither self-enhancing nor self-verifying. The feedback that was both self-enhancing and self-verifying contained comments about the positive aspects of the participants' self-descriptions, while the feedback that was only self-enhancing contained positive comments that were not related to the participants' self-descriptions. The feedback that was only self-verifying contained comments about the negative aspects of the participants' self-descriptions, while the feedback that was neither self-enhancing nor self-verifying contained negative comments that were not related to the participants' self-descriptions. Participants were then asked to rate their attraction to potential partners who had evaluated their self-descriptions. The results showed that participants rated potential partners most positively when their feedback was both self-enhancing as well as self-verifying, and least positively when their feedback was neither self-enhancing nor self-verifying. Although participants were less attracted to potential partners who provided only self-enhancing or only self-verifying information, partners who only self-verified were rated as more accurate and competent than partners who only self-enhanced.

Think critically

In Katz and Beach's (2000) research, feedback that was only self-verifying was always negative. Think back to Chapter 2 and our discussion of the negativity bias, why might negative, accurate information about the self be perceived more favorably than positive, inaccurate information?

Similarly to feedback from an interaction partner who is a stranger, feedback from a romantic relationship partner should be most well-received when it is both positive and accurate. Research performed by Lackenbauer et al. (2010) echoes Katz and Beach's (2000) results for participants currently involved in romantic relationships. These authors found that feedback from a romantic relationship partner was perceived more positively when it was both positive and accurate. These authors speculate that positive partner evaluations may eventually lead to self-fulfilling prophecies (which we discuss in detail below). The authors state that "over time people begin to perceive themselves more in line with their partner's rosy appraisals, thus making the positively biased appraisals self-verifying" (p. 488). Similarly, the authors speculate that a self-perpetuating process may be sustained in which positivity may lead to greater accuracy and greater accuracy may in turn lead to greater positivity.

However, in research with newlyweds, simultaneously exploring accuracy, positivity bias, and similarity bias (a similarity bias occurs when couples over-estimate how much they have in common with each other), Luo and Snider (2009) found that early marital relationships were most satisfying when partner perceptions were accurate and when spouses considered themselves more similar to one another than they actually were (see Chapter 5 for more information on similarity). Consistent with prior research illustrating the importance of self-verification, the positivity of a partner's evaluations was not related to marital satisfaction.

The preference for a partner who verifies your self-perceptions may be related to the type of relationship you have with that partner. For example, Swann et al. (1994) surveyed dating and married couples from the US Southwest about their own qualities as well as their partners' qualities. The researchers also measured couples' perceptions of intimacy in their relationships (relationships satisfaction, time spent together, etc.). The results revealed that among dating partners, self-enhancement was associated with greater intimacy (those who viewed their dating partners positively felt greater intimacy with them). However, among married partners, self-verification was associated with greater intimacy (those who viewed their marriage partners accurately felt greater intimacy with them). The authors also found that individuals with *negative* self-views preferred dating partners who saw them favorably, but marriage partners who saw them unfavorably. Even married partners with positive self-views preferred to be seen accurately and not more positively than they viewed themselves. Swann et al. speculate that the shift from self-enhancement to self-verification is slow and occurs gradually in marital relationships, perhaps reflecting comfort with the relative permanency of the relationship. Similarly, Letzring and Noftle (2010) found that self-verification (although evident across dating, cohabiting, and married couples) was most strongly related to relationship quality among married couples. As stated above, Kwang and Swann (2010) suggest that this preference for self-verification in marital relationships may be due to the lower risk of rejection among married couples.

Regardless of how someone prefers a partner to view him, individuals seem to prefer to view their *partners* positively rather than accurately. Research by Morry et al. (2010) suggests that individuals "partner-enhance" (p. 372), or view their romantic partners more positively than these same individuals view themselves. Similarly, Conley et al. (2009) state that individuals idealize their partners, viewing their partners more positively than their partners view themselves (sometimes referred to as "positive illusions" p. 1417). Consistent with Swann et al.'s (1994) research cited above, in Morry et al.'s research, partner enhancement was more common among dating couples than married couples. However, in Conley et al.'s research gay and lesbian as well as heterosexual cohabitating and married couples reported more relationship satisfaction when they also viewed their partners more positively than their partners viewed themselves. Researchers speculate that partner enhancement may serve to undermine the quality of alternative relationship partners, thus perpetuating current relationships (Morry et al. 2010). However, because these results are correlational, it may be the case that individuals who idealize their partners are more satisfied with their relationships or that individuals in satisfying relationships are more likely to view their partners positively (Luo et al., 2010; Murray et al., 1996a).

Furthermore, the correlates of partner enhancement may not be entirely positive. Research by Swami et al. (2012) highlights partner enhancement of physical attractiveness, suggesting that some participants are likely to view their partners as more physically attractive than themselves (these authors refer to this tendency as the "love-is-blind bias" p. 796). In Swami et al.'s research, community members from London displaying this type of partner enhancement were more prone to jealousy.

Self-fulfilling prophecy

When your partner views you positively (or when you view your partner positively), those idealistic views may actually lead to more positive relationships. For example, Murray et al. (1996b) conducted a longitudinal study of dating partners from Canada who were of college age. The romantic partners rated "themselves, their partner, their ideal partner, and the typical partner on a variety of interpersonal attributes" (p. 1158). These authors found that the couples' views of each other remained idealistic over time. Indeed, couples with more (unrealistic) positive views of their partners tended to stay together over the course of the year, especially if men idealized their female partners. Furthermore, the authors report that "idealizing a partner appeared to create the realities intimates desired as these romances developed" (p. 1169). For example, the authors recount that men and women who viewed their partners more positively experienced less conflict in their relationships. In contrast, women who more accurately understood their male partners reported being less happy over the course of the year. Although these results seem to contradict those reported above regarding the preference for a self-verifying partner rather than a self-enhancing partner, we should remember that Murray et al.'s research involves dating rather than married partners (see Swann et al., 1994, as discussed above).

Let's explore how self-fulfilling prophecy can explain how one partner's positive views might actually be manifested in the behavior of the other partner over time. Self-fulfilling prophecy is a term which often confuses students. When we begin our Social Psychology course, the students usually believe that self-fulfilling prophecy means that if you believe in yourself, you can eventually make your hopes or dreams come true. Although it is possible to refer to your own expectations and behaviors, self-fulfilling prophecy usually involves one person's expectations or beliefs about *another* person's behavior. Kassin et al. (2011) provide a great illustration of the three-step process of self-fulfilling prophecy (see p. 137). According to these authors, self-fulfilling prophecy begins when a perceiver has expectations about what a target's behavior will be like. The perceiver's expectations influence his own behavior, so that he behaves toward the target in a way that is consistent with his expectations. The target responds with corresponding behavior toward the perceiver, which in turn confirms the perceiver's initial expectation. This sounds complicated, but if you consider the following example it will elucidate the process.

Imagine that you have an expectation that librarians tend to be quiet. One day while you are eating lunch you run into your friend, Joan, the local librarian. Your expectation that librarians tend to be quiet might lead you to approach Joan quietly and timidly to say hello (even though you are outside of the library when you meet). Your quiet and timid manner will influence Joan's behavior back toward you, so she will probably respond commensurately, answering your hello quietly and gently. Her quiet behavior will then confirm your expectation that librarians tend to be quiet. So you can see the three steps of self-fulfilling prophecy through this example. The first step is your expectation, which influences your behavior toward your friend. The second step is your actual behavior toward your friend, which is consistent with your initial expectation. The third step is her behavior back toward you. (As an aside, a fourth step may also occur in which the librarian's behavior actually reinforces your expectations or strengthens your stereotypes, making you even more likely to believe that librarians tend to be quiet; see Kassin et al.'s 2011 description of how stereotypes self-perpetuate, pp. 169–170).

So how does self-fulfilling prophecy influence romantic partners' behavior? One of the early studies addressing self-fulfilling prophecy involved interpersonal attraction (Snyder et al., 1977). When I discuss this research with my students I like to refer to this study as "The Blind Date Study" because it resembles the situation that might occur when two people engage in a telephone conversation before being set up for a blind date. This research shows that men's expectations about their partners' attractiveness (step 1) influences their behavior toward their partners (step 2), which in turn influences their partners' behavior back toward them (step 3).

What the research says

Snyder et al. (1977) invited university students from the United States to participate in a study which purportedly assessed the process through which people get to know one another. The students were assigned a partner of the other sex and were asked to have a telephone conversation with that partner. Each participant completed a questionnaire assessing a little bit of background information about himself/herself to share with their partners. Additionally, men were told that a photograph would be taken of each participant to share with their partners. However, only men received photographs of their partners; women never received photographs of their partners, nor were they told that men received photographs. Further, the photographs the men received were not actually photos of their female partners. Men were randomly assigned to receive a photograph of either an attractive woman or an unattractive woman.

In order to assess the first step in the self-fulfilling prophecy process, men completed questionnaires regarding their expectations about their partners after seeing the photographs but before having the telephone conversation. The authors then assessed men's expectations about their partners. The authors found that men who received a photograph of an attractive woman expected to find their partners to be "sociable, poised, humorous, and socially adept," while men who received a photograph of an unattractive woman expected their partners to be "unsociable, awkward, serious, and socially inept" (Snyder et al., 1977, p. 661).

To assess the second and third steps in the self-fulfilling prophecy process, men and women interacted in a telephone conversation, and their conversations were recorded and played for "observer judges" who were kept blind to the photograph condition of the women (i.e., the observer judges did not know whether the men were assigned a photograph of an attractive or unattractive partner). Confirming the second step in the self-fulfilling prophecy process, the authors found that when men were assigned to talk with a woman whom they believed to be attractive, the observer judges rated men's behavior as more "sociable, sexually warm, interesting,...outgoing, humorous,...and socially adept" (Snyder et al., 1977, p. 663) than when men were assigned to talk with a woman whom they believed to be unattractive. Thus, men's behavior was influenced by their expectation about whether they would be talking with an attractive or an unattractive partner.

Finally, confirming the third step in the self-fulfilling prophecy process, the authors found that when women were believed by their partners to be attractive, they were rated by the observer judges as more "sociable, poised, sexually warm, and outgoing" (p. 661) than their peers who were believed to be unattractive. Thus men's behavior influenced women's behavior and confirmed men's expectations.

Think critically

In Chapter 5, we reviewed cross-cultural research by Gebauer et al. (2012) suggesting that similarity in romantic partnerships may more important in countries whose residents are less heavily influenced by physical attractiveness. Do you think the results of Snyder et al.'s self-fulfilling prophecy study would change if it were conducted outside the United States?

Similarly, Curtis and Miller's (1986) research also reveals how self-fulfilling prophecies can influence liking for a partner. These researchers told undergraduate participants that as part of the experimental procedures, their partners had been given false information in order to induce liking or disliking of the participant, who was to serve as the "target" person for the research project. So the experimenters manipulated the participants' expectations that they would be liked or disliked by their partners. The participants and their partners then engaged in a ten-minute conversation which was observed through a one-way mirror as well as tape-recorded. The authors found that participants who were told that their partners were led to like them used a more positive tone of voice and disclosed more information about themselves to their partners. The participants displayed behaviors consistent with their expectations that their partners would like them. As a result of their behavior, they were actually liked more by their partners who were not actually led by the researchers to like or dislike the targets. In contrast, the participants who were told that their partners were led to dislike them tended to disagree more with their partners and displayed a more negative attitude overall. Correspondingly, these targets were actually liked less by their partners. The partners also adjusted their behaviors to match those of the target, for example, participants "who believed that they were liked self-disclosed more, which led the perceivers to ask more questions of the targets and disclose more themselves" (p. 289), thus completing the self-fulfilling prophecy.

Interestingly, a meta-analysis performed by Langlois et al. (2000) suggests that in addition to expecting positive characteristics from attractive people whom we do not know, we also expect and treat attractive targets whom we do know more positively, thus leading to potential behavioral confirmation of those positive expectancies even for targets who are already familiar to us, such as our relationships partners.

Confirmatory hypothesis testing

Confirmatory hypothesis testing is similar to self-fulfilling prophecy and, indeed, more than one of these processes may be at work during any interaction. Confirmatory hypothesis testing is when we test our beliefs in a biased fashion so that we are more likely to confirm suspicions that we already hold. Consider the example of the librarian named Joan discussed above. If we were to approach Joan and ask her whether she likes the peaceful ambiance of the library and she were to respond in the affirmative, we are only testing the hypothesis that she likes quiet without testing the hypothesis that she likes noise. If we were to test the opposite hypothesis, we might ask her whether she likes the noisy raucous environment of a close football game in its final seconds.

What the research says

Snyder and Swann's (1978) classic research offers insight into how expectations can influence attraction. This research illustrates both confirmatory hypothesis testing and self-fulfilling prophecy. Snyder and Swann asked pairs of women to engage in a conversation that was supposed to be structured as an interview, with one interviewing the other. Unbeknownst to the participants, the interviewers were assigned to interview partners who were randomly designated as either introverts or extroverts. The researchers then provided the interviewers with a list of questions to choose from to begin the interview. Displaying confirmatory hypothesis testing, the authors found that when women expected to interview someone whom they believed to be introverted, the women chose to ask introverted types of questions (for example, "What factors make it hard for you to really open up to people?"). But when women expected to interview someone whom they believed to be extroverted, the women chose to ask extroverted types of questions (for example, "In what situations are you most talkative?" p. 1204). Snyder and Swann also recorded these interviews and played them for "listener-judges" who were kept blind to the introvert/extrovert condition that was randomly assigned to the interviewees. Furthermore, the judges only heard the responses of the interviewees, not the questions asked by the interviewers. Showing self-fulfilling prophecy, the judges rated the interviewees as more introverted when they were randomly designated as introverted and more extroverted when they were randomly designated as extroverted.

Think critically

Snyder and Swann's (1978) research seems to contradict Kenny's (1994) assertion that extroversion can be accurately perceived even at zero acquaintance (see Chapter 3). However, Snyder and Swann's participants interacted from separate rooms via microphones and headphones. Do you think the results of Snyder and Swann's research would change if the participants interacted in person?

This research on self-fulfilling prophecy and confirmatory hypothesis testing is important to keep in mind if you are trying to set your friends up on a blind date. You should inform your friends about some of the good qualities of each member of the pair, and then they can seek to confirm their positive expectations during the date. You should provide photographs ahead of time only if your friends are physically attractive. You could also inform your friends that the other likes him/her already, based upon the positive information, thus hopefully leading to greater liking when they meet (capitalizing on the reciprocity effect discussed in Chapter 5).

Attributions in relationships

Similar to viewing our partners positively, it is also good for our relationships to make positive attributions for our partners' behaviors. In order to illustrate this point, let us consider the case of a fictitious couple, Jonah and Cindy. Imagine they have a challenge in their relationship: they cannot agree on a division of labor for the household chores. Imagine that Jonah always takes out the trash and does the laundry and Cindy always washes the dishes and balances the checkbook, yet Jonah and Cindy cannot agree about who should sweep the floor or clear the table. Imagine that Cindy comes home late from work on a Friday night to find Jonah lounging on the sofa watching television while the kitchen table and floor are a mess. How will Cindy explain Jonah's behavior of watching television or, more specifically, of *not* cleaning the kitchen? Will she assume that he is too lazy to clear the table and sweep the floor? Will she assume that Jonah has had a long, hard week of work just as she has? Will she assume that Jonah is waiting for her to clean the kitchen? The way Cindy explains Jonah's behavior (as well as the way she explains her own behavior) is called an attribution. The type of attributions that Cindy makes for Jonah's behavior and for her own behavior can impact their relationship. You can easily imagine that if Cindy decides that Jonah did not clean the kitchen because he has had a long, hard week at work, the way she perceives their relationship will be more positive than if she decides that Jonah is too lazy to clean the kitchen.

Before we discuss the attributional research, we should explain the different types of attributions one can make for a behavior. Heider (1958) proposed one of the first theories of attribution. One of the most important features of Heider's theory was the distinction between personal and situational attributions. To explain this distinction in my Social Psychology classes, I always ask my students to imagine that I have walked across the room and tripped over a chair. Consider the reasons why I might have tripped over the chair. If my students suggest that I tripped because I am clumsy, they have made a personal attribution; that is, deciding that the cause of the behavior is due to the actor, or the person who has performed the behavior. If my students suggest that I tripped because the chair was in the middle of the walkway, then they have made a situational attribution; that is, deciding that the cause of the behavior is due to the situation or the environment, not to the actor.

Once again, consider the example of Jonah and Cindy provided above. If Cindy decides that Jonah has not cleaned the kitchen because he is lazy, she is making a personal attribution, the "lazy" part of Jonah's personality is to blame for his behavior. However, if Cindy decides that Jonah has not cleaned the kitchen because he had a long, hard week at work, she is making a situational attribution. Jonah is not to blame, but his situation at work is the reason for his current idle behavior. You can see how Cindy's attributions may impact her perception of her companion and their relationship, as well as her subsequent behaviors. If Cindy makes a personal attribution and decides that Jonah is lazy, she might berate him for not cleaning the kitchen. If Cindy makes a situational attribution and decides that Jonah has had a long, hard week at work, she might snuggle up with him on the sofa and empathize with him. However, situational attributions are not always the most beneficial to a relationship. Imagine that Jonah performs a positive behavior: he buys Cindy a bouquet of flowers. If Cindy makes a personal attribution and decides that Jonah is such a sweet guy, that bodes better for their relationship rather than if Cindy makes a situational attribution and decides that Jonah only bought the flowers to make up for leaving the kitchen a mess.

Self-serving bias

Making accurate attributions for our own as well as others' behavior can be a complicated process, and we often make errors. Some of these errors are predictable: we are vulnerable to a variety of attributional biases which can influence how we make attributions. One such bias is called the self-serving bias. The self-serving bias refers to the tendency to internalize our successes and credit them to their own good qualities (e.g., "I got an A on my Social Psychology test because I am smart, and I studied hard") while blaming negative outcomes on others (e.g., "I got a D on my Social Psychology test because the instructor is awful") or on external factors (e.g., "That test was too difficult"; see Kassin et al., 2011; Malle, 2006).

Research investigating ex-spouses' opinions about their divorces lends itself to a self-serving bias interpretation. Gray and Silver (1990) found that both members of divorced couples tended to view themselves positively and take less responsibility for their divorces while simultaneously viewing their ex-partners more negatively and maximizing their partners' accountability for the divorce. As the authors recount, although they could not objectively determine who was at fault for the demise of the relationship, "both appraisals obviously cannot be accurate" (p. 1188). Gray and Silver suggest that this self-serving bias in interpreting the marital break-up may serve to further justify the break-up. The authors state that "by biasing one's perception in this way, resolution regarding the marital termination may be bolstered" (p. 1189). In other words, couples may feel more comfortable with a break-up if they can convince themselves that the other partner either was not a good partner or was culpable for the dissolution of the relationship.

Even members of happy and intact romantic couples seem to display the self-serving bias when making attributions. Schütz (1999) interviewed German spouses separately regarding a marital conflict. Although spouses described the same dispute, both partners tended to view their spouse as the initiator of the conflict and to describe the spouse's behavior as unfair. Simultaneously, both described themselves as blameless, correct, and rational.

To what causes do you tend to attribute negative behaviors that occur in your relationship? You may have a self-serving bias, meaning you tend to interpret events in a way that makes you look good or preserves your positive feelings about yourself. In this case, if you are like Cindy, you might decide that *you* have not cleaned the kitchen because you are simply exhausted from your long, hard week at work. A self-serving bias in making attributions for your own behavior does not necessarily translate into a bias for your partner's behavior. No matter how you attribute your own behavior, you can make a similar attribution for your spouse (for example, Jonah must be tired from his week at work too) or a different attribution for your spouse (for example, I am tired from a long week at work, but Jonah is lazy). If you make a personal attribution for your spouse's negative behavior, it may have a negative impact on your relationship in the long run.

The fundamental attribution error

Another attributional bias evident in Western cultures such as that of the United States (see Krull et al., 1999) is the tendency to overestimate personal causes when judging others' behavior. This error in assigning causes to behaviors happens so often, it is referred to as the "fundamental" attribution error. So if Cindy makes the fundamental attribution error, she may decide that Jonah's behavior of not cleaning the kitchen is due to a personal cause (such as his laziness).

> A personal moment: I love teaching my classes about the fundamental attribution error because I get to tell one of my favorite stories to illustrate this bias. When my girlfriends and I were in college, we decided to take a long weekend to ski in New Hampshire. On the way to the mountain, we drove through Massachusetts and took a road New Englanders refer to as the "Mass Pike." If you have ever driven on the Massachusetts Turnpike (especially in the days before automatic tolls), you may recall that you have to take a ticket at the entrance to the highway and then return your ticket and pay your money to the toll-taker when you exit. I happened to be driving when we exited the Pike and I had to give the toll-taker 50 cents. I gave her the ticket successfully (I will make a self-serving attribution: what a good ticket-hander I am) but my two quarters fell to the ground (I will make another self-serving attribution: the toll-taker placed her hand too close to the toll booth for me to reach it). When my girlfriends saw what I had done they immediately started laughing. I had never dropped my money at a toll before, so I did not know what to do. Should I pick up the money? As I laughed with the girls and wondered what to do, the toll-taker yelled "OPEN THE DOOR, GET OUT OF THE CAR, PICK UP THE MONEY, AND PUT IT IN MY HAND." I did as I was told, drove away, and immediately made the fundamental attribution error, assuming that the toll-taker was a bitch. Although at the time I never stopped to question my personal attribution for the toll-taker's behavior, I have since learned that I may have underestimated the situational reasons for her behavior. For example, the weather was bitterly cold that day, perhaps the cold weather motivated her response, or maybe because it was windy she felt that she had to yell so that I could hear her instructions.

The fundamental attribution error is the tendency to overestimate the role of personal causes and underestimate the role of situational causes when explaining an event (Kassin et al., 2011). I am sure you can easily apply this tendency to make personal attributions to your relationships. For example, when, Malcolm, the husband of my friend, Delisha, takes care of their four children while she "works" in Aspen, I assume that Malcolm is a saint rather than focusing on other reasons that may motivate his behavior. Maybe Malcolm hopes that Delisha will use her corporate bonus to buy a new pair of skis for him, or maybe it is more economical for Malcolm to stay with the kids than to accompany Delisha on the trip. It may be useful to try to be aware of the attributions you are making in your relationships. Research shows that if you take your time and devote some thought to the matter, you can avoid the fundamental attribution error (Gilbert & Malone, 1995). If you can avoid attributing negative behaviors in your relationship to personal causes associated with your spouse, you may be able to preserve a more positive view of your relationship.

What the research says

Bradbury and Fincham (1992) invited married couples from the United States to their laboratory to discuss their marriages. While there, the couples completed a survey regarding any marital problems. On the survey, each member of the pair also indicated who was responsible for each problem. Further, while the researchers videotaped, the couples tried to discuss one marital problem and reach a consensus. The researchers found that couples who viewed their spouses as culpable for their marital problems were more likely to show negative behaviors (for example, anger) in their problem-solving sessions. Moreover, wives who blamed the problem on their husbands were more likely to reciprocate negative behaviors performed by their spouses and less likely to reciprocate the positive behaviors (such as empathy and support) performed by their spouses. As these authors state, when a partner attributes a problem to the other and thus shows more negative behavior toward the other, the problems in the relationship are likely to be perpetuated and even worsened over time.

Think critically

Bradbury and Fincham (1992) found that individuals who blamed their marital problems on their spouses were more likely to behave negatively as well and then to elicit negative behaviors from their counterparts. What type of intervention would you propose to end the cycle of negativity for these couples? And would the type of intervention you proposed depend on the severity of the marital problems?

Consistent with Bradbury and Fincham's (1992) research, Fincham et al. (1987) found that couples seeking marital therapy were more likely to make negative attributions for their partners' behavior than for their own behavior. Interestingly, the reverse was also true: couples who were not in therapy made more positive attributions for the partners' behavior than for their own behavior. Similar to the research we discuss below on the hostile attribution bias (see Sümer & Cozzarelli, 2004), Fincham et al. also suggested that viewing one's partner's behavior positively was more important to relationship satisfaction than the way one viewed one's own behavior.

Hostile attribution bias

In addition to a tendency to blame their spouses for negative events in their relationships, some people may also exhibit a tendency to perceive malevolent intent in behaviors performed by their spouses. This tendency to perceive malicious intentions is called a hostile attribution bias (see Epps & Kendall, 1995) and is not limited to the behavior of romantic companions. Epps and Kendall found that people who self-reported more angry and aggressive attitudes and behaviors tended to attribute more hostility to actors in both ambiguous and aggressive situations. Similarly, Dill et al. (1997) found that participants with a more aggressive personality tended to expect stories to end in a more aggressive fashion than did participants who were less aggressive. Further, Dill et al. also found that participants with aggressive personalities perceived more aggression in social interactions that they watched on videotape.

Using the example of the fictional couple developed above, if Cindy perceives that Jonah has deliberately left the kitchen messy in order to anger her, she may be exhibiting a hostile attribution bias. The good thing about attributions is that they often take place in your thoughts so, although they may result in different behaviors (as evidenced by Bradbury and Fincham's (1992) research discussed above), if you can become aware of your attributional biases, you can adjust your behavior accordingly so that negative attributions need not necessarily translate into negative behaviors. As Gilbert and Malone (1995) suggest, if you take the time to consider all the possible causes of the behavior, you can make fewer errors in your attributions and perhaps also exhibit more positive relationship behaviors. Interestingly, Mikulincer (1998) found that Israeli individuals with avoidant or anxious attachment styles were more likely to infer hostile intent from their partner's behavior than did those with more secure attachment styles. Additionally, men high in hostile sexism (a tendency to interpret women's ambitions as undesirable and subversive) were more likely to view their female partners' behavior negatively and to experience more negative feelings toward their partners as well as reduced relationship satisfaction (Hammond & Overall, 2013).

Sümer and Cozzarelli (2004) recruited primarily White university students from the central United States who were involved in romantic relationships for at least two months to participate in their attributional research. These researchers found that students who had positive views of the self were less likely to generate negative attributions, both for their own behavior and for their partners' behavior, and thus experienced stronger relationship satisfaction. These researchers also examined the students' attachment styles, showing that securely attached participants were more likely to make relationship-enhancing attributions, even for negative behavior performed by their partners. These authors also suggest that the type of attributions we make for our partners' behaviors are more important to our overall relationship satisfaction than attributions we make for our own behaviors.

However, trying to make positive attributions and to display positive behaviors within a romantic relationship is more likely to improve relationships which are already stronger from the outset. As McNulty (2010) reviews, more positive attributions and behaviors are useful for maintaining marital satisfaction in couples who are already relatively satisfied with their relationships and who experience fewer conflicts with one another. Surprisingly, McNulty also contends that for couples with less satisfying marriages and more severe problems, a more beneficial approach may be to focus on the negative attributions and behaviors as a means of addressing and resolving their relationship problems.

Chapter summary

In this chapter we have reviewed how our attachment styles (which may stem from our attachment to our childhood caregivers) can impact different facets of our romantic relationships, from the duration of the relationships to our satisfaction with our relationships, and to our coping with the dissolution of those relationships. We also reviewed the potential health and happiness benefits associated with romantic relationships. We presented two theories and research suggesting that when we cease to derive benefits from our romantic relationships, we are more likely to leave those relationships for more attractive alternatives. We also reviewed several dyadic processes which can influence our satisfaction with our relationships, such as self-verification, self-fulfilling prophecy, and relationship-enhancing attributions. We present our suggestions for future reading below.

Suggested reading

Hatzenbuehler, M. L., McLaughlin, K. A., Keyes, K. M., & Hasin, D. S. (2010). The impact of institutional discrimination on psychiatric disorders in lesbian, gay, and bisexual populations: A prospective study. *American Journal of Public Health*, *100*(3), 452–459. doi:10.2105/AJPH.2009.168815
    These authors make a very compelling case for the negative impact of state laws banning same-sex marriage on the emotional well-being of gay men and lesbians.
Katz, J., & Beach, S. H. (2000). Looking for love? Self-verification and self-enhancement effects on initial romantic attraction. *Personality and Social Psychology Bulletin*, *26*(12), 1526–1539. doi:10.1177/01461672002612007
    I like this article because the authors attempt to disentangle the often-confounded effects of self-verification and self-enhancement.

McNulty, J. K. (2010). When positive processes hurt relationships. *Current Directions in Psychological Science, 19*(3), 167–171.doi:10.1177/0963721410370298

This article is short, but it highlights the surprising finding that more positive behaviors and attributions may not enhance distressed relationships.

Snyder, M., Tanke, E., & Berscheid, E. (1977). Social perception and interpersonal behavior: On the self-fulfilling nature of social stereotypes. *Journal of Personality and Social Psychology, 35*(9), 656–666. doi:10.1037/0022-3514.35.9.656.

This is a classic study in social psychology. I encourage my students to read this article in order to understand the powerful role our expectations exert on our own behaviors as well as the behavior of others.

Sprecher, S. (2001). Equity and social exchange in dating couples: Associations with satisfaction, commitment, and stability. *Journal of Marriage and the Family, 63*(3), 599–613. doi:10.1111/j.1741-3737.2001.00599.x.

This article is easy to read and tests hypotheses related to both social exchange and equity theories.

Sex and Love

8

Despite the fact that some readers may consider sex and love to be mutually exclusive, we address them together in this chapter because of their shared importance to satisfying romantic relationships. As Miller (2012) declares, although "sex need not always involve romantic intimacy...for most people romantic intimacy involves sex" (p. 273). We will discuss sex first, covering topics such as sexual attitudes and behaviors as well as sexual double standards. In the latter portion of this chapter we will cover several theories and taxonomies of love as well as differences in attitudes toward love and expressions of love across gender, age, and culture. Finally, we will examine the neurological activity that occurs when we are in love. Although we discuss some gender differences related to sex and love in this chapter, we also emphasize the overall similarities between men and women with regard to sex and love.

Sex

From an evolutionary perspective (which emphasizes reproduction and the survival of offspring, see Chapter 4), sexual intercourse is one of the most important activities one can perform. However, if you ask people why they have sex, they rarely reply that they do so in order to ensure the survival of their genes. In an interesting article exploring the reasons for having sex, Meston and Buss (2007) asked a large group of undergraduate and graduate students as well as community volunteers from the US Southwest to list all the reasons they could think of for having sex. A different group of undergraduate students then evaluated the frequency with which they had engaged in sex in the past for each of those reasons. Not surprisingly, some of the most frequently cited reasons for having sex included "attraction, pleasure, affection, love, romance, emotional closeness, arousal" (p. 498). Also unsurprising (given the predominantly undergraduate student sample), few respondents indicated wanting a child as a reason for sex.

Meston and Buss (2007) also examined gender differences in the endorsement of different reasons for having sex. They found that men were more likely than women to cite reasons for sex such as the physical desirability of a partner or the availability of a partner. Although women were more likely than men to endorse reasons related to love, Meston and Buss stressed that most of the other emotional reasons for having sex were equally endorsed by men and women (such as feeling connected in their relationships or wanting to be emotionally close). Interestingly, men endorsed almost *all* of the reasons for having sex more frequently than women, perhaps reflecting their desire to have sex for a greater variety of reasons than women or perhaps reflecting their increased desire for sex for any reason. As the authors note, reasons for having sex may vary with age as well as with culture, and future research should address these potential differences in motivations for sexual intercourse.

A media moment: In the 1991 movie *City Slickers*, Billy Crystal's character, Mitch Robbins, states: "women need a reason to have sex, men just need a place" (Underwood & Crystal, 1991). The research reviewed by Meston and Buss (2007) above seems to support this idea. Men were more likely than women to state that they had engaged in sex for almost all of the 237 reasons generated by Meston and Buss's participants. Perhaps for men (or at least for the male undergraduates in Meston and Buss's research project), any reason to have sex will suffice.

Engaging in sex for different reasons may impact relationship satisfaction. Muise et al. (2013) conducted experimental as well as longitudinal studies to assess whether individuals engaged in sex for "approach goals, such as to enhance intimacy" or for "avoidance goals, such as to avoid disappointing a partner" (p. 1320) as well as the relationship satisfaction associated with those different goals. These authors found that having sex for different reasons was associated with an individual's satisfaction as well as the partner's satisfaction. For example, the researchers found that engaging in sex for approach goals resulted in self- as well as partner-reports of enhanced sexual desire and relationship satisfaction. Conversely, engaging in sex for avoidance goals resulted in less self-reported and partner-reported satisfaction as well as perceptions of decreased relationship quality over time. Interestingly, the authors found stronger negative effects for the avoidance goals leading them to interpret these results as consistent with prior research suggesting that negative experiences may exert a stronger influence over perceptions than positive experiences (see Chapter 2 for more information on negativity bias).

Sexual attitudes

Regardless of one's motivations for engaging in sex, we may hold favorable or unfavorable attitudes toward sex under different circumstances (sex with a marriage partner, sex with a loving partner, sex with a willing partner). Attitudes toward sex are typically described as conservative (traditional) or liberal (permissive). Those with more conservative attitudes toward sex are likely to view sex favorably only when it occurs within the context of an exclusive or marital relationship, while those with more liberal attitudes toward sex are likely to view sex favorably under a variety of circumstances: outside of marriage, outside of a committed relationship, or outside the context of any relationship at all.

You may expect that sexual attitudes differ by gender. Do you think that men or women tend to hold more liberal sexual attitudes? Do you think that men and women differ strongly in their sexual attitudes? Or weakly? Petersen and Hyde (2010) performed a meta-analysis of research assessing men's and women's sexual attitudes and behaviors. This analysis involved more than 800 individual studies as well as several large national data sets resulting in hundreds of thousands of individual participants and data from 87 different countries. Despite the variety of studies, Petersen and Hyde state that their combined samples were comprised predominantly of young adults from a White North American background.

We will discuss the results of Petersen and Hyde's (2010) research related to sexual attitudes here and the results related to sexual behaviors below. Similar to a meta-analysis conducted by Oliver and Hyde in 1993, Petersen and Hyde found small differences in sexual attitudes between men and women. For example, men were slightly more permissive than women in overall sexual attitudes and attitudes toward premarital sex, and men were slightly more likely to endorse sexual double standards than women (men rated sexual behaviors as more acceptable for men than for women; see the discussion of sexual double standards below). All of these effect sizes were small. One moderate gender difference emerged: men were moderately more permissive than women in their attitudes toward casual sex (see Chapter 9 for more research regarding men's and women's attitudes toward casual sex).

Petersen and Hyde (2010) also investigated some moderating variables which impacted the magnitude of the gender differences. The authors reported that gender differences in sexual attitudes tended to decrease as the age of the participants increased. Also, the gender differences weakened for data gathered more recently. (Other research supports the idea of diminishing gender differences over time, suggesting that women's sexual attitudes may be becoming more permissive, thus causing the convergence in gender differences in sexual attitudes; see Earle et al., 2007; Wells & Twenge, 2005.) Interestingly, in Petersen and Hyde's meta-analysis, gender differences were also smaller in countries with increased gender equality (as assessed by the United Nations Gender Empowerment Measure). We will return to this issue of gender equality when we discuss sociosexuality and sexual double standards below.

In sum, Petersen and Hyde suggest that men and women are very similar in their sexual attitudes and that "stereotypes about gender and sexuality provide a largely inflated view of gender differences in sexual attitudes" (p. 34). In fact, in terms of sexual attitudes, the similarities between men and women are much stronger than the differences between them.

Do you think that sexual attitudes vary across cultures? Which cultures would you expect to be most conservative? Most permissive? Widmer et al. (1998) examined attitudes toward sex in 24 different countries. Unlike other research involving convenience samples, the current researchers examined data from nationally representative samples. The authors found differences in specific sexual attitudes across nations. Of the countries studied, the Philippines was the most conservative toward all non-marital sex. Perhaps surprising to some readers, respondents from Ireland, Poland, and the United States also held relatively negative attitudes toward non-marital sex. In contrast, respondents from European countries such as Austria, Germany, Slovenia, and Sweden showed relatively liberal attitudes toward both premarital sex as well as sex among younger teenagers. Respondents from Canada, the Czech Republic, the Netherlands, Norway, and Spain were the most liberal in their attitudes toward homosexuality. Although this analysis emphasized differences among cultures, the authors indicate that there was a great degree of overlap between cultures in their sexual attitudes, perhaps due to the fact that the nations examined were primarily Western industrialized nations.

Within US culture, recent examinations of sexual attitudes suggest that African American men express the most liberal sexual attitudes, followed by White Americans, Hispanic Americans, and Asian Americans (Sprecher et al., 2013; Fugère et al., 2008). Interestingly, in the most recent research, ethnic differences were not found among women (Sprecher et al., 2013).

Sexual behaviors

In their meta-analysis (described above) Petersen and Hyde (2010) also report relatively small gender differences in sexual behaviors (as the authors note, this finding is rather intuitive because most reported sexual behaviors were heterosexual behaviors). Men were slightly more likely than women to self-report participating in more frequent sexual intercourse and having more sex partners, while women were slightly more likely than men to report engaging in same-sex sexual behavior. Moderate gender differences were reported for the incidence of casual sex, masturbation, and using pornography (with men more likely to report engaging in all of these behaviors). Similar to the findings for sexual attitudes discussed above, these gender differences also tended to decrease along with the age of the participants and with more recent data collection. Once again, the authors reported that the magnitude of gender differences was also related to the gender equality of a nation, with countries with more egalitarian gender norms showing smaller gender differences in self-reported sexual behaviors.

Kissing

Kissing is common across many different cultures (Eibl-Eibesfeldt, 1970, as cited by Gallup & Frederick, 2010) and may be employed differentially by men and women. Although not exclusively a sexual behavior, kissing is often viewed as a prelude to sex, especially by men (Gallup & Frederick, 2010; Hughes et al., 2007). Men not only expect kissing to lead to sex but may try to use kissing to increase their chances of having sex (Hughes et al., 2007). Conversely, men are also more willing than women to consent to sex without kissing or to consent to sex with someone who is not a good kisser (Hughes et al., 2007). Hughes et al. speculate that kissing may provide information to men about their partner's sexual receptivity or even fertility status.

Women may use kissing as a mate-assessment tool, to assess both the quality and the commitment of a potential mate (Gallup & Frederick, 2010; Hughes et al., 2007; Wlodarski & Dunbar, 2013). For example, Hughes et al. (2007) found that women were more likely than men to say that the taste and smell of a partner's mouth and breath were important factors in deciding to kiss. The taste and smell of a partner's kisses may provide information about whether he is healthy (Hughes et al., 2007) or information about his immune genes (Floyd et al., 2009, see Chapter 1 for more information on scent and immunity). Moreover, women in the most fertile phase of their menstrual cycle rate kissing as more important at the beginning of a relationship than women in less fertile cycle phases (Wlodarski & Dunbar, 2013). Women also show more jealousy than men do when imagining their partners kissing a rival (Hughes et al., 2007).

Kissing may be beneficial to both sexes, both in terms of selecting a mate and in terms of physical and psychological health. Floyd et al. (2009) found that married or cohabiting adults instructed to increase the amount of romantic kissing they engaged in over a six-week period showed decreased cholesterol levels as well as decreased perceived stress and increased relationship satisfaction. Gulledge et al. (2003) also report that increased kissing is associated with greater relationship satisfaction.

The frequency of sexual thoughts and behaviors

How often do you think about sex? Do you think there is a difference in the frequency with which men and women think about sex? Who thinks about sex more, men or women? As Fisher et al. (2012) review, gender stereotypes might lead one to expect that men think about sex more than women. However, Fisher et al. state that previous research has yielded mixed results, with some studies showing large gender differences, and some showing small or no gender differences. Fisher et al. also critique the previous research as unreliable because of its use of retrospective self-reports to examine potential gender differences in thoughts about sex. According to the authors, retrospective self-reports are vulnerable to a variety of biases, including inaccurate memory as well as influence by stereotypes and social desirability. In their research, the authors employed two different methods to test the frequency of thoughts about sex: the typical retrospective self-report estimate as well as a tally count. Fisher et al. found that gender differences in sexual thoughts were small and were most likely influenced by factors such as social desirability and societal expectations.

What the research says

Fisher et al. (2012) asked undergraduates from the Midwestern United States to estimate the frequency with which they thought about sex each day as well as to estimate the number of thoughts about eating and sleeping (as two other need-based thoughts). They also asked the students to carry a golf tally counter with them throughout the day. One group of students was asked to click the counter whenever they thought about sex, while two other groups tallied thoughts about food and sleep. Students recorded their thoughts in this fashion for one week. The authors found that men self-reported thoughts about sex approximately eight times per day while women self-reported thoughts about sex approximately six times per day. When examining the tally counts, the averages for both men and women increased, with men clicking on average approximately 34 times per day and women clicking on average approximately 19 times per day. Although these averages seem vastly different, averages can be highly influenced by extreme scores. Due to the extreme variability in men's tally counts, the authors also presented the medians for each group. The median for men's tally counts was almost 19 while the median for women's tally counts was close to 10. These results do suggest that men did tally more thoughts about sex than do women, but the effect size representing this sex difference was small. Additionally, men tallied more thoughts about food and sleep than women, perhaps showing that men have more need-based thoughts than their female counterparts overall, not just more thoughts about sex. Importantly, a measure of social desirability was collected for both men and women. For women, the higher they scored on the social desirability measure, the lower their tally counts of sexual thoughts, suggesting that women may be more reluctant to admit their sexual cognitions, perhaps due to social stereotypes or concern over sexual double standards.

Think critically

Fisher et al. (2012) found that both men and women increased their thoughts about sex when using the tally counter versus their retrospective estimates. Do you think that both men and women grossly underestimated how often they thought about sex? Or is there another explanation for the finding that the tally counts far exceeded the participants' estimates? (Hint: The tally counts were also higher than the retrospective estimates for thoughts about food and sleep.)

Consistent with their more liberal sexual attitudes and more frequent sexual thoughts, a variety of research shows that men desire more frequent sex than women (e.g., Buss & Schmitt, 1993; Lippa, 2009; Peplau, 2003; Smith et al.,

2011). In Lippa's cross-national research involving respondents from 53 coun-tries, he found that in every nation in which gender differences were examined, men reported stronger sex drives than women did. However, he also noted that in each nation he examined, women's sex drives were more variable than men's. Similarly, in Smith et al.'s research involving a nationally representative sample of Australian adults, although men expressed a desire to have more frequent sex than women, both men and women who were dissatisfied with their sexual relationships were also more dissatisfied with their romantic relationships. So although men may desire more frequent sex than women, a satisfying sexual relationship is important to both men and women.

In addition to gender, sexual orientation may be associated with the frequency of sexual behavior both within and outside romantic relationships. As Peplau (2003) reviews, because the frequency of sexual intercourse depends upon the desires of both partners, gay men report the most frequent sexual behavior followed by heterosexual couples and then lesbian couples. Peplau also reports that lesbians tend to have more conservative attitudes toward casual sex, similar to their heterosexual female counterparts, while gay men and hetero-sexual men tend to have more liberal sexual attitudes. Gay men also report more sexual behavior with partners other than their primary partners than do their male and female heterosexual counterparts as well as their lesbian coun-terparts (Conley et al., 2013).

Moreover, marital status seems to be associated with the frequency of sexual behavior. Married couples report having sex less often than their cohabiting counterparts (Yabiku & Gager, 2009; Rao & DeMaris, 1995). In research involving a nationally representative sample of adults from the United States, cohabiting couples reported sexual activity twice as often as their married counterparts (Yabiku & Gager 2009). These effects persisted even after researchers controlled for variables such as age, religion, ethnic background, income, health, and relationship length. This research also reveals that cohabi-tating couples who engaged in less frequent sexual intercourse were more likely to leave their relationships than their married counterparts. The authors inter-preted these results as consistent with social exchange theory (see Chapter 7), stating that "compared to marriage, cohabitation may be more heavily based on extrinsic rewards" (such as sex, p. 998) and thus cohabitating relationships may be more likely to dissolve when those rewards are less frequent.

Number of sexual partners

One of the more puzzling results consistently obtained by researchers is the fact that heterosexual men report having more sexual partners than hetero-sexual women (e.g., Alexander & Fisher, 2003; Jonason & Fisher, 2009; Petersen & Hyde, 2010; Wiederman, 1997). As stated above, this finding is counter-intuitive because each time there is a heterosexual sexual interaction, there should be both a man and a woman present. As Wiederman reviews, this difference in self-reported number of sexual partners has been documented in countries such as the United States, Great Britain, Norway, France, and New Zealand, with similar ratios of men's estimates exceeding women's estimates. Wiederman documents a number of different ways researchers have explained this gender difference and notes that none of them can adequately explain the difference. For example, some researchers have suggested that the gender difference is due to a sampling bias, in which the women who have sex with large numbers of sex partners (or even women who are prostitutes) are systematically excluded from the sample. However, according to Wiederman, nationally representative samples of individuals from Great Britain and France fail to reveal evidence of these highly active women. Some researchers have suggested that men consider more sex acts to qualify as sex than women do, however, according to Wiederman, researchers are careful to explain to participants which acts they define as constituting sex with a partner.

Wiederman (1997) concludes that the primary factor driving this gender difference is men's tendency to estimate their number of sexual partners, rather than to count them, especially when they report higher numbers of sex partners. In research using a national sample of adults from the United States, Wiederman found that respondents with larger numbers of sex partners were especially likely to report numbers of sex partners ending in a 0 or 5. Accordingly, Wiederman suggests that when unsure of the exact number of partners, men may round their estimates up while women round their estimates down. Wiederman also suggests that women may be more emotionally invested in sexual relationships than men, thus leading to greater accuracy in their recall of specific sexual partners.

Providing participants with a motivation to be accurate in their efforts to recall specific sexual partners can decrease the gender discrepancy. For example, consider Alexander and Fisher's (2003) use of a device referred to in the literature as a "bogus pipeline" (p. 27). As described by these researchers, the "bogus pipeline" is a machine which is described to participants as similar to a polygraph and purportedly capable of detecting dishonest answers. In reality, the machine does not function as a lie detector, but this technique encourages participants to answer honestly. Alexander and Fisher used this methodology to assess men's and women's self-reported sexual attitudes and behaviors.

What the research says

In Alexander and Fisher's (2003) research, undergraduates (primarily White) from the Midwestern United States were recruited to participate in a project assessing sexual attitudes and behaviors. The participants were randomly assigned to one of three conditions: (a) the bogus pipeline condition in which the participants were told that they would complete surveys while attached to a "physiological monitor" similar to a polygraph, (b) the "exposure threat condition" in which the participants were told to hand their surveys in person to the experimenter (who might then potentially view the responses), or (c) the "anonymous" (p. 30) condition in which participants were told to deposit their surveys in a locked box so that their answers could remain anonymous. Consistent with previous literature, in each condition, men reported more permissive sexual attitudes than women. However, gender differences in masturbation and exposure to pornography were smaller in the anonymous condition and even smaller in the bogus pipeline condition than in the exposure threat condition. The gender differences in the number of reported sexual partners was also the largest in the exposure threat condition, followed by the anonymous condition and then the bogus pipeline condition. Interestingly, in this research, women reported *more* sexual partners than did their male counterparts in the bogus pipeline condition. It may be the case that through encouraging men and women to be honest and accurate, the difference in number of self-reported sexual partners might be eliminated.

Think critically

When Alexander and Fisher (2003) recruited their participants, they advertised the research as involving sexual attitudes and behaviors. How might the students volunteering to participate in this research project differ from participants volunteering to participate in another type of research project? How do you think this sampling bias may have impacted the results of the research?

Sociosexuality and sexual double standards

Some researchers prefer to combine sexual attitudes and behaviors into one construct called sociosexuality (see Sprecher et al., 2013). According to these researchers, sociosexuality can be conceptualized as a continuum ranging from restricted (people who will only consent to a sexual relationship if it involves love) to unrestricted (people who readily engage in casual sex without emotional involvement). In a large international sample analyzed by Lippa (2009), the author found that across cultures men tended to be less restricted with regard to sociosexuality than their female counterparts, but that this difference varied with the gender equality of the nation. In countries with more gender equality, men's and women's sociosexuality scores were much closer to one another than in countries with less gender equality. One reason that women may report less willingness to engage in casual sex or sex without love is that they may be judged differently for engaging in the same sexual behaviors as men. In more egalitarian cultures, the tendency to derogate women for sexual behavior may be lessened, thus enabling women to more freely express their sociosexuality.

When women are viewed less favorably than men for engaging in sexual behavior, it is called a sexual double standard (Reiss, 1964). Evidence for the sexual double standard includes some research showing its continued existence (e.g., Sprecher et al., 2013) and some research showing its decline (e.g., Marks &

Fraley, 2005). Some research also shows that men are more likely than women to endorse sexual double standards (e.g., Crawford & Popp, 2003; Petersen & Hyde, 2010; Reiss, 1964; Sprecher et al., 2013). Although cross-cultural research assessing sexual double standards is practically non-existent, Sprecher and Hatfield (1996) assessed sexual double standards in convenience samples from the United States, Russia, and Japan. The researchers asked participants to rate the acceptability of sexual intercourse for men and women on a first date, when casually dating, seriously dating, pre-engaged, and engaged. The results suggested that men and women from the Russian and Japanese samples were more likely to hold "traditional" sexual double standards, regarding sex as acceptable for men but not for women in any relationship context. Men from the United States sample also rated sex as relatively more acceptable for a man than a woman across relationship contexts. Across cultures, Sprecher and Hatfield found that the double standard was strongest at the earliest dating stages, suggesting that not all sexual behaviors are subject to sexual double standards.

Variation with respect to the documentation of sexual double standards may be impacted by the type of sexual behavior presented for review by participants. For example, Sprecher et al. (2013) investigated sexual attitudes and double standards in a large sample of college students from the United States over a 23-year time span. These authors found that sexual double standards were evident for casual sex but not for sex within the context of a committed relationship. Jonason and Marks (2009) found no evidence for sexual double standards when students evaluated monogamous sexual relationships, but they found evidence that women were judged more harshly than their male counterparts for engaging in threesomes, especially with two members of the opposite sex. Future research should examine cross-cultural sexual double standards across different sexual behaviors as well as ways to eliminate sexual double standards.

Love

Love is an important part of a satisfying romantic relationship. But how is love defined? Harlow (1958) notes that "so far as love and affection is concerned, psychologists have failed in their mission. The little we know about love does not transcend simple observation, and the little we write about it has been written better by poets and novelists" (p. 673). Despite the difficulty involved in studying love scientifically, below we summarize researchers' best attempts. First, we will discuss theoretical models of love proposed by researchers, as well as attempts to define love by asking respondents for their own views. Then we will consider attitudes toward love and expressions of love across gender, age, and culture. Finally, we will examine the neurological activity which occurs when we are in love.

What is love?

If someone asked you to define love, what would you say? Would you think about your romantic partner and define love as "passion and fire," or would you think about the love that you have for your family and friends and define love as "support and commitment?" In this section, we will discuss the major theories defining love. As you will see, defining love is not an easy task; after decades of study, researchers still have not reached a consensus about the definition of love.

Love theories

Rubin's (1970) work was one of the first major studies to analyze love as an attitude measurable through the use of a psychological scale. Rubin asked college students to rate their attitudes concerning a number of items that he created based on the limited love literature of the 1950s and 1960s. He defined the three major factors of love as affiliative and dependent need (e.g., "It would be hard to get along without _____"); predisposition to help (e.g., "I would do almost anything for _____"); and exclusiveness and absorption (e.g., "I feel very possessive toward _____)" (p. 267–268). Overall, he described a difference between romantic loving and liking, and developed the notion that love is based on intimacy, need, and caring.

In response to Rubin's (1970) work, Berscheid and Walster (1978) posited that love has two distinct types, companionate love and passionate love. Companionate love is friendly love, whereas passionate love includes a sexual, physical, and emotional need for someone (as cited by Hendrick & Hendrick, 2006). Passionate love may be characterized as the love that you have towards your romantic partner versus the companionate love that you have for family members. If you have ever heard of the phrase, "I love you, but I'm not in love with you," then you understand this distinction. You can love other people and feel a strong connection to them without feeling the butterflies in your stomach and intense physical attraction associated with passionate love.

Much of the more recent love research was sparked by Lee's (1973) book *The Colours of Love*. Lee used a complex interview and sorting system to create the *colors* of love. Lee's theory focuses on the metaphor of love as a color. Like primary and secondary colors, Lee proposes primary and secondary loves. He notes that the secondary loves are not in any way inferior; they are simply created by combining the primary love styles.

According to Lee, the primary love styles are eros, storge, and ludus. Eros is having a strong physical attraction and an intense emotional connection to another person. Storge refers to friendship love, a strong emotional commitment to their partners (but no passion). Ludus occurs when someone attempts to play games and to engage a number of different love partners. Ludus also involves using deception and withholding information about yourself. The idea that playing games with a potential mate is actually considered a type of love is controversial. Although calling it love may be controversial, you may have heard about (or experienced) someone whom you might refer to as a "player."

In fact, Hendrick and Hendrick (2006) assert that there are a large number of college students who choose ludus as their principal love style.

The secondary love colors are pragma, mania, and agape (Lee, 1973). Pragma is a combination of storge and ludus. Has anyone ever asked you to describe what you want in a potential mate? If so, they were asking you to think about your pragmatic love because this love style includes a practical list of desires for a potential romantic partner. Hendrick and Hendrick (2006) use the metaphor of online dating to illustrate pragma. Online dating typically involves describing yourself (and what you want in another person) as a list of desirable attributes; these attributes illustrate your pragmatic love color. Mania combines eros and ludus and is described as a highly intense love color. When individuals feel mania, they alternate between feeling ecstatic about their relationships (an extreme high) and feeling agony over them (an extreme low). Individuals with this love style may also be very possessive of their partners. People high in mania often feel either very much in love or have strong, heated arguments with their partners. Agape results from the combination of eros and storge. Agape is sometimes referred to as altruistic and sacrificial love. When people feel agape, they put their partner's needs ahead of their own.

Lee's (1973) taxonomy and love colors are often referred to as "love styles." Hendrick and Hendrick's measure of Lee's love styles, called the Love Attitudes Scale, was pivotal in changing the discourse about love. In 1986, Hendrick and Hendrick created a 42-item scale measuring the six love styles (in their 1998 work it was revised, made relationship-specific, and shortened to 24 items). The Love Attitudes Scale has been widely used throughout the love literature. Each love style is measured using a scale to rate a person's levels of eros (e.g., "My partner and I have the right physical chemistry between us"), ludus (e.g., "I believe that what my partner doesn't know about me won't hurt him/her"), storge (e.g., "Our love is the best kind because it grew out of a long friendship"), pragma (e.g., "A main consideration in choosing my partner was how he/she would reflect on my family"), mania (e.g., "If my partner ignores me for a while, I do stupid things to try to get his/her attention back"), and agape (e.g., "I would rather suffer myself than let my partner suffer" p. 395–396).

Lee's (1973) love styles have been associated with different types of relationships and outcomes. For example, as Hammock and Richardson (2011) review, eros tends to be associated with self-disclosure, relationship satisfaction, and strong commitment to the relationship, while ludus is linked to permissiveness, more short-term relationships, and relationship dissatisfaction. Storge is related to more short-term relationships and a willingness to terminate relationships, while pragma is associated with longer-term relationships. Mania is connected with jealousy, obsession, and reduced relationship satisfaction, while agape is associated with greater satisfaction and commitment to relationships (Hammock & Richardson 2011).

Sternberg (1986) critically examined Lee's (1977) taxonomy of love. Although Sternberg highlights the similarities of some of Lee's love styles with his own typology of love (e.g., eros or mania could be considered as similar to infatuation, while storge could be considered as similar to companionate love), Sternberg's examination of the empirical data failed to confirm the six types of love suggested by Lee. Alternatively, Sternberg developed a theory of love which explained the components and types of love as a triangular shape. According to Sternberg, the three components of love are intimacy (at the top of the triangle), passion (the lower left corner of the triangle), and commitment (the lower right corner of the triangle). Sternberg writes that intimacy involves feelings of closeness and bonding with a partner; passion is the physical attraction or sexual behavior in a relationship; and commitment refers to deciding that one is in love and feeling committed to maintaining that loving relationship. Sternberg states that by combining these different components, one may arrive at eight different types of love (or non-love).

Including none of the components or just one component at a time, four different types of love may result. Non-love is the absence of all three components. Liking is intimacy alone without passion and commitment. Infatuation is passion alone without intimacy or commitment ("love at first sight," Sternberg, 1986, p. 124). Empty love is commitment alone without intimacy or passion. If we combine two components of love, three more types of love can result. Romantic love is a combination of intimacy and passion without commitment. Companionate love is a combination of intimacy and commitment without passion. Fatuous love is a combination of passion and commitment without intimacy. Finally, the combination of all three components of intimacy, passion, and commitment results in consummate love. Sternberg contends that consummate love is the type of love people try to achieve in their romantic relationships.

A personal moment: When teaching about Sternberg's love triangle, students often ask how you can have fatuous love – passion and commitment, without intimacy. My students think that you must know a person and have intimate knowledge of them in order to be committed to that relationship. Not true. I (Leszczynski) have a perfect example of fatuous love from my teenage years. I was in the generation of teenage girls obsessed with New Kids on the Block. By obsession, I mean that I had pictures of Joey McIntyre on every inch of my bedroom walls. In class, my friends and I passed notes about how we were destined to marry each of the New Kids; our daily worlds revolved around watching them on television, planning for their next concert, and dreaming about our lives with them. I now know that I had a great deal of fatuous love for Joey McIntyre. Did I know him? No. Even though I could tell you his favorite color and the name of his pets (memorized from *Teen Beat Magazine*), I didn't really know him. However, I was very committed to him and felt a lot of passion for him. It seems as if every generation has a Joey McIntyre; elder generations had Frank Sinatra, and younger generations, 'N Sync and Justin Bieber.

Importantly, Sternberg notes in his article (1986) that in a loving relationship there are two people, and each person may have his or her own unique triangular blend of the love components. Failing to measure love in both relationship members is a major shortcoming of much of the love literature. Sternberg posits that the degree of satisfaction in a loving relationship is related to the degree of matching between the triangles of each member of the pair. Sternberg likens this matching to the similarity research discussed in Chapter 5. He speculates that similarity in attitudes and backgrounds may make the couple's love triangles more similar to one another, thus enhancing their likelihood of having a satisfying romantic relationship. Indeed, research by Morrow et al. (1995) suggests that discrepancies between romantic partners in love styles are associated with reduced relationship satisfaction.

Sternberg (1986) even provides some suggestions for maintaining consummate love in romantic relationships. To enhance intimacy, he suggests introducing some change and variation in a relationship in order to cultivate intimacy over time. In terms of passion, he suggests considering the needs the relationship is filling and trying to make sure those needs continue to be fulfilled while simultaneously evaluating the needs that are not being fulfilled and trying to develop ways to address those new needs. For commitment, he suggests highlighting the importance of the romantic relationship and expressing the couple's commitment to one another.

The last major love theory discussed in the literature conceptualizes love as attachment styles similar to those displayed by infants toward their caregivers (Hazan & Shaver, 1987). As discussed in Chapter 7, Hazan and Shaver contend that we have similar attachment styles to our romantic partners as we had to our primary caregivers. These researchers argue that our attachment styles are congruent with Lee's love styles mentioned earlier in this chapter. They posit that secure attachment corresponds with the love style eros, while avoidant attachment is similar to ludus, and anxious/ambivalent attachment corresponds with mania (Shaver et al., 1988). However, Hendrick and Hendrick (2006) disagree with the characterization of love styles as attachment styles and assert that attachment styles and romantic love are two completely different systems which evolved independently of each other.

Now that we have reviewed the literature related to the definitions of love, take a moment and think about your opinion. How would you categorize different types of love? Do you think that there is more utility in referring to general categories of love, such as romantic and companionate love, or do you find more specific love styles (e.g., eros, mania, and pragma) as more useful? Do you think that your attachment style corresponds to your love style for your romantic partner?

What the research says

In 1989, Hendrick and Hendrick performed a comprehensive analysis of the psychometric properties of several measures of love. They were interested in similarities and differences among the scales. Undergraduates attending a university in the southwestern US participated in the study. Students completed five different measures: The General Relationship Attitude Scale measuring romantic attachment (Hazan & Shaver, 1987), the Love Attitude Scale (Hendrick & Hendrick, 1986), Sternberg's Triangular Theory of Love Scale (Sternberg, 1986), the Passionate Love Scale (Hatfield & Sprecher, 1986), and the Relationship Rating Form (Davis & Todd, 1982). After conducting a factor analysis, Hendrick and Hendrick (1989) identified two major factors (or types of love) and three additional factors. Interestingly, the two major factors echo back to a theory introduced in the early 1970s and discussed earlier in this chapter. Remember our discussion of Berscheid and Hatfield's (1974) original conceptualization of passionate and companionate love? The first factor in Hendrick and Hendrick's (1989) study was very similar to passionate love (e.g., eros, passion), and the second factor was similar to companionate love (e.g., intimacy, care). However, the authors contend that a two-factor model of love is really not adequate because they also found three other minor factors: an anxious-ambivalent/manic love, secure and avoidant attachment, and storge/pragma love. Nevertheless, the majority of the items could be explained using the first two factors and the notions of passionate and companionate love. Therefore, after all the years and discussions of different theories, it really may be just that simple! You either feel passion and physical attraction toward a person, or you are in "the friend zone."

Think critically

Hendrick and Hendrick (1989) found that defining love may really may be as simple as feeling either passionate or companionate love for another person. You either feel passion and physical attraction towards a person or you are in "the friend zone." However, students often ask "Where would friends with benefits (FWB) fit into these models?" Do you think that people who have these arrangements would describe their relationships as loving? How should future researchers attempt to address these questions?

Passionate and romantic love

If one of the major types of love is romantic or passionate, what does that really mean? I (Leszczynski) always think of this type of love as the fire and passion in a relationship – the butterflies in your stomach when you see the person that you love. Hatfield and Sprecher (1986) set out to measure passionate love by developing the Passionate Love Scale. The Passionate Love Scale defines passionate love as having a cognitive component (e.g., "Sometimes I feel I can't control my thoughts; they are obsessively on_____"); an emotional component (e.g., "I possess a powerful attraction for _____"); and a behavioral component (e.g., "I eagerly look for signs indicating _____'s desire for me," p. 391).

Similarly, in 1989 Sprecher and Metts (1989) created the Romantic Beliefs Scale. The scale includes such items as: "I believe to be truly in love is to be in love forever"; "I expect that in my relationship, romantic love will last; it won't fade with time"; and "I believe that if another person and I love each other, we can overcome any differences and problems that may arise" (p. 399). There may in fact be gender differences in how romance and intimacy are defined. For instance, men are more likely to define intimacy in terms of physical proximity and women in terms of self-disclosure (Rubin, 1993). If this is true, men and women may define romance differently as well (see Chapter 9).

Romantic love is very strongly related to falling in love. People who feel passionate and romantic love are most likely experiencing eros or mania (Hendrick & Hendrick, 2006). People in relationships high in romantic love are less permissive in their sexual attitudes, have higher self-esteem, and feel more erotic (physical attraction) and agapic (altruistic) types of love compared to those who are not "in love" (Hendrick & Hendrick, 1988).

Researchers have also explored the way romantic love impacts perceptions of partners. For example, Förster et al. (2010) asked undergraduates and older adult participants to think about a loving relationship partner or a one-night stand. Those participants primed to think about love were more likely to evaluate their partners positively across all traits, while those primed to think about the one-night stand were more likely to differentiate among traits when rating their partners. The authors posit that this lack of differentiation when thinking about love might enhance the positivity bias that respondents often display when evaluating their romantic partners (see Chapter 7 for more information concerning partner enhancement). Hendrick and Hendrick contend that people who are in love "wear rose colored glasses" (1988, p. 161).

Although some researchers suggest that passionate love wanes over time (e.g., Ahmetoglu et al., 2010; Sternberg, 1986), other research suggests that in some couples passionate love can persist over the long term (Langer, 2009; O'Leary et al., 2012). O'Leary et al. surveyed a random sample of adults from the United States who had been married for at least 10 years, finding that 40 percent of those individuals reported that they were "very intensely in love" with their partners (p. 241). Moreover, those who reported being intensely in love with their partners also reported greater overall life happiness, more positive thoughts about their partners, more affection, more frequent sexual intercourse, and more shared leisure activities. Engaging in new and exciting leisure activities together may actually inspire more relationship satisfaction (Aron et al., 2000). Aron et al. found that men and women who reported engaging in more exciting activities with their partners also reported better relationship quality. Also, these authors created experimental conditions exposing men and women to an exciting or a boring task, and then measuring perceived relationship quality. Men and women who engaged in the more exciting task together reported enhanced relationship quality versus the more boring task and versus a control condition in which the couples did not perform either of the tasks.

A media moment: Shakespeare's Sonnet CXVI (116) suggests that passionate love remains intense over time. For example, lines 2–6: "Love is not love/Which alters when it alteration finds,/Or bends with the remover to remove:/O no! It is an ever-fixed mark/That looks on tempests and is never shaken." Lines 9–12 further declare: "Love's not Time's fool, though rosy lips and cheeks/Within his bending sickle's compass come:/Love alters not with his brief hours and weeks,/But bears it out even to the edge of doom" (Burto, 1988, p. 156). Passionate love which wanes over time may never have been love at all.

Companionate and practical love

It is wonderful to have passionate relationships, but if you choose to remain in a long-term relationship, it may also be important to be friends with your partner – to like each other and get along on a daily basis. Kephart's (1967) classic research sought to determine just how important passion (versus practicality) was when determining who was "marriage material." He asked 1,079 White college students from the Eastern United States: "If a boy (girl) had all the other qualities you desired, would you marry this person if you were not in love with him (her)?" In his sample, 35 percent of men said that they would marry someone in the absence of love. Do you think that women would be more or less practical compared to men? The answer to the question of marrying someome in the absence of love was "yes" for 76 percent of the women in his sample, suggesting that romantic love was less important to women than was practicality. Do you think that this trend has changed since the 1960s? Allgeier and Wiederman (1991) found a clear change across generations. In their sample, 86 percent of men and 91 percent of women actually answered "no" to the question (as cited in Lieberman & Hatfield, 2006). This result not only suggests a clear change over time in the preference for romantic love in the United States, but also reverses the gender difference found earlier: women are less practical than men in the more recent research. Do you anticipate cross-cultural differences in response to this same question? Levine et al. (1995) asked this question of college students in 11 countries. They found that a need for love prior to marriage was important in many Western countries (e.g., Australia, Brazil, England, United States) but not as important in Eastern countries (e.g., India, Pakistan).

What happens when companionate love intersects with passion? This means that you have a friend to whom you also have a strong physical attraction. In the United States we refer to this blend as "friends with benefits" (FWB). FWB relationships are becoming quite common on college campuses in the United States. Hughes et al. (2005) defined friends with benefits as two people who have sex together, but would not say that they feel romantic love for each other. People who have not had these types of relationships may wonder: What are the reasons why someone would get involved in this type of relationship? Hughes et al. found that students reported that they had FWB relationships to avoid other romantic relationships, for the sex, to simplify the relationship, and for the emotional connection. When asked about how their love attitudes related to their motivations, they reported more ludic love (game-playing) and less storge love (friendship). Therefore, people are more likely to have friends with benefits relationships if they see romance as a game, if they want sex without the commitment, and enjoy the challenge of trying to get it.

Compassionate love

Compassionate love (similar to agape in Lee's 1977 model) has been defined by Sprecher and Fehr (2005) as caring and concern for others, including romantic partners, close friends or family members, and all of humanity. In their research, Sprecher and Fehr found that increased feelings of compassionate love were associated with increased empathy, religiosity, social support, and prosocial behavior. Although higher scores on the Compassionate Love Scale toward others in general were associated with higher scores on the scale when specifically considering a romantic partner, compassionate love scores toward romantic partners were higher for women than men (in a college student sample from the Midwestern US). Rauer et al. (2013) found no difference in compassionate love scores based upon gender for older married adults (who were on average approximately 70 years of age). Importantly, the adults in Rauer et al.'s research were measured as couples, not individually as in Sprecher and Fehr's research. It may be the case that those who feel more compassionate love *for* their partners also receive more compassionate love *from* their partners. An additional strength of Rauer et al.'s research was that the authors were able to determine that feeling compassionate love was linked to better health outcomes for female partners, but receiving compassionate love was linked with worse health outcomes for both male and female partners (perhaps because those with poor health were in need of more compassionate love).

Compassionate love for a partner may also influence the break-up strategies one uses to end a relationship. Sprecher et al. (2010) asked undergraduate students to imagine breaking up with a partner and to choose which type of strategy they might use to break-up. Not surprisingly, students with higher compassionate love scores for their real partners were more likely to choose more compassionate break-up strategies for their hypothetical break-ups (such as emphasizing the good things about a partner, trying to prevent "hard feelings," and avoiding blaming the partner, p. 75).

Our own ideas about love

Instead of theorizing about hypothetical love, some researchers ask participants directly about their experiences with love. In an investigation of respondents' ideas of what constituted liking, loving, and being in love, Lamm and Wiesmann (1997) asked participants from Germany (primarily women) to convey how they knew they liked, loved, or were in love with someone. These researchers found that participants most frequently mentioned, as indicators of love, a positive mood induced by the other, trust, and a desire for the other's presence. The most frequently mentioned factor for liking was a desire for interaction. The most frequently mentioned factor for being in love was physiological arousal. The authors noted the difference between loving and being in love was strongly related to the notions of physiological arousal and sexual desire, suggesting the co-occurrence of romantic love and sexual attraction.

Cross-cultural research exploring respondents' own ideas about romantic love shows a great deal of consensus across cultures. In research assessing participants from Lithuania, Russia, and the United States, de Munck et al. (2011) asked respondents to indicate what they thought romantic love was.

These authors found that, although there was not complete consensus about what constituted romantic love, respondents tended to agree that "romantic love is a strong feeling and being together is the main desired state" (p. 144). Furthermore, respondents from all three countries tended to associate romantic love with strong feelings, sexual attraction, recurring thoughts about a partner, happiness, passion, altruistic feelings toward a partner, and trying to promote the partner's well-being. The frequency with which participants mentioned these factors varied by culture (e.g., Russians did not consider altruism toward a partner as important as Americans did). Interestingly, these authors also found that Lithuanian and Russian respondents were more likely than American respondents to see love as "unreal" and "temporary" (p. 129). Despite these more practical impressions of love, Lithuanians reported falling in love earlier (within days or weeks) than their American counterparts (a number of months to a year).

Expressions of love

If you wanted to express your love for your romantic partner, what would you do? What would you say? Wade et al. (2009) asked undergraduates and community members from the Northeastern United States to list the actions one might use to express love toward a partner. These researchers found that actions highlighting the exclusivity of the relationship (such as getting married or proposing marriage, not cheating on one another) were rated as the most typical. Sharing feelings, honesty, and saying "I love you" were also frequently mentioned.

Harrison and Shortall (2011) also studied expressions of love and specifically whether men or women say "I love you" first within a relationship. The authors surveyed students from a university in the Northeastern United States and asked men and women to report when they first fell in love and when they first told their partners that they loved them. Interestingly, although the students assumed that women would tend to fall in love and express that love before men, Harrison and Shortall's data revealed the opposite trend. Men reported falling in love earlier and saying that they loved their partners earlier than their female counterparts. However, in this research the male and female participants were not involved in relationships with each other; future research should examine these findings in men and women involved in romantic relationships with each other to assess whether the same trend holds.

Galperin and Haselton (2010) also investigated whether men or women fall in love first. These authors surveyed respondents via an Internet questionnaire. They found that the men in their sample were not more likely to report falling in love before the women, but that most couples reported falling in love at the same time. (Once again, only one member of a romantic partnership participated in this research project.) Galperin and Haselton did find that men reported falling in love at first sight more often than women. These authors posited that men may fall in love at first sight more often because of their stronger emphasis on physical attractiveness (see Chapter 1) or because expressing love serves as a signal of commitment to women, who then might be more willing to enter into a relationship.

Schoenfeld et al. (2012) researched expressions of love within marital relationships in adults from the Eastern United States. They interviewed both husbands and wives four times over the course of 13 years of marriage. They found that men expressed their love through initiating sex and through participating in shared activities, such as leisure activities and household tasks. Wives tended to express their love through providing affection and refraining from criticism. However, both husbands and wives tended to express affection and intimacy toward each other. One intriguing finding presented by these researchers was that men who were more in love with their spouses were more likely to initiate sex, while women who were more in love with their spouses were less likely to initiate sex.

Gareis and Wilkins (2011) investigated expressions of love in German and American students and community members. These authors found that American spouses tended to say, "I love you," frequently while German spouses used the phrase only occasionally. American participants reported using the phrase more casually while, for German respondents, saying "I love you" was more deeply symbolic and private. While German and American participants both reported using more nonverbal than verbal expressions of love, German participants reported nonverbal expressions, such as sincerity and loyalty, while American participants reported physical expressions, such as hugging and kissing.

Diversity in love research

You may have noticed throughout the discussion of the love literature that much of the research in this area, especially the research exploring different types of love, has been performed using college students from the United States as participants. In the following section, we highlight literature exploring love across culture as well as across the lifespan. We also highlight gender differences and similarities where they occur.

Cross-cultural love attitudes

In an examination of 166 different cultures, Jankowiak and Fisher (1992) found evidence for the experience of romantic love in over 88 percent of the cultures investigated, suggesting that romantic love is nearly universal. These researchers coded personal accounts, love songs or folklore, elopements, and ethnographic accounts to determine whether romantic love was evidenced. In 147 of the 166 cultures, there was at least one indicator of romantic love. African cultures tended to be those lacking evidence for romantic love. In some of the cultures without evidence for romantic love, the authors speculate that these cases were oversights, rather than evidence that romantic love was not present in those cultures.

Culture may be a stronger determinant of attitudes toward love than gender. Sprecher and Toro-Morn (2002) gathered samples of college students from North America (the United States and Canada) as well as China. In the North American sample, both men and women believed that love was an important precursor to marriage, with women rating it as more important than men. However, men and women from the North American sample considered love as more important for marriage than did men and women from the Chinese sample. The North American students were also more likely than their Chinese counterparts to deem physical pleasure as important in marriage. The Chinese students displayed more romantic attitudes toward love, showing a stronger endorsement of the belief in "one" true love as well as more partner idealization.

Similarly, Neto et al. (2000) explored the attitudes of undergraduates from different cultures using Lee's (1977) typology of love as measured by Hendrick and Hendrick's (1986) Love Attitudes Scale. Participants from Angola, Brazil, Cape Verde, France, Macao, Mozambique, Portugal, and Switzerland participated. First it is important to note that the six factors identified by Hendrick and Hendrick and postulated by Lee were confirmed in each of these cultures. Second, congruent with Sprecher and Toro-Morn's (2002) results, there were few gender differences in love styles. Across cultures, men did tend to report slightly more ludic (game-playing) and agapic (altruistic) attitudes than women. Third, as predicted, endorsement of the love styles of eros (romantic love), mania (possessive love), and agape were relatively consistent across cultures. However, undergraduates from Angola, Cape Verde, and Mozambique demonstrated both more pragmatic (practical) and storgic (friendship-based) love styles than those from France and Switzerland. The authors interpret these results as consistent with differences between more individualistic and more collectivistic cultures. For example, in more collectivistic cultures the choice of a spouse might be a family decision and therefore individuals might display a more pragmatic love style.

Schmitt et al. (2009) investigated love using a measure of emotional investment (including questions related to passion, intimacy, and commitment) in college and community samples from 48 different nations. He found that, cross-culturally, greater emotional investment was associated with personality traits, such as increased extroversion and agreeableness, but not other traits such as neuroticism, suggesting that the experience of love is associated with certain personality characteristics across different cultures. Interestingly, Schmitt et al. also found that in nations with harsh living conditions (e.g., lack of resources, malnutrition) adults were less emotionally invested in their romantic relationships.

In another examination of cultural influences on attitudes toward love, Twamley (2013) described love and feelings of intimacy among Indian couples born in the United Kingdom or born in India. She found that for those born in India, love at first sight was derogated and not expected to last. Those born in India also expected to wait to have sex until they were married, even if their marriages were not arranged. For those born in the United Kingdom, however, love at first sight and physical attraction were valued, and these participants expected to engage in sex with their partners before marriage.

Age and love

Do you think that people's ideas and definitions of love change throughout their lives? If you are a college student now or a young adult, have your ideas about love and romance changed since you were a teenager? If you are an older adult, have your ideas about love changed since your twenties? As you read this chapter, you may have noticed that much of the research on love has been developed by asking college students their views. Few studies have asked married adults what they think love is, and even fewer studies have tapped into the wisdom of older adults on the subject.

The literature that does assess age and perceptions of love has mainly focused on age differences in passion and friendship. Typical results show that passion and sexual intimacy are more important to young adults, and that emotional security, loyalty, and commitment are more important to middle-aged adults (Ahmetoglu et al., 2010; Reedy et al., 1981). However, others have asserted that as people age, they do not lose the sexual passion and fire in their relationships (Langer, 2009; O'Leary et al. 2012).

The majority of the literature assessing age and love has used cross-sectional research designs. In a cross-sectional study, researchers compare different people from two or more age groups. The problem with using this type of design is that the research only reveals age differences (which may be confounded with generational differences); it does not reveal how love changes over time. It is only by using a longitudinal design (in which researchers follow one group of people throughout their lives) that we know how people's ideas about love change across the lifespan. Using cross-sectional research, the literature cannot give us a clear understanding about whether we will become less passionate as we age.

Therefore, although sexual intimacy may not be as important later in life as it is earlier in youth, older adults may still be passionate in their love relationships. In fact, Reeder (1996) found that, regardless of age, people defined romantic love in the same way. Older participants mentioned sex as an aspect of passion just as often as their younger counterparts did. Stereotypes that passion wanes when we get older and that love becomes friendship and companionship may not be accurate. We may feel passionate love throughout our lives, and we may want to continue to experience sexual intimacy into older adulthood.

The neurological experience of love

Early feelings of romantic love may be stimulated by the release of oxytocin. Oxytocin is a neuropeptide which facilitates relaxation and bonding (Meyer, 2007). Research conducted by Schneiderman et al. (2012) showed that levels of oxytocin (as measured by blood samples) were higher among new romantic partners (who had been together from two weeks to four months) than among single individuals. Furthermore, in this study, men's and women's levels of oxytocin did not differ from one another and stayed stable over a six-month period. Interestingly, baseline oxytocin levels of romantic couples who were still together six months later were higher than baseline levels from couples who had broken up. Although these findings seem to suggest that romantic love and bonding increases oxytocin levels, as the authors suggest, it may also be the case – because of the correlational nature of the data – that people with higher levels of oxytocin are more likely to fall in love or form romantic relationships. Researchers postulate that oxytocin may even help to maintain fidelity in monogamous relationships. Scheele et al. (2012) found that men involved in monogamous romantic relationships who were administered oxytocin intra-nasally maintained a greater distance between themselves and an attractive female confederate versus men in a placebo condition and versus single men.

The neurotransmitters dopamine and serotonin may also be involved in the experience of love. Kurup and Kurup (2003) found that, among adults from India, those who had fallen in love and had non-arranged marriages exhibited increased levels of dopamine and decreased levels of serotonin, while the reverse was true for individuals who had never fallen in love and who had arranged marriages. However, Langeslag et al. (2012), who collected data in the Netherlands, found that serotonin levels for men in love were lower than for men who were not in love. Women in love showed higher serotonin levels than women who were not in love. Furthermore, participants in Langeslag's research were "in love" for nine months or less and had an average age of 20, while Kurup and Kurup's participants were in marital relationships and ranged in age from 30–40. Future research will be necessary to elucidate the relationship between serotonin and romantic love.

A personal moment: My friends who are happily wedded in arranged marriages would want me to point out that the participants for Kurup and Kurup's (2003) study referenced above were particularly chosen to meet the criteria of being both in love and in "choice" marriages, or not in love and in arranged marriages. My friends in arranged marriages do love their partners, and this anecdotal evidence is supported by research. For example, Regan et al. (2012) found, in either arranged or "love-based" marriages, no difference in love, commitment, or marital satisfaction among Indian participants living in the United States (p. 915). Similarly, Myers et al. (2005) failed to find any differences in marital satisfaction or love among their samples of adults in arranged marriages in India versus adults in marriages of choice in the United States. Furthermore, Yelsma and Athappilly (1988) found that Indian couples in arranged marriages expressed greater marital satisfaction than did their Indian and American counterparts in marriages of choice. However, Xiaohe and Whyte (1990) found that wives in arranged marriages in China were less satisfied with their marriages than wives in love marriages. Future research should investigate whether couples in arranged marriages who love each other resemble couples in choice marriages in their levels of dopamine and serotonin.

Researchers have posited that the areas of the brain involved with emotion and reward might also be involved in the experience of intense, passionate love. Stoessel et al. (2011) conducted research using an fMRI which showed that

German participants who were currently intensely in love with their romantic partners (as compared to those who had recently endured a break-up) and were shown photographs of their romantic partners showed stronger activation in brain regions related to emotion and reward: such as the anterior cingulate cortex, bilateral insula, and the posterior cingulate cortex. These authors posited that the face of a romantic partner was pleasant and rewarding to those intensely in love, but not to those who had recently parted with their loved ones. Interestingly, in this research the authors also asked participants to view erotic photographs. The authors found that similar areas of the brain were activated when viewing (non-erotic) photographs of their own romantic partners and when viewing erotic photographs of strangers. The authors suggest that brain areas associated with sexual arousal are also activated by the experience of romantic love. Aron et al. (2005) found similar results using a similar methodology.

What the research says

Aron et al. (2005) explored the areas of the brain that were activated while research participants (who reported being intensely in love with their partners) underwent an fMRI. In this research project, undergraduate as well as community participants were sought who were from the region around New York City and who reported being intensely in love with their partners for 1 to 17 months. The respondents completed a questionnaire to measure passionate love as well as underwent the fMRI procedure. Photographs of romantic partners as well as photographs of friends of the same sex and approximately the same age as their partners were used as stimuli during the fMRI procedure. The participants were asked to think about a positive (but not sexual) experience they experienced with their romantic partners while viewing their partners' photographs. When presented with photographs of their friends, participants were also asked to think about a positive event involving those friends. To prevent contamination, in between trials the participants were asked to count backwards from a four-digit number, by sevens, either for 40 seconds (following the photo of a loved one) or 20 seconds (following the photo of a friend). The authors found that viewing photographs of romantic partners (coupled with thinking about positive events with those partners) produced activation in the ventral tegemental area as well as the caudate body and tail. The authors concluded that early romantic love is characterized by strong activation of areas of the brain associated with reward. The authors also posited that the neurological evidence reveals that, rather than being an emotion itself, love is more like a *motivation* to be with a specific person, which then leads to emotions such as euphoria.

Think critically

Aron et al. instructed their participants to count backward from a four-digit number by sevens for either 40 or 20 seconds. Furthermore, the participants were not asked to count out loud, but just to count mentally. Do you think that the differing time intervals may have influenced the results? Do you think that the participants were more distracted from the counting task following photos of their romantic partners or friends?

Acevedo et al. (2012) investigated the areas of the brain that were active in married adults who reported being intensely in love with their long-term partners (couples' relationships had to span at least ten years). Interestingly, of the 17 participants in this research project, 10 were in relationships in which at least one partner had been previously divorced. Similar to the results for early-stage romantic love reported above (Aron et al., 2005), this research also revealed "neural activity in response to images of their partners...in mesolimbic, dopamine-rich regions important for reward-processing and motivation" (p. 153). Consistent with the results for early-stage romantic love, there was increased activation in the ventral tegmental area and caudate when looking at a photograph of a romantic partner rather than a photograph of a close friend. These authors also found that greater scores on the Passionate Love Scale as well as the love style of eros were associated with increased activation in the caudate. Once again, these authors interpreted the results to suggest that romantic love is similar to a motivational state rather than a particular emotion.

Using this fMRI technique, romantic love may be distinguished from other types of love. Ortigue et al. (2010) conducted a meta-analysis showing that romantic love involves areas such as the ventral tegemental area and caudate nucleus, while maternal love involves the periaqueductal gray matter of the brain. These authors also echo the suggestion of Aron et al. (2005) that romantic love is a "reward-based goal-directed motivation toward a specific partner" (p. 3549).

Although expressed feelings about love may vary with cultures, the neural experience of love seems consistent across cultures. Xu et al. (2011) found that Chinese undergraduates who reported being in love and who were looking at photographs of their romantic partners showed activation in the ventral tegmental area, the caudate nucleus, and the cerebellum, suggesting that similar neural activity occurs when gazing at photographs of love partners in China and in the United States.

Interestingly, fMRI research by Wager et al. (2013) suggests that the pain of a romantic break-up activates many of the same areas of the brain as does the physical pain experienced by high heat applied to the forearm of the participants. These researchers asked participants to view photographs of their ex-partners or photographs of friends, and to endure warmth or painful heat delivered to the forearm while their brain activity was measured through fMRI. Although the activation for the physical pain was stronger than the activation when viewing photographs of their exes, the same areas of the brain were activated under each type of painful scenario.

Chapter summary

In this chapter, we have highlighted the importance to overall relationship satisfaction of satisfying sexual relationships and love. Although men and women differ somewhat in terms of self-reported sexual attitudes and behaviors, with regard to sex we are more similar to one another than different from one another. Men and women also tend to share similar attitudes toward love. Researchers' attempts to study love have yielded a variety of similar models of love, most of which emphasize the difference between feeling love and being "in love." The experience of romantic love seems to be nearly universal, although attitudes toward love and expressions of love vary with culture. Age can also impact our views of love, but many adults report passionate feelings for their partners. The neurological experience of love seems to be rooted in the areas of the brain associated with emotion and rewards. We present our suggestions for future reading below.

Suggested reading

Fisher, T. D., Moore, Z. T., & Pittenger, M. (2012). Sex on the brain? An examination of frequency of sexual cognitions as a function of gender, erotophilia, and social desirability. *Journal of Sex Research*, 49(1), 69–77. doi:10.1080/00224499.2011.5 65429
   I recommend this article because of the unique way the researchers measure sexual thoughts.
Muise, A., Impett, E. A., & Desmarais, S. (2013). Getting it on versus getting it over with: Sexual motivation, desire, and satisfaction in intimate bonds. *Personality and Social Psychology Bulletin*, 39(10), 1320–1332. doi:10.1177/0146167213490963
   This article was easy to understand, and I recommend it because it considers the perspectives of both members of the romantic partnership.
Petersen, J. L., & Hyde, J. (2010). A meta-analytic review of research on gender differences in sexuality, 1993–2007. *Psychological Bulletin*, 136(1), 21–38. doi:10.1037/a0017504
   I enjoyed this article because it presents information about gender differences while highlighting similarities among men and women as well.
Sprecher, S., Treger, S., & Sakaluk, J. K. (2013). Premarital sexual standards and socio-sexuality: Gender, ethnicity, and cohort differences. *Archives of Sexual Behavior*, doi:10.1007/s10508-013-0145-6
   This article utilizes a relatively unique trend research design exploring sexual double standards within the same population over time.
Sternberg, R. J. (1986). A triangular theory of love. *Psychological Review*, 93(2), 119–135. doi:10.1037/0033-295X.93.2.119
   Sternberg's original description of the triangular model is easy to read and interesting. I enjoy the critique of the previous models of love as well as his suggestions for achieving and maintaining consummate love.

Gender

9

The similarity hypothesis

Although most gender research focuses on gender differences rather than similarities, while reading this chapter, keep in mind that the majority of research shows men and women are actually more similar than they are different. Most gender effects are small and, thus, there is more overlap between the sexes than is typically discussed. Throughout this chapter we will discuss some well-known individuals who have argued that men and women are from different planets (Gray, 1992), or that they have different linguistic cultures based on communication (Tannen, 1990; 1994). However, Hyde (2005) conducted an intensive meta-analysis of the gender literature and found that the majority of gender effects were quite small; her research has sparked others to look for similarities between the sexes. For example, Thompson and O'Sullivan (2012) found that both women and men showed strong implicit preferences for romantic stimuli compared to sexual stimuli. Perrin et al. (2011) did not find gender differences in self-reported desirable and actual romantic behaviors. Gender similarities like these are often overlooked.

Gender similarities are important because of the real-world influences of gender stereotyping. Imagine you are going to therapy with your spouse and want to discuss communication difficulties. The therapist tells you that you will never understand each other because men and women communicate differently. You may leave thinking, "Therapy is pointless. I'll never understand my partner." Furthermore, it may not be a person's sex that is necessarily influencing dating scripts, communication, and romance, but a person's level of masculinity and femininity. Unlike biological sex, characteristics of masculinity and femininity can vary in different situations (Leszczynski, 2009); for example, you may act more sensitively when you are with your romantic partner and more competitively when at work.

Gender differences in communication style

A media moment: In 1992, Gray wrote an international bestselling book entitled, *Men are from Mars, Women are from Venus*. This book has sold over 50 million copies and has been translated into 42 languages. His premise is that men and women have so many problems communicating in relationships that they might as well be from different planets. If you have ever had the thought, "Is he even listening to me?" or "Why doesn't she think that I listen to her?" – then you understand Gray's point. Some believe that these communication differences are the key to relationship difficulties. In fact, a common complaint of couples in relationship counseling is a problem with communication. Gray established the Mars Venus Institute in 1996 to offer workshops for individuals with trouble communicating in their relationships (www.marsvenusinsitute.com). The website includes contact information for counselors and a list of workshops facilitated by Gray and his colleagues. However, we advise waiting to book an appointment until after reading this entire chapter. Alternative views regarding Gray's theory are discussed throughout this chapter.

Think back to when you were in early elementary school – let us say second grade. Who were your friends? If you cannot remember, can you identify the gender of your closest friends? If you are a woman, it is most likely that you had a lot of friends who were girls. If you are a man, it is most likely that you had many friends who were boys. Maccoby has done extensive work throughout her career examining gender and peer relationships within the developmental context. In her 1998 book, *The Two Sexes: Growing Up Apart, Coming Together*, she discusses how our same-sex relationships during childhood later affect our other-sex relationships during adolescence. In developmental psychology, we refer to this phenomenon as gender segregation. Girls prefer to spend time with girls and boys with boys (if this was not you, do not fret; there are advantages to other-sex interactions). This phenomenon is specific to childhood, is quite robust, and is seen in different cultures across the world.

Why is gender segregation important to future romantic relationships? It is important because we know that boys' and girls' interactions are different from one another. Through same-sex relationships during childhood, females develop a communication style that is expressive, dependent, and communal; the main goal of communication is to make connections and to facilitate relationships. Girls are more likely to self-disclose to their friends, spend time in supportive conversations, and learn to communicate in these ways. On the other hand, boys' friendships are often less emotional and more likely to be based on similar activity preferences rather than on sharing personal information. Men's communication style is dominant, controlling, and directive; the main goal of male communication is to be assertive and independent (Maccoby, 1998). Leaper and Smith (2004) conducted a meta-analysis to analyze gender differences in communication styles in children. They analyzed 155 studies published between 1958 and 2000. Overall, they found that girls tended to be more talkative and more affiliative in their speech, while boys tended to be more assertive in their conversations.

The idea, then, is that we spend so much time during childhood segregated from the other sex, that when we emerge in our teen years and become interested in other-sex interactions, we have different communication styles. Maccoby (1998) contends that gender segregation during childhood establishes two different (gendered) cultures. Tannen takes a similar approach in that she asserts that men and women are from different linguistic cultures. She makes these claims in her 1987 book, *That's Not What I Meant! How Conversational Style Makes or Breaks Relationships*. Her follow-up book, entitled, *You Just Don't Understand: Women and Men in Conversation* (1991), was on the *New York Times* bestseller list for four years and has been translated into 31 languages (www.georgetown.edu/faculty/tannend).

Tag questions and verbal interruptions

Let me give you an example of how gender differences in conversational style can influence a romantic relationship. A man and a woman are trying to figure out where to go for dinner on their first date. The man asks the woman where she prefers to eat; she answers "It seems like the new Thai place on Main Street might be good, right? I really love Chinese food, but Italian would be really nice too ... whatever you think." This example illustrates a number of ways that women communicate. She is using emotional words (e.g., "love"), intensive adverbs (e.g., "really"), passive speech and uncertainty (e.g., "whatever you think" Lakoff, 1975). She is also using tag questions – questions at the end of a sentence that make the speaker sound tentative. For example, she may say "That was a great movie, wasn't it?" Some researchers suggest that this style is less assertive (Newcombe & Arnkoff, 1979). Men are less familiar with this type of answer. When men were growing up they were around other boys who were direct and controlling in their speech. Given the question of where to eat, a man is more likely to answer: "The Thai place on Main Street is good." His answer is very simple and to the point. He is exhibiting confidence and assertiveness. Later, I will discuss gendered dating scripts. Some argue that these communication differences are not problematic because men are supposed to be the initiators and women the passive responders.

There are other gender differences in verbal communication that may lead to problems on a date. For example, men are more likely to use intrusive interruptions in conversations. If a man's date begins to tell a story about her weekend, he is more likely to interrupt what she is saying (Athenstaedt et al., 2004) and assert his own topic. These controlling interruptions are related to men's higher status in a patriarchal society. Interestingly, the research displays that men are more likely to interrupt women than they are other men (Smith-Lovin & Brody, 1989). How do you think women deal with these interruptions during a date? Would you hypothesize that women get annoyed and angry when men interrupt?

What the research says

Farley et al. (2010) assessed how gender impacted reactions to being interrupted. They had 150 college students from the United States participate in experimental research utilizing two female and two male confederates. In the control and experimental conditions, participants discussed a *USA Today* article about remedial education with a partner (the partner was actually a confederate who followed a script). One of the sample scripted statements given was, "I always thought that the reasoning was, people who pay their tuition deserve to sit in on classes, but if they don't pass the class, then oh well, they don't deserve that piece of paper" (p. 198). In the control condition, the confederate was told to let the participant discuss his/her opinion about the article. In the experimental condition, the confederate interrupted the participant between 8–10 times. In fact, if the participant did not stop talking, the confederates were told to keep repeating the first few words of their statement several times until they fully interrupted what the participant was saying. Coders rated participants' nonverbal behaviors in response to the interruptions (smiling, posture, laughing, nodding, interruption, disagreements, laughing, and latency). In response to interruptions by a male confederate, women tended to exhibit more laughter. Did you hypothesize that a woman would get annoyed when a dating partner interrupted her? Farley et al.'s findings do not support this hypothesis. In fact, they found that, overall, regardless of condition, women were more likely to smile, agree, nod, and laugh than were men. The authors interpret these behaviors as a way in which women attempt to make a conversation run smoothly. This can be seen as a way for women to assert themselves nonverbally in the conversation because they are actively engaged.

Think critically

Farley et al. (2010) interpreted their findings as saying that women smile, nod, and laugh when interrupted by men because they remain engaged in the conversation. Do you think that women's responses are always interpreted in a positive way? What are the alternative interpretations of this data? Think about whether women could also be viewed as unassertive and overly agreeable. If so, what are the implications of this for the couple's future together?

How "Women's Speech" helps communication

As Farley et al.'s (2010) study shows us, women's nonverbal behaviors can actually help a conversation along. This may be especially important on a first date when easy conversation can be a struggle. I remember first dates (and some second dates too!) with many awkward silences. Once you get past discussing some of the surface information (e.g., Where did you grow up? What is your favorite movie?), conversations sometimes stall. Thus, "Women's Speech" can actually help during a date. During conversations, a woman is more likely to pay attention to her partner's intonation and body language (sometimes this is called the meta-message; Tannen, 1987). She is more likely to be sensitive to nonverbal cues and to interpret emotional information more easily. If she interrupts the conversation, she will use affiliative interruption to show interest and affirm what the other person is saying. For example, women tend to interrupt by saying "that's interesting ..." or "really!" To show interest in a conversation, women tend to use one of the most important gendered techniques in communication – "interaction work."

Interaction work

Women are taught in their same-sex interactions during childhood to show interest in the conversation; women work during the interaction. Fishman introduced the notion of "interaction work" in her 1978 study. She listened to 52 hours of conversations among three couples and developed 5 communication differences that she termed "interaction work." She found that women were much more likely to ask questions of their partners instead of simply stating a fact. Taking this research into the context of a date, it suggests that women might be the ones who facilitate the conversation (e.g., "Did you have fun at the party yesterday?"). Similarly, Fishman found that women are twice as likely to ask "Do you know what?" questions compared to men (p. 401). If you are stuck in an awkward silence during a date, one technique to start the conversation is by asking a question – you are almost always guaranteed a response! If you are still struggling, Fishman discusses attention beginnings. She describes how the phrase "This is interesting" or "You know" is used much more by women than men. Lastly, Fishman's theory is most well-known for the interaction strategy of minimal responses. These are the "yeah," "mmm-hmm," and "huhs" that people say throughout their conversations. Women are much more likely to use these phrases, and these phrases are the most descriptive of the term "interaction work." Take a moment to think back to how this relates to gender segregation during childhood and why Tannen contends that men and women have different linguistic cultures. Boys' and men's conversations do not include this interaction work. They were not taught as children to acknowledge what their partner is saying, the way girls were. In fact, Fishman found that the most commonly used phrase by men in her study was a statement (e.g., "I had a good time at the party"). Interestingly, she found that when the female partner made a statement about herself, the man ignored her until she turned her attention back to his topic of the conversation. Thus, if a woman is keeping the conversation going during a date, she is most likely talking only about the topics of interest to the man!

A personal moment: When I (Leszczynski) talk to my mom on the phone, I know that she is actively engaged in the conversation. How do I know that? Because I hear "mmm-hmmm," "yeah," "really," and "oh" throughout the conversation. I am confident that my mom is listening, and the conversation flows easily. Phone conversations with my husband are quite different. I talk for some time and tell him something that happened that day and then realize after a few minutes that he hasn't said anything. I usually stop and say, "Are you still there?" He says, "Of course I'm here," and then I usually ask him what I just said. He asks me why am I asking him to recount a story he just heard? When I use this example in my Psychology of Gender class, I hear a lot of laughing and see many nods of agreement. One semester, about a week after I finished teaching the communication section, a student approached me after class. He told me that my class helped him to understand why his girlfriend was constantly telling him that he was not listening to her. He said that after learning about interaction work, he integrated it into his conversations with his girlfriend over the course of a week. He thanked me for saving their relationship because she had told him the night before: "I can't believe how much you have changed. You are really listening to me now!"

What the research says

Edwards and Hamilton (2004) contend that communication is more complicated than a simple gender difference. Compared to men, women are more likely to interpret situations as cooperative (Tannen, 1990). Edwards and Hamilton tested Tannen's ideas of different linguistic gendered cultures by asking college students to rate four ambiguous scenarios by level of cooperativeness. The majority of their sample was European-American (from the United States). The authors created four ambiguous scenarios based upon Tannen's (1990) book. The scenarios involved co-workers, friends, colleagues, and spouses. The relationship scenario was: "A husband and wife are painting their living room. When the husband (wife) trips over a ladder, the wife (husband) says, 'you need to be more careful.' How would you react?" (p. 496). After reading each scenario, participants rated how cooperative the actors were in each scenario. The authors also assessed other variables. Participants rated their own dominance and nurturance, and their beliefs about the speaker's motivations. Interestingly, participants were also asked about their beliefs regarding cross-sex communication (e.g., "I think that men and women communicate in different ways" p. 497). Edwards and Hamilton found that interpretations of interactions are very complex. Contrary to Tannen's theory (1990; 1994), a person's gender alone did not predict his/her interpretation of the situation. Rather, participants who were more nurturing were more likely to interpret situations as being more cooperative compared to participants who were more dominant. They did find that the scenario which included a husband and a wife was the only one to show a cross-sex communication difference. When spouses warned, "You need to be more careful," they were viewed as being less cooperative than when the message came from a same-sex actor.

Think critically

It is rather interesting that Edwards and Hamilton (2004) found that if a same-sex person tells you to be careful, you think they are helping, but if your spouse says it, you interpret it as less cooperative. What are the possible reasons why, in this situation, a romantic partner is viewed as being less helpful than a same-sex peer? What other variables could the researchers have examined to assess these possibilities?

Gender and dating

Before we review the literature on dating, it is important to understand to whom we can generalize these findings. The majority of the research in this area is based on college student samples. Keep in mind that individuals in their twenties (we call this age group emerging adults) differ in what they look for in a romantic partner compared to people who are young adults (30–40 year-olds), middle-aged adults (50–65 year-olds), and older adults (over the age of 65). Thus, one of the weaknesses of this literature is that we simply do not know a lot about dating in older populations. As a life-span developmental psychologist, I have a hard time believing that what college students want in a romantic partner is the same as what someone who is older desires.

For this section, imagine two heterosexual people, Tom and Linda, who are interested in each other. I want you to take a moment to think about your gendered expectations. For example, who do you think will be the one to initiate the date? Will it be Tom, who approaches Linda at a nightclub and uses a bad pick-up line? How do you imagine Linda's response? Does she play hard to get? Where do you picture them going on their date? Is it dinner and a movie or a drink at a local bar or coffeehouse? Who is most likely to initiate the first move when it comes to physical intimacy? I am asking you to think about your scripts for dating. Dating scripts are preconceived expectations for what happens on a date – often they involve the sequence of events and typical actions by both men and women.

What do women (and men) want?

What are your ideas about what men and women want from an intimate relationship? Do they just want someone to hang out with? Is Tom only dating Linda because he hopes it will lead to a sexual encounter? Is Linda only looking for a man who is "marriage material?" Clark et al. (1999) asked college students to list their goals for dating; their participants reported that love, sex, fun, learning about their partner, impressing others, and gaining access to a partner's resources were the most important reasons for dating. Even though they found that the majority of emerging adults reported that love was an important goal, there were some gender differences in reasons for dating. Did you hypothesize that Tom would be more focused on the possibility of having sex after the date? Is Linda focused on what Tom can offer her in terms of a long-term relationship? If so, your opinion agrees with what the research shows. Researchers across the globe have found that men are highly focused on sex. As discussed in Chapter 4, men look for physically attractive women, whereas women look for financial security in a mate. Men report sex as a reason for dating more often than do women, and men have more permissive attitudes about casual sex and dating (Oliver & Hyde, 1993).

What the research says

One of my favorite studies illustrating how men are more liberal about casual sex was conducted by Clark and Hatfield (1989). Clark and Hatfield trained nine confederates (five women and four men, approximately 22 years of age) to approach students on a college campus. The confederates were slightly to moderately physically attractive. The researchers instructed the confederates to approach other-sex students on the campus and say, "I have been noticing you around campus. I find you to be very attractive." Each participant was then asked "Would you go out with me tonight?" "Would you come over to my apartment tonight?" or "Would you go to bed with me tonight?" Fifty-six percent of women accepted the invitation for a date that evening, 6 percent the request to go to his apartment, and 0 percent the invitation for sex. For men, 50 percent accepted the invitation for a date (notice that this is fewer than the women), 69 percent of the men accepted the women's request to go to her apartment, and 75 percent accepted the invitation to have sex – that evening! The female confederates reported that men who rejected them provided excuses and indicated that they felt bad refusing them saying such statements as: "I cannot tonight, but tomorrow would be fine," or "I'm married." This is in contrast to women's responses to the sexual invitation, for instance: "You've got to be kidding," or "What is wrong with you? Leave me alone." (p. 52). Is it not interesting that fewer men accepted a strange women's offer to go on a date with her than agreed to have sex with her in a few hours?

Think critically

The original study was conducted in 1978, and the authors replicated the findings in 1982 and 1990. Do you think that the findings could be replicated today? Hald and Høgh-Olesen (2010) did just that when they replicated the study in Denmark. They used 21 male and female confederates who were approximately 21 years of age and ranged in physical attractiveness. Individuals in relationships and not in relationships were analyzed separately. Women who were in a relationship (4 percent) were *more* likely to agree to have sex with a stranger than women not in a relationship (0 percent). Men in a relationship (18 percent) were *less* likely to agree to have sex compared to men not a relationship (59 percent).

Initiating a date

If you notice a stranger on the other side of the room and want to meet that person, how do you approach him/her? It may depend on whether you are interested in a long-term partnership, a short-term partnership, sex, or more than one of these possibilities. Research in this area has focused on either nonverbal behaviors that can elicit a response or on direct propositions (for a more thorough review, see Cunningham & Barbee, 2008). The layman's term for these behaviors is "flirting." Think back to Tom and Linda and create some suggestions for them. What behaviors are considered flirting by a woman versus a man? What would you tell Tom and Linda to look for in order to determine whether the other is interested?

Before potential dating partners approach each other, they may use nonverbal cues to indicate their interest. Moore (1985) observed 200 women in a singles bar and identified 52 different solicitation behaviors. For most women, the first step is checking out the entire room. After that, women become more discerning and may glance quickly at a particular man and then fixate their eye contact on him for more than three seconds. As reviewed in Chapter 5, eye contact is an important indicator of attraction. I often refer to this as the "come hither look" because it is usually an invitation to the man to initiate a verbal interaction. Men look for repeated eye contact by women to show interest and do not often approach women who do not perform that particular behavior. Other solicitation behaviors that Moore (1985) found to be common included: the head toss, hair flip, smile, laugh, whisper, primp, giggle, lip lick, lean, and neck presentation (where the woman tilts her head sideways at a 45-degree angle). These solicitation cues are important when reading interest in a potential mate. What are other ways that women can indicate attraction? Gueguen (2009) examined individuals taking part in speed dating. He found that men rated a woman higher in physical attractiveness if she mimicked his nonverbal behaviors.

Who performs more nonverbal flirting behaviors, men or women? McCormick and Jones (1989) observed 70 couples ranging in age from 18–39 in several busy singles bars. Whereas Moore (1985) looked at the solicitation behaviors prior to meeting, McCormick and Jones (1989) focused on recording heterosexual couples' behaviors after talking for a few minutes. A female confederate posing as someone asking about consumer behavior approached each couple. The confederate asked the couple about their familiarity with each other. The researchers found that women were pivotal in either escalating or deescalating the flirtation at the beginning of the interaction. Overwhelmingly, women were more likely to give the "come hither" look. They spent more time gazing towards a potential partner, engaged in more brief touching, were more likely to use positive facial expressions, and spent more time on grooming behaviors. However, after the interaction became more sexual, men were more likely to initiate intimate touching (this is consistent with the gendered dating scripts that we will discuss later).

Do you think that you can correctly read nonverbal cues? Place et al. (2009) researched whether people could correctly perceive the romantic interest of a dating couple based on their nonverbal behavior. They found that both men and women were accurate; however, participants tended to incorrectly perceive women's interest. That is, women were perceived to be more sexually interested than they actually were (see Chapter 3 for more research on the overestimation of women's sexual interest).

Verbal initiation

You may be more familiar with the term "pick-up" lines, but the literature refers to these as "direct propositions." Do you have any examples of pick-up lines?

Maybe you have one that is your stand-by and you use it when you are at a loss for words. Maybe you have heard several cheesy ones that you later laughed about with a friend or family member. If you are a woman, you may prefer innocuous lines which elicit conversations (e.g., "You look really familiar") or direct lines self-disclosing interest (e.g., "I'm kind of shy, but I'd really like to get to know you"). If you are man, you may prefer cute, flippant lines meant to break the ice with sexual humor (e.g., "Your place or mine?" "Isn't it cold? Let's make some body heat," Kleinke et al., 1986, p. 588). In a real-world setting, even though men prefer flippant lines, Cunningham (1989) found that women are more likely to reject these types of advances. Men were likely to be receptive to any type of pick-up line.

Think back to Tom and Linda. Who is most likely to approach the other and verbally initiate the relationship? Research examining dating initiation is highly stereotypical. Clark et al. (1999) found that men were more likely to verbally initiate relationships. Women tend to be more passive and wait for the man to make the first move. But what if he does not? If you are a woman, have you ever asked a guy out? It may shock you (it did me!) that men are more likely to expect intimate sexual behavior if the woman asks him on a date (Mongeau et al., 1997). Similarly, Morr Serewicz and Gale (2008) found that men expected sexual intimacy beyond kissing when the date was female-initiated.

Given this discussion, what advice do we have for Linda and Tom? It seems like we should tell Tom to wait until Linda gives him a long glance – indicating interest. Then he should approach her and use either direct or flattering pick-up lines. He should look for behaviors that indicate her continued interest in him. For instance, does she lick her lips? Is her head tilted to the side? Is she whispering in his ear? If she is not showing those behaviors, she may be telling him that she is no longer interested, and he should back off. What do we tell Linda? Tom is going to look for her to initiate contact with a few glances, and she needs to indicate her continued interest using those nonverbal solicitation cues. At the beginning of the encounter, Linda will either escalate or deescalate the romantic interaction. She can either accept him or "shoot him down." At the beginning, she also has a lot of control over where and how far the interaction goes. If she is looking for a long-term relationship, she needs to wait for Tom to approach her. However, remember Clark and Hatfield's (1989) work. If she is looking for a one-night stand, she need only say, "Hi, you're cute. My place or yours?"

A media moment: Some of my favorite pick-up lines come from movies. In the movie *Hitch* (Tennant, 2005), the main character states, "I couldn't help but notice that you look a lot like my next girlfriend." In the movie *Couples Retreat* (Billingsley, 2009), shortly after introducing himself, a character named Dave asks, "Do you have a cell phone that I can use? Someone has to call God and tell him that one of his angels is missing." Think back to the research described above on pick-up lines. Although men prefer to use these types of pick-up lines, is a woman likely to respond positively to these pick-up lines?

Dating scripts

Gender differences in what men and women want in a relationship are related to traditional dating scripts. Popular culture would lead you to believe that romance, dating, and sex are highly gender stereotypical. For instance, you may have heard of the *New York Times* bestselling book, *The Rules: Time-Tested Secrets for Capturing the Heart of Mr. Right*, by Fein and Schneider (1995), which has been translated into 18 languages. The authors have created follow-up books discussing the rules for marriage, online dating, and generational differences, including *Not Your Mother's Rules: The New Secrets for Dating* in 2013. Their website (www.therules-book.com) includes links to consultations, courses, and dating coaches (each with fees of course). To illustrate the rules, the website has a quiz with the following scenario (See how you do!): "Amy got a text at 5:20 p.m. on a Friday night from a guy at work asking if she wanted to meet up later for drinks. Amy thought that he was really cute, just her type, and was actually not doing anything later." What should she do? According to the website, she should text him back on Monday and say thank you, but that she already had plans over the weekend. Did you answer that she should text him back that evening? If your answer was that you should text him back and accept the offer, Fein and Schneider say that you need to purchase their book right away! Why? The notion is that women should play hard to get and that men should put in more effort.

Let us assume that Tom and Linda have now met and are on their first date; take a moment to do an activity. Put two columns on paper – one for men and one for women. Now list the actions that you believe men and women should do on a first date. When you are done with your list, continue reading this section. Rose and Frieze's (1989) classic research asked college students to do this activity. They found dating scripts to be reactive for women and proactive for men. Men's dating scripts were proactive in terms of initiating the date (e.g., asking the woman out and planning the date), the public domain (e.g., driving), and initiating sexual intimacy (e.g. making the first move). Women's dating scripts were reactive in terms of the private domain (e.g., focus on physical appearance before the date), following the man's lead (e.g., having doors opened for her), and reacting to sexual intimacy (e.g., stopping the man from kissing her). Rose and Frieze's (1993) follow-up study examined whether college students actually acted out these scripts. They not only asked participants to report their ideas about typical actions on a first date, but also to describe their most recent date. They found that participants' reports of their actual dates followed the gendered scripts.

Let us critically examine these findings. I hope that you noticed when these studies were conducted – during the late 1980s and early 1990s. Are you wondering whether times have changed? Eaton and Rose (2011) conducted an archival analysis of both popular and scholarly literature. The authors analyzed seven self-help books focusing on dating advice and found that they all endorsed traditional reactive and proactive gendered scripts. For example, they analyzed Dr. Phil McGraw's (2005) *Love Smart: Find the One You Want – Fix the One You Got*. Dr. Phil tells women that they need to let men feel like they are in charge, and that men are intimated by strong women. Eaton and Rose (2011) concluded that ideas about dating scripts have not changed in the last 20–30 years. As mentioned earlier, *The Rules* is a perfect example of these scripts (even though this particular book was not mentioned in the article). To analyze the scholarly literature, Eaton and Rose looked at 94 articles published in the journal, *Sex Roles*, and sorted them by decade. Similar to what was in the popular media, research articles also reported that dating scripts have not changed. Thus, even if men and women feel that they can ask someone out, men actually report initiating relationships more often than women (Clark et al., 1999). Men are also still more likely to initiate sexual activities. Women's responsibility is to be the gatekeepers and tell the men how far they are allowed to go. However, in the current generation, college students who are older and involved in fraternities and sororities (especially men) often include sex in their typical dating scripts (Bartoli & Clark, 2006).

Certain exceptions to the traditional dating scripts are becoming more normative, especially for young people. Group dating is becoming more common; this occurs when a group of teenagers or college students hang out together in hopes of pairing off later on during the evening. During adolescence, girls and guys are more likely to spend time in mixed-gender groups and to interact with other-gender peers whom they may later date (Connolly et al., 2004). Speed dating, online dating, and "hook-ups" are also becoming more common.

Current research trends

Overall, our scripts for first dates are very consistent and have not changed over time. Current research is examining whether these scripts vary according to contextual differences. For example, Morr Serewicz and Gale (2008) asked college students at a US Midwest university to read hypothetical dating initiation scripts. The scripts varied in whether the date occurred at a keg party or a coffee shop. Not surprisingly, they found that participants expected more sexual intimacy when alcohol was involved in the dating scenario. However, there was a gender difference. Research shows that alcohol leads to decreased anxiety and more self-disclosure for men, but increased anxiety and decreased self-disclosure in women (George & Norris, 1991). Perhaps women are less likely to be intimate when they have consumed alcohol because they fear that the men will misinterpret their nonverbal cues.

Current research also examines where these gendered scripts of first dates come from. One of the most likely sources is the media. Holz Ivory et al. (2009) analyzed 12 heterosexual or homosexual couples on seven television shows that aired between 2001 and 2004 (e.g., *Sex and the City*, *Queer as Folk*, *The Sopranos*, *The L Word*). In straight couples, men were found to be more dominant and women more submissive. This is consistent with the stereotypical gendered scripts we discussed earlier. For same-sex couples, each partner was portrayed as being either "the dominant one" or "the submissive one" in the relationship. The take-home message is that, gay or straight, everyone is assigned a gendered role in a relationship according to the media.

What the research says

If gender scripts prescribe that all men should be dominant and controlling in a relationship, what happens when a man does not fit that stereotype? In layman's terms, the question then becomes, "Do nice guys finish last?" Jensen-Campbell et al. (1995) asked just that of female college students attending an introductory psychology class at a university in Texas. Female participants watched a videotaped interaction between an experimenter and a participant (these were actually two confederates). In one interaction, the supposed participant exhibited highly dominant behaviors. He chose a chair close to the experimenter, spoke loudly and rapidly, and showed a relaxed sitting posture. In the low-dominance condition, the confederate pushed the chair away from the experimenter, and leaned slightly forward and spoke in a soft and slow manner. "Niceness" was manipulated by varying the level of altruism that the confederate exhibited. In the high altruistic condition, the confederate talked about helping others, and in the low altruistic condition about only looking out for himself. Each female participant then viewed one of the videos and was given either a physically attractive or physically unattractive picture of the confederate purportedly in order to enable her to see him more clearly. The participants rated each confederate on his level of physical attractiveness, dating desirability, social desirability, and external resources. Their findings showed that the altruistic man was rated as being more physically and sexually attractive, and the women rated him as being a more desirable dating partner than the non-altruistic man. In the follow-up study, participants watched interactions similar to those in the first study; however, the confederate was either dominant (assertive, bold, talkative) or non-dominant (introverted, quiet, reserved) and either agreeable (considerate, kind, generous) or disagreeable (rude, selfish, uncooperative). Again, nice guys fared very well. Highly agreeable confederates were perceived as being more physically attractive and more socially desirable than the disagreeable confederates. However, these agreeable men were rated even better in terms of dating desire and long-term relationships if they were also dominant. As I ask my students – what is the take-home message? Nice guys finish first – especially if they are confident!

Think critically

Jensen-Campbell et al. (1995) operationally defined "niceness" as speaking softly and talking about helping others. If you were to conduct this experiment, how would you define "niceness?" Would you define niceness differently in a dating scenario compared to simply talking to a stranger? Do you think that your operational definitions could lead to different findings?

Gender and romance

A personal moment: Looking at my Netflix account, I find their suggested programs for my family entertainment. The suggested categories are often either "Romantic movies with a strong female lead," "Horror and suspense," or "Educational programs for children under age 5." You may be able to easily guess which suggestions are for me, for my husband, and for my two young children. I spend most of the time during scary movies with my eyes closed. My husband spends most of his time during romantic comedies looking at me, smiling, and asking, "Are you crying yet?" My two favorite movies are *Say Anything?* (a classic romantic comedy from the 1990's) and *The Notebook* (Cassavetes, 2004). Both of these movies harken back to the "Do nice guys finish last?" question. I remember during my teenage years saying to my best friends, "Why can't I find a Lloyd Dobler?" (the main character in *Say Anything*). Because I am a woman, I feel that society expects me to cry during romantic comedies, to want flowers and poetry, and to believe in the power of love. In this section, we will discuss whether the highly stereotypical gender differences in romance are accurate in the real world. Am I really more romantic than my husband just because I cried during *Titanic* and love to read Jane Austen novels?

Gender differences in emotionality

Stereotypically, we consider women to be highly emotional and men to be logical and rational. Remember Gray's (1992) notion of separate worlds for men and women? Although we discussed this idea in relation to communication, Gray (1992) contends that this difference also relates to emotion and romance. Rubin (2007) illustrates this concept when discussing an exchange between a man and a woman in a relationship: "he complains, 'she's so emotional, there's no point in talking to her.' She protests, 'It's him you can't talk to, he's always so darned rational.' ... Thought, defined as the ultimate good, has been assigned to men; feeling, considered at best a problem, has fallen to women" (p. 322). The notion from these authors is that women feel and express emotion, and that men do not. What do you think? Do you think that men do not feel emotions? Or is it that they are taught from a very young age to hide their emotions? If a young boy falls and skins his knee it is likely that his parent will tell him to stand up and shrug it off – boys are supposed to be tough both physically and emotionally. Many other researchers argue that it is not that men do not feel emotions, but that they do not display them. Display rules are set by societal and cultural demands and tell men and women when they can and cannot display emotions (and which emotions are socially acceptable and unacceptable to display). Women are more likely to display sadness, fear, shame, and guilt, whereas men are more likely to display anger (LaFrance & Banaji, 1992).

Fischer et al. (2004) examined display rules for both powerful emotions (anger and disgust) and powerless emotions (sadness, fear, shame, and guilt). The most interesting aspect of their study is that they analyzed data from university students in 37 different countries on five continents. They looked at participants' reports of emotions in relation to the countries' Gender Empowerment Measure (GEM). GEM is an indicator of how actively women participate in the country's political and economic system. Cross-cultural analyses are an excellent test of Gray's (1992) contention that men and women are from different planets. Would you hypothesize that they found that the gender differences in emotions were universal or culturally specific? Let us start with the more universal aspects of emotion. Fischer and colleagues found that crying in women seemed to be consistent across countries. However, there were some cross-cultural differences. They found that the restrictive emotionality for powerless emotions (e.g., sadness, fear) was reserved for Western countries. Women in higher GEM countries felt like they could express anger more than women in lower GEM countries. That is, Western countries are becoming more accepting of women showing some stereotypically masculine emotions; however, men are still highly limited by their emotional display rules. I want you to think back to my original example of crying during romantic comedies. If crying is an emotional response exhibited by women cross-culturally, it is not at all shocking that women are more likely to cry during romantic comedies. Knowing this literature, I feel much better in displaying my emotions – my husband can keep laughing at me. The question still remains – are women more romantic? Or is it just more socially acceptable for them to show their desire for romance?

Who is more romantic?

A personal moment: So far, we have discussed display rules and the gender stereotypes associated with particular emotions. Now, I want you to think about the stereotypes regarding communication, dating, and emotions, and hypothesize whether women or men are more romantic. This seems like a no-brainer. In my Psychology of Gender class one of my exam questions asks: "According to the literature, who is more romantic, men or women?" I need only look at the answer to this question to determine which students have been attending class and which students have not. You may find out throughout your studies that the most interesting findings in social psychology are counter to your expectations – students only receive points on this question if their answer is that *men* are more romantic than women. In case you are still skeptical, let us review the literature.

Sprecher and Metts (1989) created the Romantic Beliefs Scale. This 15-item measure has been widely used throughout the love and gender literature. Let me give you some example items to see whether you would rate yourself as romantic: "I believe that to be truly in love is to be in love forever"; "I expect that in my relationship, romantic love will really last; it won't fade with time"; and "The person I love will make a perfect romantic partner" (p. 398–399). The scale measures four distinct beliefs: love finds a way, one and only, idealization, and love at first sight. As we have discussed, many people would expect that women would score higher on this scale than men. Interestingly, the researchers found the opposite. Men were more likely to believe in love at first sight, in an idealized notion of love, that love is the basis for marriage, and that love can overcome all obstacles. Men are also more likely to report falling in love earlier in the relationship than women (Harrison & Shortall, 2011). If I were to ask who says, "I love you," first in a relationship, what would you answer? As reviewed in Chapter 7, Harrison and Shortall (2011) found that although 70 percent of people believe that women say "I love you" first in a relationship, their data showed that three times as many men than women said "I love you" first.

If you are still not convinced that men are more romantic than women, let me refer back to women's love for romantic comedies. Harris et al. (2004) completed an autobiographical study of men's and women's memories for romantic movies watched on a date. Stereotypically, women enjoyed, and reported that they fantasized about inserting themselves into, the movies more than the men. However, men also reported enjoying the romantic films. The authors suggest that, contrary to common opinion, men are not always unwillingly dragged to these films – they may in fact enjoy them.

All of this research highlights that men are more likely to have traditional views of long-term relationships. For example, even though gender roles have become more egalitarian in terms of the workplace, men are still likely to report that they believe that "women tease men sexually" (Glick & Fiske, 1996, p. 500). Note that recent research shows that men become progressively more egalitarian throughout their marriages (Kalmijn, 2005). The literature also shows that those more traditional views are optimistic. Across the globe, men tend to think more positively about romantic relationships than do women. In a Taiwanese sample, Lin and Raghubir (2005) found that men were optimistic when it came to positive situations (e.g., a happy marriage) and thought that negative situations (e.g., divorce) were less likely to happen to them than to someone else. Men are more likely to have negative reactions to a romantic breakup (Choo et al., 1996). All of this literature is in line with the evolutionary view of romantic relationships. Men's emphasis on physical attraction and love at first sight has some evolutionary underpinnings. Remember that evolutionary theory proposes that women are more interested in their potential partner's financial security (see Chapter 4). Women may be more pragmatic when entering romantic relationships and are more realistic and aware of relationship difficulties. In their Taiwanese sample, Lin and Raghubir (2005) indicated that women were more realistic about relationship dissolution than were men. Women are also more likely to initiate a breakup. In fact, an Australian study (Hewitt, 2009) found that women initiate two-thirds of the break-ups of heterosexual couples (but this is less likely if there are children involved).

You may have noticed that the majority of the studies discussed in this section were completed in Western countries. Do these gender differences hold true across all cultures? As reviewed in Chapter 7, Sprecher and Toro-Morn (2002) compared men and women's romantic beliefs in North America and in China.

They found that culture related more to romantic beliefs than did a person's gender. For instance, Chinese participants were found to be more idealistic and practical compared to participants from North America. Similarly, Simmons et al. (1986) found no gender differences when comparing college students in Japan, West Germany, and the United States. Thus, keep in mind that much of what we reviewed above may only be true for Western cultures. Future cross-cultural studies will reveal whether that is the case.

What the research says

Can romantic notions relate to women feeling less personal power in their lives? Rudman and Heppen (2003) examined whether romantic fairy tales elicit a glass-slipper effect for women. Because the gender stereotypes are so prevalent in the media, many young girls feel the pull of the "princess" dream. The romantic notions engendered in princess fairy tales idealize femininity and women's reliance on men for economic needs. Women attending a university in the United States. participated in the first part of this experiment. Participants indicated their interest in 12 occupations that had been ranked by the researchers in terms of personal power. To assess romantic fantasies, the women rated their agreement to the following statements: "I think of my lover as a Prince Charming"; "I think of my lover as a White Knight"; "My romantic partner is very protective of me"; "I think of my love as a hero"; and "My romantic partner is an average man" (p. 1359). Participants also completed an implicit romantic task assessing beliefs in fantasy (e.g., Prince Charming, castle, protector) and reality (e.g., average Joe, regular guy, ordinary) for both romantic and non-romantic people in their lives. They found that women's implicit fantasies were negatively correlated with power. Therefore, the more implicit romantic fantasies the women had, the less likely they were to choose high-status occupations. In their second experiment Rudman and Heppen also looked at gender differences involving men and women. Again, implicit romantic fantasies for women related to lower feelings of power. However, they found the opposite effect for men – the more romantic fantasies they had, the more interested they were in high-status jobs.

Think critically

Take a moment to critically interpret the findings. Even though these findings are interesting, they are correlational. Because the findings are correlational, we do not know the direction of the relationship. It could very well be that the more women idealize princess fairy tales, the less likely they are to seek personal power in the workforce. However, it could also be that women who would have chosen less powerful jobs anyway (possibly because of some personality characteristics) also have more romantic ideals.

Chapter summary

Overall, the gender literature shows that men and women are actually more similar than they are different. Some researchers assert that men and women differ in their communication styles, and that these differences have a significant influence on romantic relationships. In particular, women are more likely to use tag questions and to perform "interaction work," and men are more likely to interrupt during a conversation. Men and women sometimes report different reasons for dating. Men are more likely to have liberal attitudes regarding sex. When initiating a date, women are often the ones using the nonverbal cues; men are more likely to verbally initiate a date. Dating scripts have not changed much over the past 20–30 years and men are still more likely to assume a proactive role, women a reactive role, during a date. Emotional display rules set by society tell men that they are limited in their emotional expression, whereas women can show their emotions freely. Perhaps as a result, people have the stereotype that women are more romantic than men. Interestingly, studies have found the opposite – men report more romantic notions, are more likely to say "I love you" first and are more traditional in their beliefs. We present our suggestions for future reading below.

Suggested reading

Clark, R. D., & Hatfield, E. (1989). Gender differences in receptivity to sexual offers. *Journal of Psychology and Human Sexuality*, 2(1), 39–55.
This is the classic research discussing how men will accept an invitation for sex from a woman, even if they have just met. Students find this research extremely interesting, and it often sparks great class discussions.

Fishman, P. M. (1978). Interaction: The work women do. *Social Problems*, 25(4), 397–406.
This research shows that women are more likely to actively engage in an interaction compared to men. Students respond well to these ideas and relate them to their own life experiences.

Hald, G., & Høgh-Olesen, H. (2010). Receptivity to sexual invitations from strangers of the opposite gender. *Evolution and Human Behavior*, 31(6), 453–458.
It is important for students to read the classic research, but also to ask themselves whether or not the findings would change today. This is the follow-up study to Clark and Hatfield's (1989) work.

Hyde, J. (2005). The gender similarities hypothesis. *American Psychologist*, 60(6), 581–592.
This article was one of the culminating pieces that changed our thinking as gender researchers. Hyde discusses the findings from a meta-analysis outlining how small gender differences in research really are and emphasizing the similarities between men and women.

Rudman, L. A., & Heppen, J. B. (2003). Implicit romantic fantasies and women's interest in personal power: A glass slipper effect? *Personality and Social Psychology Bulletin*, 29(11), 1357–1370.
This article addresses the question of how contemporary women fit into the princess fantasy.

References

Acevedo, B. P., Aron, A., Fisher, H. E., & Brown, L. L. (2012). Neural correlates of long-term intense romantic love. *Social Cognitive and Affective Neuroscience, 7*(2), 145–159. doi:10.1093/scan/nsq092

Adams, J. S. (1965). Inequity in social exchange. *Advances in Experimental Social Psychology, 2*, 267–299.

Adams, J. F., & Sprenkle, D. H. (1990). Self-perception and personal commitment: A challenge to current theory of marital dissolution and stability and implications for marital therapy. *American Journal of Family Therapy, 18*(2), 131–140. doi:10.1080/01926189008250797

Ahmetoglu, G., Swami, V., & Chamorro-Premuzic, T. (2010). The relationship between dimensions of love, personality, and relationship length. *Archives of Sexual Behavior, 39*(5), 1181–1190. doi:10.1007/s10508-009-9515-5

Ainsworth, M., Blehar, M., Waters, E., & Wall, S. (1978). *Patterns of attachment: A psychological study of the strange situation*. Oxford: Lawrence Erlbaum. Retrieved from PsycINFO database.

Albright, L., Malloy, T. E., Dong, Q., Kenny, D. A., Fang, X., Winquist, L., & Yu, D. (1997). Cross-cultural consensus in personality judgments. *Journal of Personality and Social Psychology, 72*(3), 558–569. doi:10.1037/0022-3514.72.3.558

Alexander, M. G. & Fisher, T. D. (2003). Truth and consequences: Using the bogus pipeline to examine sex differences in self-reported sexuality. *The Journal of Sex Research, 40*(1), 27–35.

Allgeier, E. R., & Wiederman, M. W. (1991). Love and mate selection in the 1990s. *Free Inquiry, 11*, 25–27.

Aloni, M., & Bernieri, F. J. (2004). Is Love Blind? The effects of experience and infatuation on the perception of love. *Journal of Nonverbal Behavior, 28*(4), 287–295. doi:10.1007/s10919-004-4160-0

Alterovitz, S. S., & Mendelsohn, G. A. (2009). Partner preferences across the life span: Online dating by older adults. *Psychology and Aging, 24*(2), 513–517. doi:10.1037/2160-4134.1.S.89

Ambady, N., Hallahan, M., & Conner, B. (1999). Accuracy of judgments of sexual orientation from thin slices of behavior. *Journal of Personality and Social Psychology, 77*(3), 538–547. doi:10.1037/0022-3514.77.3.538

Ambady, N., Hallahan, M., & Rosenthal, R. (1995). On judging and being judged accurately in zero-acquaintance situations. *Journal of Personality and Social Psychology, 69*(3), 518–529. doi:10.1037/0022-3514.69.3.518

Ambady, N., & Rosenthal, R. (1993). Half a minute: Predicting teacher evaluations from thin slices of nonverbal behavior and physical attractiveness. *Journal of Personality and Social Psychology, 64*(3), 431–441. doi:10.1037/0022-3514.64.3.431

Anderson, E. (2010). "At least with cheating there is an attempt at monogamy": Cheating and monogamism among undergraduate heterosexual men. *Journal of Social and Personal Relationships, 27*(7), 851–872. doi:10.1177/0265407510373908

Anderson, N. H. (1965). Averaging versus adding as a stimulus-combination rule in impression formation. *Journal of Experimental Psychology, 70*(4), 394–400. doi:10.1037/h0022280

Apatow, J. (Producer & Director). (2007). *Knocked up.* (Motion Picture). USA: Apatow Productions.

Aron, A., Dutton, D. G., Aron, E. N., & Iverson, A. (1989).Experiences of falling in love. *Journal of Social and Personal Relationships, 6*(3), 243–257. doi:10.1177/0265407589063001

Aron, A., Fisher, H., Mashek, D. J., Strong, G., Li, H., & Brown, L. L. (2005). Reward, motivation, and emotion systems associated with early-stage intense romantic love. *Journal of Neurophysiology, 94*(1), 327–337. doi:10.1152/jn.00838.2004

Aron, A., Norman, C. C., Aron, E. N., McKenna, C., & Heyman, R. E. (2000). Couples' shared participation in novel and arousing activities and experienced relationship quality. *Journal of Personality and Social Psychology, 78*(2), 273–284. doi:10.1037/0022-3514.78.2.273

Aronson, E., & Mills, J. (1959).The effect of severity of initiation on liking for a group. *The Journal of Abnormal and Social Psychology, 59*(2), 177–181. doi:10.1037/h0047195

Asch, S. (1946). Forming impressions of personality. *The Journal of Abnormal and Social Psychology, 41*(3), 258–290. doi:10.1037/h0055756

Athenstaedt, U., Haas, E., & Schwab, S. (2004). Gender role self-concept and gender-typed communication behavior in mixed-sex and same-sex dyads. *Sex Roles, 50,* 37–52.

Austen, J. (2001). Pride and prejudice. In *The Works of Jane Austen.* Ann Arbor, MI: State Street Press.

Back, M. D., Penke, L., Schmukle, S. C., Sachse, K., Borkenau, P., & Asendorpf, J. B. (2011). Why mate choices are not as reciprocal as we assume: The role of personality, flirting and physical attractiveness. *European Journal of Personality, 25*(2), 120–132. doi:10.1002/per.806

Back, M. D., Schmukle, S. C., & Egloff, B. (2008). Becoming friends by chance. *Psychological Science, 19*(5), 439–440. doi:10.1111/j.1467-9280.2008.02106.x

Back, M., Stopfer, J., Vazire, S., Gaddis, S., Schmukle, S., Egloff, B., et al. (2010). Facebook profiles reflect actual personality, not self-idealization. *Psychological Science, 21*(3), 372–374. doi:10.1177/0956797609360756

Baldwin, M., & Fehr, B. (1995).On the instability of attachment style ratings. *Personal Relationships, 2*(3), 247–261. doi:10.1111/j.1475-6811.1995.tb00090.x

Barber, N. (2003). Divorce and reduced economic and emotional interdependence: A cross-national study. *Journal of Divorce and Remarriage, 39*(3–4), 113–124. doi:10.1300/J087v39n03_06

Barelds, D. H., & Barelds-Dijkstra, P. (2007). Love at first sight or friends first? Ties among partner personality trait similarity, relationship onset, relationship quality, and love. *Journal of Social and Personal Relationships, 24*(4), 479–496. doi:10.1177/0265407507079235

Bargh, J. A., McKenna, K. A., & Fitzsimons, G. M. (2002). Can you see the real me? Activation and expression of the 'true self' on the Internet. *Journal of Social Issues, 58*(1), 33–48. doi:10.1111/1540-4560.00247

Bartholomew, K. & Horowitz, L. M. (1991). Attachment styles among young adults: A test of a four-category model. *Journal of Personality and Social Psychology, 61*(2), 226-244. doi: 10.1037/0022-3514.61.2.226

Bartoli, A. M., & Clark, M. (2006). The dating game: Similarities and differences in dating scripts among college students. *Sexuality and Culture: An Interdisciplinary Quarterly, 10*, 54–80. doi:10.1007/s12119-006-1026-0

Baumeister, R. F., Bratslavsky, E., Finkenauer, C., & Vohs, K. D. (2001). Bad is stronger than good. *Review of General Psychology, 5*(4), 323–370. doi:10.1037/1089-2680.5.4.323

Bègue, L., Bushman, B. J., Zerhouni, O., Subra, B., & Ourabah, M. (2013). 'Beauty is in the eye of the beer holder': People who think they are drunk also think they are attractive. *British Journal of Psychology, 104*(2), 225–234. doi:10.1111/j.2044-8295.2012.02114.x

Beins, B. C. (2013). *Research methods: A tool for Life* (3rd ed.). New York: Pearson.

Bem, D. (1967). Self-perception: An alternative interpretation of cognitive dissonance phenomena. *Psychological Review, 74*(3), 183–200. Retrieved September 9, 2008, doi:10.1037/h0024835

Berscheid, E., & Walster, E. (1978) *Interpersonal Attraction* (2nd ed). Reading, MA: Addison-Wesley.

Billingsley, P. (Director). (2009). *Couples Retreat*. (Motion Picture). USA: Universal Pictures.

Bornstein, R. (1989). Exposure and affect: Overview and meta-analysis of research, 1968–1987. *Psychological Bulletin, 106*(2), 265–289. doi:10.1037/0033-2909.106.2.265

Bowlby, J. (1969). *Attachment and loss*. New York: Basic Books. Retrieved from PsycINFO database.

Bradbury, T., & Fincham, F. (1992).Attributions and behavior in marital interaction. *Journal of Personality and Social Psychology, 63*(4), 613–628. doi:10.1037/0022-3514.63.4.613

Brassard, A., Péloquin, K., Dupuy, E., Wright, J., & Shaver, P. R. (2012). Romantic attachment insecurity predicts sexual dissatisfaction in couples seeking marital therapy. *Journal of Sex and Marital Therapy, 38*(3), 245–262. doi:10.1080/00926 23X.2011.606881

Brehm, J. (1956). Postdecision changes in the desirability of alternatives. *The Journal of Abnormal and Social Psychology, 52*(3), 384–389. doi:10.1037/h0041006

Brehm, S. S., Kassin, S. M., & Fein, S. (2005). *Social Psychology* (6th ed.) New York: Houghton Mifflin Company.

Bressler, E. R., & Balshine, S. (2006). The influence of humor on desirability. *Evolution and Human Behavior, 27*(1), 29–39. doi:10.1016/j.evolhumbehav.2005.06.002

Brown, W. M., Cronk, L., Grochow, K., Jacobson, A., Liu, C., Popović, Z., & Trivers, R. (2005). Dance reveals symmetry especially in young men. *Nature, 438*(7071), 1148–1150. doi:10.1038/nature04344

Burchell, J. L. & Ward, J. (2011). Sex drive, attachment style, relationship status and previous infidelity as predictors of sex differences in romantic jealousy. *Personality and Individual Differences, 51*, 657–661. Doi: 10.1016/j.paid.2011.06.002

Burns, R., & Machin, M. (2013). Psychological wellbeing and the diathesis-stress hypothesis model: The role of psychological functioning and quality of relations in promoting subjective well-being in a life events study. *Personality and Individual Differences, 54*(3), 321–326. doi:10.1016/j.paid.2012.09.017

Burriss, R. P., Roberts, S., Welling, L. M., Puts, D. A., & Little, A. C. (2011). Heterosexual romantic couples mate assortatively for facial symmetry, but not masculinity. *Personality and Social Psychology Bulletin, 37*(5), 601–613. doi:10.1177/0146167211399584

Burto, W. (Ed.) (1988). *William Shakespeare: The Sonnets.* New York: NAL Penguin, Inc.

Buss, D. M. (2012). *Evolutionary psychology: The new science of the mind.* New York: Allyn and Bacon.

Buss, D.M. (2002). Human mate guarding. *Neuroendocrinology Letters, 23,* 23–29.

Buss, D. M. (1989). Sex differences in human mate preferences: Evolutionary hypotheses tested in 37 cultures. *Behavioral and Brain Sciences, 12*(1), 1–49. doi:10.1017/S0140525X00023992

Buss, D. M. & Barnes, M. F. (1986). Preferences in human mate selection. *Journal of Personality and Social Psychology, 50,* 559–570.

Buss, D. M., Larsen, R. J., Westen, D., & Semmelroth, J. (1992). Sex differences in jealousy: Evolution, physiology, and psychology. *Psychological Science, 3,* 251–255.

Buss, D. M., & Schmitt, D. P. (1993). Sexual strategies theory: An evolutionary perspective on human mating. *Psychological Review, 100*(2), 204–232. doi:10.1037/0033-295X.100.2.204

Buss, D., Shackelford, T., Kirkpatrick, L., & Larsen, R. (2001). A half century of mate preferences: The cultural evolution of values. *Journal of Marriage and the Family, 63*(2), 491–503. doi:10.1111/j.1741-3737.2001.00491.x

Buunk, B. P., Angleitner, A., Oubaid, V., Buss, D. M. (1996). Sex differences in jealousy in evolutionary and cultural perspective: Tests from the Netherlands, Germany, and the United States. *Psychological Science, 7,* 359–363.

Buunk, B. P., & Dijkstra, P. (2001). Evidence from a homosexual sample for a sex-specific rival-oriented mechanism: Jealousy as a function of a rival's physical attractiveness and dominance. *Personal Relationships, 8*(4), 391–406. doi:10.1111/j.1475-6811.2001.tb00047.x

Buunk, A. P., Park, J. H., Zurriaga, R., Klavina, L., & Massar, K. (2008). Height predicts jealousy differently for men and women. *Evolution and Human Behavior, 29*(2), 133–139. doi:10.1016/j.evolhumbehav.2007.11.006

Buunk, A. P., & Solano, A. (2010). Conflicting preferences of parents and offspring over criteria for a mate: A study in Argentina. *Journal of Family Psychology, 24*(4), 391–399. doi:10.1037/a0020252

Buunk, B. P. & van Driel, B. (1989). *Variant lifestyles and relationships.* Newbury Park, CA: Sage.

Byrne, D. (1961a). Interpersonal attraction and attitude similarity. *The Journal of Abnormal and Social Psychology, 62*(3), 713–715. doi:10.1037/h0044721

Byrne, D. (1961b). The influence of propinquity and opportunities for interaction on classroom relationships. *Human Relations, 14,* 63–69. doi:10.1177/001872676101400106

Byrne, D. D. (1971). The ubiquitous relationship: Attitude similarity and attraction: A cross-cultural study. *Human Relations, 24*(3), 201–207. doi:10.1177/001872677102400302

Byrne, D., & Blaylock, B. (1963). Similarity and assumed similarity of attitudes between husbands and wives. *The Journal of Abnormal and Social Psychology, 67*(6), 636–640. doi:10.1037/h0045531

Byrne, D., Clore, G., & Smeaton, G. (1986). The attraction hypothesis: Do similar attitudes affect anything? *Journal of Personality and Social Psychology, 51*(6), 1167–1170. doi:10.1037/0022-3514.51.6.1167

Caldwell, M. A., & Peplau, L. A. (1984). The balance of power in lesbian relationships. *Sex Roles, 10*(7–8), 587–599. doi:10.1007/BF00287267

Campbell, A. (2005). Aggression. In D. M. Buss (Ed.), *The handbook of evolutionary psychology*. Hoboken, NJ: John Wiley & Sons Inc.

Cárdenas, R., & Harris, L. (2006). Symmetrical decorations enhance the attractiveness of faces and abstract designs. *Evolution and Human Behavior, 27*(1), 1–18. doi:10.1016/j.evolhumbehav.2005.05.002

Carmalt, J. H., Cawley, J., Joyner, K., & Sobal, J. (2008). Body weight and matching with a physically attractive romantic partner. *Journal of Marriage and Family, 70*(5), 1287–1296. doi:10.1111/j.1741-3737.2008.00566.x

Chastel, O., Barbraud, C., Weimerskirch, H., Lormée, H., Lacroix, A., & Tostain, O. (2005). High levels of LH and testosterone in a tropical seabird with an elaborate courtship display. *General and Comparative Endocrinology, 140*, 33–40.

Choo, P., Levine, T., & Hatfield, E. (1996). Gender, love schemas, and reactions to romantic breakups. *Journal of Social Behavior and Personality, 11*, 143–160.

Clark, C. L., Shaver, P. R., & Abrahams, M. F. (1999). Strategic behaviors in romantic relationship initiation. *Personality and Social Psychology Bulletin, 25*(6), 707–720.

Clark, M. S., & Mills, J. (1979). Interpersonal attraction in exchange and communal relationships. *Journal of Personality and Social Psychology, 37*(1), 12–24. doi:10.1037/0022-3514.37.1.12

Clark, R. D., & Hatfield, E. (1989). Gender differences in receptivity to sexual offers. *Journal of Psychology and Human Sexuality, 2*(1), 39–55.

Clarkwest, A. (2007). Spousal dissimilarity, race, and marital dissolution. *Journal of Marriage and Family, 69*(3), 639–653. doi:10.1111/j.1741-3737.2007.00397.x

Cohen, A. B., & Tannenbaum, I. J. (2001). Lesbian and bisexual women's judgments of the attractiveness of different body types. *Journal of Sex Research, 38*(3), 226–232. doi:10.1080/00224490109552091

Collins, S. (2009). *Catching fire*. New York: Cengage Learning.

Collins, S. (2010). *Mockingjay*. New York: Scholastic Press.

Collins, S., & Missing, C. (2003). Vocal and visual attractiveness are related in women. *Animal Behaviour, 65*(5), 997–1004. doi:10.1006/anbe.2003.2123

Connelly, J., Craig, W., Goldberg, A., & Peplar, D. (2004). Mixed-gender groups, dating, and romantic relationships in early adolescence. *Journal of Research on Adolescence, 14*, 185–207.

Cooper, J. (1971). Personal responsibility and dissonance: The role of foreseen consequences. *Journal of Personality and Social Psychology, 18*(3), 354–363. doi:10.1037/h0030995

Conley, T. D., Roesch, S. C., Peplau, L., & Gold, M. S. (2009). A test of positive illusions versus shared reality models of relationship satisfaction among gay, lesbian, and heterosexual couples. *Journal of Applied Social Psychology, 39*(6), 1417–1431. doi:10.1111/j.1559-1816.2009.00488.x

Cornwell, B. B., & Lundgren, D. C. (2001). Love on the Internet: Involvement and misrepresentation in romantic relationships in cyberspace vs. realspace. *Computers in Human Behavior, 17*(2), 197–211. doi:10.1016/S0747-5632(00)00040-6

Cousins, A. J., & Fugère, M. A. (unpublished). Development of the Resistance to Mate Guarding Scale. Under review.

Cousins, A. J., Fugère, M. A., & Franklin, M. (2009). Digit ratio (2D:4D), mate guarding, and physical aggression in dating couples. *Personality and Individual Differences, 46*, 709–713. doi:10.1016/j.paid.2009.01.029

Cousins, A. J., & Gangestad, S. W. (2007). Perceived threats of female infidelity, male proprietariness and violence in college dating couples. *Violence and Victims, 22*, 651–668.

Crawford, M., & Popp, D. (2003). Sexual double standards: A review and methodological critique of two decades of research. *Journal of Sex Research*, 40(1), 13–26. doi:10.1080/00224490309552163

Cunningham, M. R. (1989). Reactions to heterosexual opening gambits: Female selectivity and male responsiveness. *Personality and Social Psychology Bulletin*, 15, 27–41. doi:10.1177/0146167289151003

Cunningham, M. R., & Barbee, A. P. (2008). Prelude to a kiss: Nonverbal flirting, opening gambits, and other communication dynamics in the initiation of romantic relationships. In S. Sprecher, A. Wenzel, & J. Harvey (Eds.), *Handbook of relationship initiation* (pp. 97–120). New York: Psychology Press.

Cunningham, M. R., Barbee, A. P., & Pike, C. L. (1990). What do women want? Facialmetric assessment of multiple motives in the perception of male facial physical attractiveness. *Journal of Personality and Social Psychology*, 59(1), 61–72. doi:10.1037/0022-3514.59.1.61

Cunningham, M. R., Roberts, A. R., Barbee, A. P., Druen, P. B., & Wu, C. (1995). "Their ideas of beauty are, on the whole, the same as ours": Consistency and variability in the cross-cultural perception of female physical attractiveness. *Journal of Personality and Social Psychology*, 68(2), 261–279. doi:10.1037/0022-3514.68.2.261

Cunningham, W. A., Johnson, M. K., Gatenby, J., Gore, J. C., & Banaji, M. R. (2003). Neural components of social evaluation. *Journal of Personality and Social Psychology*, 85(4), 639–649. doi:10.1037/0022-3514.85.4.639

Curtis, R. C., & Miller, K. (1986). Believing another likes or dislikes you: Behaviors making the beliefs come true. *Journal of Personality and Social Psychology*, 51(2), 284–290. doi:10.1037/0022-3514.51.2.284

Daly, M., & Wilson, M. (1988). *Homicide*. Hawthorne, NY: Aldine de Gruyter.

Daly, M., Wilson, M., & Weghorst, S. J. (1982). Male sexual jealousy. *Ethology and Sociobiology*, 3, 11–27.

Davis, D., Shaver, P. R., & Vernon, M. L. (2003). Physical, emotional, and behavioral reactions to breaking up: The roles of gender, age, emotional involvement, and attachment style. *Personality and Social Psychology Bulletin*, 29(7), 871–884. doi:10.1177/0146167203029007006

Davis, K. E., & Todd, M. J. (1982). Friendship and love relationships. *Advances in Descriptive Psychology*, 279–122.

Davis, J. L., & Rusbult, C. E. (2001). Attitude alignment in close relationships. *Journal of Personality and Social Psychology*, 81(1), 65–84. doi:10.1037/0022-3514.81.1.65

DeKeseredy, W. S., & Schwartz, M. D. (1998). *Woman abuse on campus: Results from the Canadian national survey*. Thousand Oaks, CA: Sage Publications.

de Munck, V. C., Korotayev, A., de Munck, J., & Khaltourina, D. (2011). Cross-cultural analysis of models of romantic love among U.S. residents, Russians, and Lithuanians. *Cross-Cultural Research: The Journal of Comparative Social Science*, 45(2), 128–154. doi:10.1177/1069397110393313

DeWall, C., Lambert, N. M., Slotter, E. B., Pond, R. R., Deckman, T., Finkel, E. J., & ... Fincham, F. D. (2011). So far away from one's partner, yet so close to romantic alternatives: Avoidant attachment, interest in alternatives, and infidelity. *Journal of Personality and Social Psychology*, 101(6), 1302–1316. doi:10.1037/a0025497

Diener, E., Gohm, C. L., Suh, E., & Oishi, S. (2000). Similarity of the relations between marital status and subjective well-being across cultures. *Journal of Cross-Cultural Psychology*, 31(4), 419–436. doi:10.1177/0022022100031004001

Dill, K., Anderson, C., & Deuser, W. (1997). Effects of aggressive personality on social expectations and social perceptions. *Journal of Research in Personality, 31*(2), 272–292. doi:10.1006/jrpe.1997.2183

Dillon, W. A. & Von Tilzer, H. (1911). *I want a girl just like the girl that married dear old dad.* Camden, NJ. Victor.

Dion, K., Berscheid, E., & Walster, E. (1972). What is beautiful is good. *Journal of Personality and Social Psychology, 24*(3), 285–290. doi:10.1037/h0033731

Dixson, B. J., Grimshaw, G. M., Linklater, W. L., & Dixson, A. F. (2011). Eye-tracking of men's preferences for waist-to-hip ratio and breast size of women. *Archives of Sexual Behavior, 40*(1), 43–50. doi:10.1007/s10508-009-9523-5

Draper, P. (1975). *!Kung Women: Contrasts in Sexual Egalitarianism in Foraging and Sedentary Contexts. Toward an anthropology of women.* R. R. Reiter (Ed.) New York: Monthly Review Press, pp. 77–109.

Durante, K. M., Li, N. P., & Haselton, M. G. (2008). Changes in women's choice of dress across the ovulatory cycle: Naturalistic and laboratory task-based evidence. *Personality and Social Psychology Bulletin, 34*, 1451–1460. doi: 10.1177/0146167208323103

Dutton, D., & Aron, A. (1974). Some evidence for heightened sexual attraction under conditions of high anxiety. *Journal of Personality and Social Psychology, 30*(4), 510–517. doi:10.1037/h0037031

Earle, J., Perricone, P., Davidson, J., Moore, N., Harris, C., & Cotten, S. (2007). Premarital sexual attitudes and behavior at a religiously-affiliated university: Two decades of change. *Sexuality & Culture: An Interdisciplinary Quarterly, 11*(2), 39–61. doi:10.1007/s12119-007-9001-y

Eaton, A., & Rose, S. (2011). Has dating become more egalitarian? A 35 year review using Sex Roles. *Sex Roles, 64*, 843–862. doi:10.1007/s11199-011-9957-9

Eastwick, P. W., Finkel, E. J., & Eagly, A. H. (2011). When and why do ideal partner preferences affect the process of initiating and maintaining romantic relationships? *Journal of Personality and Social Psychology, 101*(5), 1012–1032. doi:10.1037/a0024062

Eastwick, P. W., Eagly, A. H., Finkel, E. J., & Johnson, S. E. (2011). Implicit and explicit preferences for physical attractiveness in a romantic partner: A double dissociation in predictive validity. *Journal of Personality and Social Psychology, 101*(5), 993–1011. doi:10.1037/a0024061

Eastwick, P. W., & Finkel, E. J. (2008). Sex differences in mate preferences revisited: Do people know what they initially desire in a romantic partner? *Journal of Personality and Social Psychology, 94*(2), 245–264. doi:10.1037/0022-3514.94.2.245

Ebbesen, E. B., Kjos, G. L., & Konecni, V. J. (1976). Spatial ecology: Its effects on the choice of friends and enemies. *Journal of Experimental Social Psychology, 12*(6), 505–518. doi:10.1016/0022-1031(76)90030-5

Eberhard, W.G. (1990). Animal genitalia and female choice. *American Scientist, 78*, 134–141.

Edwards, R., & Hamilton, M. A. (2004). You need to understand my gender role: An empirical test of Tannen's model of gender and communication. *Sex Roles, 50*, 491–504. doi:10.1023/B:SERS.0000023069.93583.8b

Egan, L., Santos, L., & Bloom, P. (2007). The origins of cognitive dissonance: Evidence from children and monkeys. *Psychological Science, 18*(11), 978–983. doi:10.1111/j.1467-9280.2007.02012.x

Elliot, A. J., Greitemeyer, T., & Pazda, A. D. (2012). Women's use of red clothing as a sexual signal in intersexual interaction. *Journal of Experimental Social Psychology, 49*(3), 599–602. doi:10.1016/j.jesp.2012.10.001

Elliot, A. J., & Niesta, D. (2008). Romantic red: Red enhances men's attraction to women. *Journal of Personality and Social Psychology, 95*(5), 1150–1164. doi:10.1037/0022-3514.95.5.1150

Elliot, A. J., Niesta Kayser, D., Greitemeyer, T., Lichtenfeld, S., Gramzow, R. H., Maier, M. A., & Liu, H. (2010). Red, rank, and romance in women viewing men. *Journal of Experimental Psychology: General, 139*(3), 399–417. doi:10.1037/a0019689

Elliot, A. J., Tracy, J. L., Pazda, A. D., & Beall, A. T. (2013). Red enhances women's attractiveness to men: First evidence suggesting universality. *Journal of Experimental Social Psychology, 49*(1), 165–168. doi:10.1016/j.jesp.2012.07.017

Elliot, A. M. (2011). Ten fascinating YouTube facts that may surprise you. Retrieved from http://mashable.com/2011/02/19/youtube-facts/

Epps, J., & Kendall, P. (1995). Hostile attributional bias in adults. *Cognitive Therapy and Research, 19*(2), 159–178. doi:10.1007/BF02229692

Farley, S. D., Ashcraft, A. M., Stasson, M. F., & Nusbaum, R. L. (2010). Nonverbal reactions to conversational interruption: A test of complementarity theory and the status/gender parallel. *Journal of Nonverbal Behavior, 34*, 193–206. doi:10.1007/s10919-010-0091-0

Farley, S. D., Hughes, S. M., & LaFayette, J. N. (2013). People will know we are in love: Evidence of differences between vocal samples directed toward lovers and friends. *Journal of Nonverbal Behavior, 37*(3), 123–138. doi:10.1007/s10919-013-0151-3

Fazio, R., Zanna, M., & Cooper, J. (1977). Dissonance and self-perception: An integrative view of each theory's proper domain of application. *Journal of Experimental Social Psychology, 13*(5), 464–479. doi:10.1016/0022-1031(77)90031-2

Feingold, A. (1990). Gender differences in effects of physical attractiveness on romantic attraction: A comparison across five research paradigms. *Journal of Personality and Social Psychology, 59*(5), 981–993. doi:10.1037/0022-3514.59.5.981

Feingold, A. (1988). Matching for attractiveness in romantic partners and same-sex friends: A meta-analysis and theoretical critique. *Psychological Bulletin, 104*(2), 226–235. doi:10.1037/0033-2909.104.2.226

Festinger, L. (1957). *A theory of cognitive dissonance.* Stanford, CA: Stanford University Press. Retrieved from PsycINFO database.

Festinger, L., & Carlsmith, J. (1959, March). Cognitive consequences of forced compliance. *The Journal of Abnormal and Social Psychology, 58*(2), 203–210. Retrieved September 9, 2008, doi:10.1037/h0041593

Festinger, L., Schachter, S., & Back, K. (1950). *Social pressures in informal groups; a study of human factors in housing.* Oxford: Harper. Retrieved from PsycINFO database

Fincham, F. D., Beach, S. R., & Baucom, D. H. (1987). Attribution processes in distressed and nondistressed couples: IV. Self–partner attribution differences. *Journal of Personality and Social Psychology, 52*(4), 739–748. doi:10.1037/0022-3514.52.4.739

Fink, B., Hugill, N., & Lange, B. P. (2012). Women's body movements are a potential cue to ovulation. *Personality and Individual Differences, 53*(6), 759–763. doi:10.1016/j.paid.2012.06.005

Fink, B., Neave, N., Brewer, G., & Pawlowski, B. (2007). Variable preferences for sexual dimorphism in stature (SDS): Further evidence for an adjustment in relation to own height. *Personality and Individual Differences, 43*(8), 2249–2257. doi:10.1016/j.paid.2007.07.014

Fink, B., Weege, B., Flügge, J., Röder, S., Neave, N., & McCarty, K. (2012). Men's personality and women's perception of their dance quality. *Personality and Individual Differences, 52*(2), 232–235. doi:10.1016/j.paid.2011.10.008

Finkel, E. J., Eastwick, P. W., Karney, B. R., Reis, H. T., & Sprecher, S. (2012). Online dating: A critical analysis from the perspective of psychological science. *Psychological Science In The Public Interest, 13*(1), 3–66. doi:10.1177/1529100612436522

Fischer, A. H., Rodriguez Mosquera, P. M., van Vianen, A. M., & Manstead, A. R. (2004). Gender and culture differences in emotion. *Emotion, 4,* 87–94. doi:10.1037/1528-3542.4.1.87

Fisher, T. D., Moore, Z. T., & Pittenger, M. (2012). Sex on the brain? An examination of frequency of sexual cognitions as a function of gender, erotophilia, and social desirability. *Journal of Sex Research, 49*(1), 69–77. doi:10.1080/00224499.2011.565429

Fishman, P. M. (1978). Interaction: The work women do. *Social Problems, 25*(4), 397–406.

Fletcher, G. O., Simpson, J. A., & Thomas, G. (2000). Ideals, perceptions, and evaluations in early relationship development. *Journal of Personality and Social Psychology, 79*(6), 933–940. doi:10.1037/0022-3514.79.6.933

Floyd, K., Boren, J. P., Hannawa, A. F., Hesse, C., McEwan, B., & Veksler, A. E. (2009). Kissing in marital and cohabiting relationships: Effects on blood lipids, stress, and relationship satisfaction. *Western Journal of Communication, 73*(2), 113–133. doi:10.1080/10570310902856071

Förster, J., Özelsel, A., & Epstude, K. (2010). How love and lust change people's perception of relationship partners. *Journal of Experimental Social Psychology, 46*(2), 237–246. doi:10.1016/j.jesp.2009.08.009

Foster, C. A., Witcher, B. S., Campbell, W., & Green, J. D. (1998). Arousal and attraction: Evidence for automatic and controlled processes. *Journal of Personality and Social Psychology, 74*(1), 86–101. doi:10.1037/0022-3514.74.1.86

Fraccaro, P. J., Jones, B. C., Vukovic, J., Smith, F. G., Watkins, C. D., Feinberg, D. R., & ... DeBruine, L. M. (2011). Experimental evidence that women speak in a higher voice pitch to men they find attractive. *Journal of Evolutionary Psychology, 9*(1), 57–67. doi:10.1556/JEP.9.2011.33.1

Fraley, R., & Marks, M. J. (2010). Westermarck, Freud, and the incest taboo: Does familial resemblance activate sexual attraction? *Personality and Social Psychology Bulletin, 36*(9), 1202–1212. doi:10.1177/0146167210377180

Fugère, M. A., Escoto, C., Cousins, A. J., Riggs, M. L., & Haerich, P. (2008). Sexual attitudes and double standards: A literature review focusing on participant gender and ethnic background. *Sexuality and Culture: An Interdisciplinary Quarterly, 12*(3), 169–182. doi:10.1007/s12119-008-9029-7

Furnham, A., Petrides, K. V., & Constantinides, A. (2005). The effects of body mass index and waist-to-hip ratio on ratings of female attractiveness, fecundity, and health. *Personality and Individual Differences, 38*(8), 1823–1834. doi:10.1016/j.paid.2004.11.011

Furnham, A., Swami, V., & Shah, K. (2006). Body weight, waist-to-hip ratio and breast size correlates of ratings of attractiveness and health. *Personality and Individual Differences, 41*(3), 443–454. doi:10.1016/j.paid.2006.02.007

Gallup, G. R., & Frederick, D. A. (2010). The science of sex appeal: An evolutionary perspective. *Review of General Psychology, 14*(3), 240–250. doi:10.1037/a0020451

Galperin, A., & Haselton, M. (2010). Predictors of how often and when people fall in love. *Evolutionary Psychology, 8*(1), 5–28.

Gangestad, S. W., Thornhill, R., & Yeo, R. A. (1994). Facial attractiveness, developmental stability, and fluctuating asymmetry. *Ethology & Sociobiology, 15*(2), 73–85. doi:10.1016/0162-3095(94)90018-3

Gangestad, S.W., Thornhill, R., & Garver, C.E. (2002). Changes in women's sexual interests and their partners' mate retention tactics across the menstrual cycle: Evidence for shifting conflicts of interest. *Proceedings of the Royal Society of London, B, 269,* 975–982.

Gareis, E., & Wilkins, R. (2011). Love expression in the United States and Germany. *International Journal of Intercultural Relations, 35*(3), 307–319. doi:10.1016/j.ijintrel.2010.06.006

Gebauer, J. E., Leary, M. R., & Neberich, W. (2012). Big two personality and big three mate preferences: Similarity attracts, but country-level mate preferences crucially matter. *Personality and Social Psychology Bulletin, 38*(12), 1579–1593. doi:10.1177/0146167212456300

Geher, G., Bloodworth, R., Mason, J., Stoaks, C., Downey, H. J., Renstrom, K. L., & Romero, J. F. (2005). Motivational underpinnings of romantic partner perceptions: Psychological and physiological evidence. *Journal of Social and Personal Relationships, 22*(2), 255–281. doi:10.1177/0265407505050953

Geiselman, R., Haight, N., & Kimata, L. (1984). Context effects on the perceived physical attractiveness of faces. *Journal of Experimental Social Psychology, 20*(5), 409–424. doi:10.1016/0022-1031(84)90035-0

George, W. H., & Norris, J. (1991). Alcohol, disinhibition, sexual arousal, and deviant sexual behavior. *Alcohol Health and Research World,* 133–138.

Gere, J., & Schimmack, U. (2013). When romantic partners' goals conflict: Effects on relationship quality and subjective well-being. *Journal of Happiness Studies, 14*(1), 37–49. doi:10.1007/s10902-011-9314-2

Gilbert, D., & Malone, P. (1995). The correspondence bias. *Psychological Bulletin, 117*(1), 21–38. doi:10.1037/0033-2909.117.1.21

Gill, A. J., Oberlander, J., & Austin, E. (2006). Rating e-mail personality at zero acquaintance. *Personality and Individual Differences, 40*(3), 497–507. doi:10.1016/j.paid.2005.06.027

Glick, P., & Fiske, S. T. (1996). The ambivalent sexism inventory: Differentiating hostile and benevolent sexism. *Journal of Personality and Social Psychology,* 491–512. doi:10.1037/0022-3514.70.3.491

Guéguen, N. (2012). Gait and menstrual cycle: Ovulating women use sexier gaits and walk slowly ahead of men. *Gait and Posture, 35,* 621–634. 10.1016/j.gaitpost.2011.12.011

Gulledge, A. K., Gulledge, M. H., & Stahmann, R. F. (2003). Romantic physical affection types and relationship satisfaction. *American Journal of Family Therapy, 31*(4), 233–242. doi:10.1080/01926180390201936

Gray, J. (1992). *Men are from Mars. Women are from Venus: The classic guide to understanding the other-sex.* New York: Harper Collins Publisher.

Gray, J. D., & Silver, R. C. (1990). Opposite sides of the same coin: Former spouses' divergent perspectives in coping with their divorce. *Journal of Personality and Social Psychology, 59*(6), 1180–1191. doi:10.1037/0022-3514.59.6.1180

Greenwald, A. G., & Banaji, M. R. (1995). Implicit social cognition: Attitudes, self-esteem, and stereotypes. *Psychological Review, 102*(1), 4–27.

Greenwald, A. G., McGhee, D. E., & Schwartz, J. K. (1998). Measuring individual differences in implicit cognition: The implicit association test. *Journal of Personality and Social Psychology, 74*(6), 1464–1480. doi:10.1037/0022-3514.74.6.1464

Griffin, A. M., & Langlois, J. H. (2006). Stereotype directionality and attractiveness stereotyping: Is beauty good or is ugly bad? *Social Cognition, 24*(2), 187–206. doi:10.1521/soco.2006.24.2.187

Grote, N., & Clark, M. (2001). Perceiving unfairness in the family: Cause or consequence of marital distress? *Journal of Personality and Social Psychology, 80*(2), 281–293. doi:10.1037/0022-3514.80.2.281.

Guthrie, G. M., & Bennett, A. B. (1971). Cultural differences in implicit personality theory. *International Journal of Psychology, 6*(4), 305–312. doi:10.1080/00207597108246697

Halberstadt, J., & Rhodes, G. (2003). It's not just average faces that are attractive: Computer-manipulated averageness makes birds, fish, and automobiles attractive. *Psychonomic Bulletin & Review, 10*(1), 149–156. doi:10.3758/BF03196479

Halberstadt, J., & Rhodes, G. (2000). The attractiveness of nonface averages: Implications for an evolutionary explanation of the attractiveness of average faces. *Psychological Science, 11*(4), 285–289. doi:10.1111/1467-9280.00257

Hald, G., & Høgh-Olesen, H. (2010).Receptivity to sexual invitations from strangers of the opposite gender. *Evolution and Human Behavior, 31*(6), 453–458.

Hammock, G., & Richardson, D. (2011). Love attitudes and relationship experience. *The Journal of Social Psychology, 151*(5), 608–624. doi:10.1080/00224545.2010.5 22618

Hammond, M. D., & Overall, N. C. (2013). Men's hostile sexism and biased perceptions of intimate partners. *Personality and Social Psychology Bulletin, 39(12) 1585–1599.* doi: 10.1177/0146167213499026

Harris, R., Hoekstra, S. J., Scott, C. L., Sanborn, F. W., & Dodds, L. A. (2004). Autobiographical memories for seeing romantic movies on a date: Romance is not just for women. *Media Psychology, 6,* 257–284. doi:10.1207/s1532785xmep0603_2

Harrison, M. A., & Shortall, J. C. (2011). Women and men in love: Who really feels it and says it first? *The Journal of Social Psychology, 151,* 727–736. doi:10.1080/002 24545.2010.522626

Hassin, R., & Trope, Y. (2000). Facing faces: Studies on the cognitive aspects of physiognomy. *Journal of Personality and Social Psychology, 78*(5), 837–852. doi:10.1037/0022-3514.78.5.837

Hatfield, E., & Sprecher, S. (1986). Measuring passionate love in intimate relationships. *Journal of Adolescence, 9,* 383–410. doi:10.1016/S0140-1971(86)80043-4

Hatzenbuehler, M. L., McLaughlin, K. A., Keyes, K. M., & Hasin, D. S. (2010). The impact of institutional discrimination on psychiatric disorders in lesbian, gay, and bisexual populations: A prospective study. *American Journal of Public Health, 100*(3), 452–459. doi:10.2105/AJPH.2009.168815

Hazan, C., & Shaver, P. (1987). Romantic love conceptualized as an attachment process. *Journal of Personality and Social Psychology, 52*(3), 511–524. doi:10.1037/0022-3514.52.3.511

HBO (Producer) & Starr, D. (Creator). (1998–2004). *Sex and the city* (Television Series). USA.

Heider, F. (1958).*The psychology of interpersonal relations*. Hoboken, NJ: John Wiley & Sons Inc. doi:10.1037/10628-000

Heine, S. J., & Renshaw, K. (2002). Interjudge agreement, self-enhancement, and liking: Cross-cultural divergences. *Personality and Social Psychology Bulletin, 28*(5), 578–587. doi:10.1177/0146167202288002

Heller, J., Pallak, M., & Picek, J. (1973). The interactive effects of intent and threat on boomerang attitude change. *Journal of Personality and Social Psychology, 26*(2), 273–279. doi:10.1037/h0034461

Hendrick, C.,& Hendrick, S. S. (2006). Styles of romantic love. In R. J. Sternberg & K. Weis (Eds.) *The New Psychology of Love* (pp. 149–170). New Haven, CT: Yale University Press.

Hendrick, C., & Hendrick, S. S. (1989). Research on love: Does it measure up? *Journal of Personality and Social Psychology, 56*, 784–794. doi:10.1037/0022-3514.56.5.784

Hendrick, C., & Hendrick, S. S. (1988). Lovers wear rose colored glasses. *Journal of Social and Personal Relationships, 5*, 161–183.

Hendrick, C., & Hendrick, S. S. (1986). A theory and method of love. *Journal of Personality and Social Psychology, 50*, 392–402. doi:10.1037/0022-3514.50.2.392

Herz, R. S., & Inzlicht, M. (2002). Sex differences in response to physical and social factors involved in human mate selection: The importance of smell for women. *Evolution and Human Behavior, 23*(5), 359–364. doi:10.1016/S1090-5138(02)00095-8

Hewitt, B. (2009). Which spouse initiates marital separation when there are children involved? *Journal of Marriage and Family, 71*, 362–372. doi:10.1111/j.1741-3737.2009.00603.x

Hill, K. & Hurtado, A.M. (1996). *Ache life history: The ecology and demography of a foraging people.* New York: Aldine De Gruyter.

Hixon, J., & Swann, W. (1993). When does introspection bear fruit? Self-reflection, self-insight, and interpersonal choices. *Journal of Personality and Social Psychology, 64*(1), 35–43. doi:10.1037/0022-3514.64.1.35

Hofstede, G. (1980). *Culture's consequences: International differences in work-related values.* Beverly Hills CA: Sage Publications.

Holland, A. S., Fraley, R., & Roisman, G. I. (2012). Attachment styles in dating couples: Predicting relationship functioning over time. *Personal Relationships, 19*(2), 234–246.

Holz Ivory, A., Gibson, R., & Ivory, J. D. (2009). Gendered relationships on television: Portrayals of same-sex and heterosexual couples. *Mass Communication and Society, 12*, 170–192. doi:10.1080/15205430802169607

Hughes, S. M., Harrison, M. A., & Gallup, G. R. (2007). Sex differences in romantic kissing among college students: An evolutionary perspective. *Evolutionary Psychology, 5*(3), 612–631.

Hughes, S. M., Harrison, M. A., & Gallup, G. R. (2002). The sound of symmetry: Voice as a marker of developmental instability. *Evolution and Human Behavior, 23*(3), 173–180. doi:10.1016/S1090-5138(01)00099-X

Hughes, M., Morrison, K., & Asada, K. K. (2005). What's love got to do with it? Exploring the impact of maintenance rules, love attitudes, and network support on friends with benefits relationships. *Western Journal of Communication, 69*, 49–66. doi:10.1080/10570310500034154

Hugill, N., Fink, B., Neave, N., & Seydel, H. (2009). Men's physical strength is associated with women's perceptions of their dancing ability. *Personality and Individual Differences, 47*(5), 527–530. doi:10.1016/j.paid.2009.04.009

Hyde, J. (2005). The gender similarities hypothesis. *American Psychologist, 60*(6), 581–592.

Imhoff, R., & Banse, R. (2011). Implicit and explicit attitudes toward ex-partners differentially predict breakup adjustment. *Personal Relationships, 18*(3), 427–438. doi:10.1111/j.1475-6811.2010.01308.x

Jankowiak, W. R., & Fischer, E. F. (1992). A cross-cultural perspective on romantic love. *Ethnology, 31*(2), 149.

Jarcho, J. M., Berkman, E. T., & Lieberman, M. D. (2011). The neural basis of rationalization: Cognitive dissonance reduction during decision-making. *Social Cognitive and Affective Neuroscience, 6*(4), 460–467. doi:10.1093/scan/nsq054

Jensen-Campbell, L. A., Graziano, W. G., & West, S. G. (1995). Dominance, prosocial orientation, and female preferences: Do nice guys really finish last? *Journal of Personality and Social Psychology, 68,* 427–440. doi:10.1037/0022-3514.68.3.427

Jia, L., & Singh, R. (2009). Asymmetrical attention allocation to dissimilar and similar attitudes. *Journal of Experimental Social Psychology, 45*(6), 1259–1265. doi:10.1016/j.jesp.2009.07.012

Joel, S., Gordon, A. M., Impett, E. A., MacDonald, G., & Keltner, D. (2013). The things you do for me: Perceptions of a romantic partner's investments promote gratitude and commitment. *Personality and Social Psychology Bulletin, 39*(10), 1333–1345.

Johnco, C., Wheeler, L., & Taylor, A. (2010). They do get prettier at closing time: A repeated measures study of the closing-time effect and alcohol. *Social Influence, 5*(4), 261–271. doi:10.1080/15534510.2010.487650

Johnson, D. J., & Rusbult, C. E. (1989). Resisting temptation: Devaluation of alternative partners as a means of maintaining commitment in close relationships. *Journal of Personality and Social Psychology, 57*(6), 967–980. doi:10.1037/0022-3514.57.6.967

Johnston, V., Hagel, R., Franklin, M., Fink, B., & Grammer, K. (2001). Male facial attractiveness: Evidence for hormone-mediated adaptive design. *Evolution and Human Behavior, 22*(4), 251–267. doi:10.1016/S1090-5138(01)00066-6

Jonason, P. K., & Fisher, T. D. (2009). The power of prestige: Why young men report having more sex partners than young women. *Sex Roles, 60*(3–4), 151–159. doi:10.1007/s11199-008-9506-3

Jonason, P. K., & Marks, M. J. (2009). Common vs. uncommon sexual acts: Evidence for the sexual double standard. *Sex Roles, 60*(5–6), 357–365. doi:10.1007/s11199-008-9542-z

Jones, B. C., DeBruine, L. M., Little, A. C., Conway, C. A., & Feinberg, D. R. (2006). Integrating gaze direction and expression in preferences for attractive faces. *Psychological Science, 17*(7), 588–591. doi:10.1111/j.1467-9280.2006.01749.x

Jones, D., & Hill, K. (1993). Criteria of facial attractiveness in five populations. *Human Nature, 4*(3), 271–296. doi:10.1007/BF02692202

Jones, J., Pelham, B., Carvallo, M., & Mirenberg, M. (2004). How do I love thee? Let me count the Js: Implicit egotism and interpersonal attraction. *Journal of Personality and Social Psychology, 87*(5), 665–683. doi:10.1037/0022-3514.87.5.665

Kaighobadi, F., Shackelford, T. K., & Goetz, A. T. (2009). From mate retention to murder: Evolutionary psychological perspectives on men's partner-directed violence. *Review of General Psychology, 13*(4), 327–334. doi:10.1037/a0017254

Kalmijn, M. (2005). Attitude alignment in marriage and cohabitation: The case of sex-role attitudes. *Personal Relationships, 12,* 521–535. doi:10.1111/j.1475-6811.2005.00129.x

Kampe, K. W., Frith, C. D., Dolan, R. J., & Frith, U. (2001). Reward value of attractiveness and gaze. *Nature, 413*(6856), 589.

Karremans, J. C., Verwijmeren, T., Pronk, T. M., & Reitsma, M. (2009). Interacting with women can impair men's cognitive functioning. *Journal of Experimental Social Psychology, 45*(4), 1041–1044. doi:10.1016/j.jesp.2009.05.004

Kassin, S. M., Fein, S., & Markus, H. R. (2011). *Social Psychology* (8th ed.). Belmont, CA: Wadsworth, Cengage Learning.

Katz, J., & Beach, S. H. (2000). Looking for love? Self-verification and self-enhancement effects on initial romantic attraction. *Personality and Social Psychology Bulletin, 26*(12), 1526–1539. doi:10.1177/01461672002612007

Keller, M. C., & Young, R. K. (1996). Mate assortment in dating and married couples. *Personality and Individual Differences, 21*(2), 217–221. doi:10.1016/0191-8869(96)00066-9

Kellerman, J., Lewis, J., & Laird, J. D. (1989). Looking and loving: The effects of mutual gaze on feelings of romantic love. *Journal of Research in Personality, 23*(2), 145–161. doi:10.1016/0092-6566(89)90020-2

Kelly, R. L. (1995). *The foraging spectrum: Diversity in hunter-gatherer lifeways.* Washington, DC: Smithsonian Institution Press.

Kenny, D. A. (2004). PERSON: A general model of interpersonal perception. *Personality and Social Psychology Review, 8*(3), 265–280. doi:10.1207/s15327957pspr0803_3

Kenny, D. A. (1994). *Interpersonal perception: A social relations analysis.* New York: Guilford Press.

Kenny, D. A., & Acitelli, L. K. (2001). Accuracy and bias in the perception of the partner in a close relationship. *Journal of Personality and Social Psychology, 80*(3), 439–448. doi:10.1037/0022-3514.80.3.439

Kenny, D. A., Horner, C., Kashy, D. A., & Chu, L. (1992). Consensus at zero acquaintance: Replication, behavioral cues, and stability. *Journal of Personality and Social Psychology, 62*(1), 88–97. doi:10.1037/0022-3514.62.1.88

Kenrick, D., & Gutierres, S. (1980). Contrast effects and judgments of physical attractiveness: When beauty becomes a social problem. *Journal of Personality and Social Psychology, 38*(1), 131–140. doi:10.1037/0022-3514.38.1.131

Kephart, W. M. (1967). Some correlates of romantic love. *Journal of Marriage and the Family, 29*, 470–474. doi:10.2307/349585

Kirkpatrick, L., & Hazan, C. (1994). Attachment styles and close relationships: A four-year prospective study. *Personal Relationships, 1*(2), 123–142. doi:10.1111/j.1475-6811.1994.tb00058.x.

Kitayama, S., Markus, H., Matsumoto, H., & Norasakkunkit, V. (1997). Individual and collective processes in the construction of the self: Self-enhancement in the United States and self-criticism in Japan. *Journal of Personality and Social Psychology, 72*(6), 1245–1267. doi:10.1037/0022-3514.72.6.1245

Kitayama, S., Snibbe, A., Markus, H., & Suzuki, T. (2004). Is there any 'free' choice? Self and dissonance in two cultures. *Psychological Science, 15*(8), 527–533. doi:10.1111/j.0956-7976.2004.00714.x

Kleinke, C. L., Meeker, F. B., & Staneski, R. A. (1986). Preference for opening lines: Comparing ratings by men and women. *Sex Roles, 15*, 585–600. doi:10.1007/BF00288216

Kniffin, K. M., & Wilson, D. (2004). The effect of nonphysical traits on the perception of physical attractiveness: Three naturalistic studies. *Evolution and Human Behavior, 25*(2), 88–101. doi:10.1016/S1090-5138(04)00006-6

Krantz, D. S., & McCeney, M. K. (2002). Effects of psychological and social factors on organic disease: A critical assessment of research on coronary heart disease. *Annual Review of Psychology, 53*(1), 341–369. doi:10.1146/annurev.psych.53.100901.135208

Krull, D., Loy, M., Lin, J., Wang, C., Chen, S., & Zhao, X. (1999). The fundamental attribution error: Correspondence bias in individualist and collectivist cultures. *Personality and Social Psychology Bulletin, 25*(10), 1208–1219. doi:10.1177/0146167299258003

Kurup, R., & Kurup, P. (2003). Hypothalamic digoxin, hemispheric dominance, and neurobiology of love and affection. *International Journal of Neuroscience, 113*(5), 721–729. doi:10.1080/00207450390200107

Kurzban, R., & Weeden, J. (2005). HurryDate: Mate preferences in action. *Evolution and Human Behavior, 26*(3), 227–244. doi:10.1016/j.evolhumbehav.2004.08.012

Kwang, T., & Swann, W. R. (2010). Do people embrace praise even when they feel unworthy? A review of critical tests of self-enhancement versus self-verification. *Personality and Social Psychology Review, 14*(3), 263–280. doi:10.1177/1088868310365876

Lackenbauer, S. D., Campbell, L., Rubin, H., Fletcher, G. O., & Troister, T. (2010). The unique and combined benefits of accuracy and positive bias in relationships. *Personal Relationships, 17*(3), 475–493. doi:10.1111/j.1475-6811.2010.01282.x

LaFrance, M., & Banaji, M. (1992). Toward a reconsideration of the gender–emotion relationship. In M. S. Clark (Ed.), *Emotion and social behavior* (pp. 178–201). Thousand Oaks, CA: Sage Publications, Inc.

Lakoff, R. (1975). Linguistic theory and the real world. *Language Learning, 25*, 309–338.

Lamm, H., & Wiesmann, U. (1997). Subjective attributes of attraction: How people characterize their liking, their love, and their being in love. *Personal Relationships, 4*(3), 271–284. doi:10.1111/j.1475-6811.1997.tb00145

Langer, N. (2009). Late life love and intimacy. *Educational Gerontology, 38*, 752–764. doi:10.1080/0360127080270845

Langeslag, S. E., van der Veen, F. M., & Fekkes, D. (2012). Blood levels of serotonin are differentially affected by romantic love in men and women. *Journal of Psychophysiology, 26*(2), 92–98. doi:10.1027/0269-8803/a000071

Langlois, J. H., Kalakanis, L., Rubenstein, A. J., Larson, A., Hallam, M., & Smoot, M. (2000). Maxims or myths of beauty? A meta-analytic and theoretical review. *Psychological Bulletin, 126*(3), 390–423. doi:10.1037/0033-2909.126.3.390

Langlois, J. H., Ritter, J. M., Roggman, L. A., & Vaughn, L. S. (1991). Facial diversity and infant preferences for attractive faces. *Developmental Psychology, 27*(1), 79–84. doi:10.1037/0012-1649.27.1.79

Larson, C. M., Haselton, M. G., Gildersleeve, K. A., & Pillsworth, E. G. (2013). Changes in women's feelings about their romantic relationships across the ovulatory cycle. *Hormones and Behavior, 63*(1), 128–135. doi:10.1016/j.yhbeh.2012.10.005

Laurenceau, J., Troy, A. B., & Carver, C. S. (2005). Two distinct emotional experiences in romantic relationships: Effects of perceptions regarding approach of intimacy and avoidance of conflict. *Personality and Social Psychology Bulletin, 31*(8), 1123–1133. doi:10.1177/0146167205274447

Lavner, J. A., Karney, B. R., & Bradbury, T. N. (2012). Do cold feet warn of trouble ahead? Premarital uncertainty and four-year marital outcomes. *Journal of Family Psychology, 26*(6), 1012–1017. doi:10.1037/a0029912

Leaper, C., & Smith, T. E. (2004). A meta-analytic review of gender variations in children's language use: Talkativeness, affiliative speech, and assertive speech. *Developmental Psychology, 40*, 993–1027.

LeBel, E. P., & Campbell, L. (2009). Implicit partner affect, relationship satisfaction, and the prediction of romantic breakup. *Journal of Experimental Social Psychology, 45*(6), 1291–1294. doi:10.1016/j.jesp.2009.07.00

Ledbetter, A. M., Stassen- Ferrara, H. M., & Dowd, M. M. (2013). Comparing equity and self-expansion theory approaches to relational maintenance. *Personal Relationships, 20*(1), 38–51. doi:10.1111/j.1475-6811.2012.01395.x

Lee, J. A. (1973). *The colours of love*. Don Mills, ON.: New Press.

Lee, R. B. (2003). *The Dobe Jul'hoansi*. Cengage Learning.

Lenton, A. P., & Francesconi, M. (2010). How humans cognitively manage an abundance of mate options. *Psychological Science, 21*(4), 528–533. doi:10.1177/0956797610364958

Leon, D., Rotunda, R., Sutton, M., & Schlossman, C. (2003). Internet forewarning effects on ratings of attraction. *Computers in Human Behavior, 19*(1), 39–57. doi:10.1016/S0747-5632(02)00017-1

Leszczynski, J. (2009). A state conceptualization: Are individuals' masculine and feminine personality traits situationally influenced? *Personality and Individual Differences, 47*, 157–162.

Letzring, T. D., & Noftle, E. E. (2010). Predicting relationship quality from self-verification of broad personality traits among romantic couples. *Journal of Research in Personality, 44*(3), 353–362. doi:10.1016/j.jrp.2010.03.008

Letzring, T. D., Wells, S. M., & Funder, D. C. (2006). Information quantity and quality affect the realistic accuracy of personality judgment. *Journal of Personality and Social Psychology, 91*(1), 111–123. doi:10.1037/0022-3514.91.1.111

Levesque, M. J., & Kenny, D. A. (1993). Accuracy of behavioral predictions at zero acquaintance: A social relations analysis. *Journal of Personality and Social Psychology, 65*(6), 1178–1187. doi:10.1037/0022-3514.65.6.1178

Levesque, M., Nave, C., & Lowe, C. (2006). Toward an understanding of gender differences in inferring sexual interest. *Psychology of Women Quarterly, 30*(2), 150–158. doi:10.1111/j.1471-6402.2006.00278.x

Levine, R. , Sato, S., Hashimoto, T., & Verma, J. (1995). Love and marriage in eleven cultures. *Journal of Cross-Cultural Psychology, 26*, 554–571.

Lewandowski, G. R., Aron, A., & Gee, J. (2007). Personality goes a long way: The malleability of opposite-sex physical attractiveness. *Personal Relationships, 14*(4), 571–585. doi:10.1111/j.1475-6811.2007.00172.x

Li, N. P., Bailey, J., Kenrick, D. T., & Linsenmeier, J. W. (2002). The necessities and luxuries of mate preferences: Testing the tradeoffs. *Journal of Personality and Social Psychology, 82*(6), 947–955. doi:10.1037/0022-3514.82.6.947

Li, N. P., Griskevicius, V., Durante, K. M., Jonason, P. K., Pasisz, D. J., & Aumer, K. (2009). An evolutionary perspective on humor: Sexual selection or interest indication? *Personality and Social Psychology Bulletin, 35*(7), 923–936. doi:10.1177/0146167209334786

Li, N. P., Yong, J. C., Tov, W., Sng, O., Fletcher, G. J. O., Valentine, K. A., Jiang, Y. F., & Balliet, D. (2013). Mate preferences do predict attraction and choices in the early stages of mate selection. *Journal of Personality and Social Psychology, 105*, 757–776. doi:10.1037/a0033777

Lieberman, D., & Hatfield, E. (2006). Passionate love: cross-cultural and evolutionary perspectivesIn R. J. Sternberg & K. Weis (Eds.).*The New Psychology of Love* (pp. 274–297). New Haven, CT: Yale University Press.

Lieberman, D., Pillsworth, E. G., Haselton, M. G. (2011). Kin affiliation across the ovulatory cycle: Females avoid fathers when fertile. *Psychological Science, 22*, 13–18.

Lin, Y., & Raghubir, P. (2005). Gender differences in unrealistic optimism about marriage and divorce: Are men more optimistic and women more realistic? *Personality and Social Psychology Bulletin, 31*, 198–207.

Lippa, R. A. (2009). Sex differences in sex drive, sociosexuality, and height across 53 nations: Testing evolutionary and social structural theories. *Archives of Sexual Behavior, 38*(5), 631–651. doi:10.1007/s10508-007-9242-8

Lippa, R. A. (2007). The preferred traits of mates in a cross-national study of hetero-sexual and homosexual men and women: An examination of biological and cultural influences. *Archives of Sexual Behavior, 36*(2), 193–208. doi:10.1007/s10508-006-9151-2

Little, A. C., DeBruine, L. M., & Jones, B. C. (2013). Sex differences in attraction to familiar and unfamiliar opposite-sex faces: Men prefer novelty and women prefer familiarity. *Archives of Sexual Behavior,* doi:10.1007/s10508-013-0120-2

Little, A., Jones, B., & DeBruine, L. (2008). Preferences for variation in masculinity in real male faces change across the menstrual cycle: Women prefer more mascu-line faces when they are more fertile. *Personality and Individual Differences, 45*(6), 478–482. doi:10.1016/j.paid.2008.05.024.

Little, A. C., Penton-Voak, I. S., Burt, D. M., & Perrett, D. I. (2003). Investigating an imprinting-like phenomenon in humans: Partners and opposite-sex parents have similar hair and eye colour. *Evolution and Human Behavior, 24*(1), 43–51. doi:10.1016/S1090-5138(02)00119-8

Lloyd, S. A., & Emery, B. C. (2000). *The dark side of courtship: Physical and sexual aggression.* Thousand Oaks, CA: Sage Publications.

Lorenzo, G. L., Biesanz, J. C., & Human, L. J. (2010). What is beautiful is good and more accurately understood: Physical attractiveness and accuracy in first impressions of personality. *Psychological Science, 21*(12), 1777–1782. doi:10.1177/0956797610388048

Lundy, D. E., Tan, J., & Cunningham, M. R. (1998). Heterosexual romantic preferences: The importance of humor and physical attractiveness for different types of rela-tionships. *Personal Relationships, 5*(3), 311–325. doi:10.1111/j.1475-6811.1998.tb00174.x

Luo, S., & Klohnen, E. C. (2005). Assortative mating and marital quality in newlyweds: A couple-centered approach. *Journal of Personality and Social Psychology, 88*(2), 304–326. doi:10.1037/0022-3514.88.2.304

Luo, S., & Snider, A. G. (2009). Accuracy and biases in newlyweds' perceptions of each other: Not mutually exclusive but mutually beneficial. *Psychological Science, 20*(11), 1332–1339. doi:10.1111/j.1467-9280.2009.02449.x

Luo, S., & Zhang, G. (2009). What leads to romantic attraction: Similarity, reciprocity, security, or beauty? Evidence from a speed-dating study. *Journal of Personality, 77*(4), 933–964. doi:10.1111/j.1467-6494.2009.00570.x

Luo, S., Zhang, G., Watson, D., & Snider, A. G. (2010). Using cross-sectional couple data to disentangle the causality between positive partner perceptions and marital satisfaction. *Journal of Research in Personality, 44*(5), 665–668. doi:10.1016/j.jrp.2010.08.006

Luxen, M. F., & Buunk, B. P. (2006). Human intelligence, fluctuating asymmetry and the peacock's tail: General intelligence (g) as an honest signal of fitness. *Personality and Individual Differences, 41*(5), 897–902. doi:10.1016/j.paid.2006.03.015

Lyvers, M., Cholakians, E., Puorro, M., & Sundram, S. (2011). Beer goggles: Blood alcohol concentration in relation to attractiveness ratings for unfamiliar opposite sex faces in naturalistic settings. *The Journal of Social Psychology, 151*(1), 105–112. doi:10.1080/00224540903366776

Ma-Kellams, C., Blascovich, J., & McCall, C. (2012). Culture and the body: East–West differences in visceral perception. *Journal of Personality and Social Psychology, 102*(4), 718–728. doi:10.1037/a0027010

Maccoby, E. E. (1998). *The two sexes: Growing up apart, coming together*. Cambridge, MA: Harvard University Press.

Malle, B. F. (2006). The actor-observer asymmetry in attribution: A (surprising) meta-analysis. *Psychological Bulletin, 132*(6), 895–919. doi:10.1037/0033-2909.132.6.895

Mann, B. (2007). 100 days, 100 nights. On 100 Days, 100 Nights. New York: Daptone Records.

Manning, J. T. (1995). Fluctuating asymmetry and body weight in men and women: Implications for sexual selection. *Ethology & Sociobiology, 16*(2), 145–153. doi:10.1016/0162-3095(94)00074-H

Marcus, D. K., & Lehman, S. J. (2002). Are there sex differences in interpersonal perception at zero acquaintance? A social relations analysis. *Journal of Research in Personality, 36*(3), 190–207. doi:10.1006/jrpe.2001.2346

Marks, M. J., & Fraley, R. (2005). The sexual double standard: Fact or fiction? *Sex Roles, 52*(3–4), 175–186. doi:10.1007/s11199-005-1293-5

Mason, M. F., Tatkow, E. P., & Macrae, C. (2005). The look of love: Gaze shifts and person perception. *Psychological Science, 16*(3), 236–239. doi:10.1111/j.0956-7976.2005.00809.x

Massar, K., Buunk, A. P., & Dechesne, M. (2009). Jealousy in the blink of an eye: Jealous reactions following subliminal exposure to rival characteristics. *European Journal of Social Psychology, 39*(5), 768–779. doi:10.1002/ejsp.579

Mautz, B. S., Wong, B. M., Peters, R. A., & Jennions, M. D. (2013). Penis size interacts with body shape and height to influence male attractiveness. *Proceedings of the National Academy of Sciences of the United States of America, 110*(17), 6925–6930. doi:10.1073/pnas.1219361110

McCormick, N. B., & Jones, A. J. (1989). Gender differences in nonverbal flirtation. *Journal of Sex Education and Therapy, 15*, 271–282.

McGee, E., & Shevlin, M. (2009). Effect of humor on interpersonal attraction and mate selection. *Journal of Psychology: Interdisciplinary and Applied, 143*(1), 67–77. doi:10.3200/JRLP.143.1.67-77

McKenna, K., Green, A., & Gleason, M. (2002). Relationship formation on the Internet: What's the big attraction?. *Journal of Social Issues, 58*(1), 9–31. doi:10.1111/1540-4560.00246

McNulty, J. K. (2010). When positive processes hurt relationships. *Current Directions in Psychological Science, 19*(3), 167–171. doi:10.1177/0963721410370298

Meier, B. P., Robinson, M. D., Carter, M. S., & Hinsz, V. B. (2010). Are sociable people more beautiful? A zero-acquaintance analysis of agreeableness, extraversion, and attractiveness. *Journal of Research in Personality, 44*(2), 293–296. doi:10.1016/j.jrp.2010.02.002

Meston, C. M., & Buss, D. M. (2007). Why humans have sex. *Archives of Sexual Behavior, 36*(4), 477–507. doi:10.1007/s10508-007-9175-2

Meston, C., & Frohlich, P. (2003). Love at first fright: Partner salience moderates roller-coaster-induced excitation transfer. *Archives of Sexual Behavior, 32*(6), 537–544. doi:10.1023/A:1026037527455.

Meyer, D. (2007). Selective serotonin reuptake inhibitors and their effects on relationship satisfaction. *The Family Journal, 15*(4), 392–397. doi:10.1177/1066480707305470

Mikulincer, M. (1998). Adult attachment style and individual differences in functional versus dysfunctional experiences of anger. *Journal of Personality and Social Psychology, 74*(2), 513–524. doi:10.1037/0022-3514.74.2.513

Miller, R. S. (2012). *Intimate relationships* (6th ed.). New York: McGraw-Hill.

Miller, G., Tybur, J. M., & Jordan, B. D. (2007). Ovulatory cycle effects on tip earnings by lap dancers: Economic evidence for human estrus? *Evolution and Human Behavior, 28*(6), 375–381. doi:10.1016/j.evolhumbehav.2007.06.002

Miller, S. L. & Maner, J. K. (2010). Scent of a woman: Men's testosterone responses to olfactory ovulation cues. *Psychological Science, 21,* 276–283.

Mongeau, P. A., Aselage, C., Ficara, L., & Hart, M. (1997, November).*Communication and sexual expectancies for first dates.*Paper presented to the National Communication Association, Chicago, IL.

Montoya, R. (2008). I'm hot, so I'd say you're not: The influence of objective physical attractiveness on mate selection. *Personality and Social Psychology Bulletin, 34*(10), 1315–1331. doi:10.1177/0146167208320387

Montoya, R., & Horton, R. S. (2013). A meta-analytic investigation of the processes underlying the similarity-attraction effect. *Journal of Social and Personal Relationships, 30*(1), 64–94. doi:10.1177/0265407512452989

Moore, M. M. (1985). Nonverbal courtship patterns in women: Context and consequences. *Ethology and Sociobiology, 6,* 237–247. doi:10.1016/0162-3095(85)90016-0

Morr Serewicz, M., & Gale, E. (2008). First-date scripts: Gender roles, context, and relationship. *Sex Roles, 58*(3–4), 149–164. doi:10.1007/s11199-007-9283-4

Moreland, R., & Beach, S. (1992). Exposure effects in the classroom: The development of affinity among students. *Journal of Experimental Social Psychology, 28*(3), 255–276. doi:10.1016/0022-1031(92)90055-O

Morrow, G. D., Clark, E. M., & Brock, K. F. (1995). Individual and partner love styles: Implications for the quality of romantic involvements. *Journal of Social and Personal Relationships, 12*(3), 363–387. doi:10.1177/0265407595123003

Morry, M. M., Reich, T., & Kito, M. (2010). How do I see you relative to myself? Relationship quality as a predictor of self- and partner-enhancement within cross-sex friendships, dating relationships, and marriages. *The Journal of Social Psychology, 150*(4), 369–392. doi:10.1080/00224540903365471

Muise, A., Impett, E. A., & Desmarais, S. (2013). Getting it on versus getting it over with: Sexual motivation, desire, and satisfaction in intimate bonds. *Personality and Social Psychology Bulletin, 39*(10), 1320–1332. doi:10.1177/0146167213490963

Murray, S. L., Holmes, J. G., & Griffin, D. W. (1996a). The benefits of positive illusions: Idealization and the construction of satisfaction in close relationships. *Journal of Personality and Social Psychology, 70*(1), 79–98. doi:10.1037/0022-3514.70.1.79

Murray, S. L., Holmes, J. G., & Griffin, D. W. (1996). The self-fulfilling nature of positive illusions in romantic relationships: Love is not blind, but prescient. *Journal of Personality and Social Psychology, 71*(6), 1155–1180. doi:10.1037/0022-3514.71.6.1155

Myers, J. E., Madathil, J., & Tingle, L. R. (2005). Marriage satisfaction and wellness in India and the United States: A preliminary comparison of arranged marriages and marriages of choice. *Journal of Counseling and Development, 83*(2), 183–190. doi:10.1002/j.1556-6678.2005.tb00595.x

Naumann, L., Vazire, S., Rentfrow, P., & Gosling, S. (2009). Personality judgments based on physical appearance. *Personality and Social Psychology Bulletin, 35*(12), 1661–1671. doi:10.1177/0146167209346309.

NBC (Producer) & David, L. (Creator). (1989–1998). *Seinfeld* (Television Series). USA.

Neto, F., Mullet, E., Deschamps, J., Barros, J., Benvindo, R., Camino, L., & ... Machado, M. (2000). Cross-cultural variations in attitudes toward love. *Journal of Cross-Cultural Psychology, 31*(5), 626–635. doi:10.1177/0022022100031005005

Newcombe, N., & Arnkoff, D. B. (1979). Effects of speech style and sex of speaker on person perception. *Journal of Personality and Social Psychology, 37*, 1293–1303. doi:10.1037/0022-3514.37.8.1293

Nisbett, R. E., & Wilson, T. D. (1977). The halo effect: Evidence for unconscious alteration of judgments. *Journal of Personality and Social Psychology, 35*(4), 250–256. doi:10.1037/0022-3514.35.4.250

Norton, M. I., Frost, J. H., & Ariely, D. (2007). Less is more: The lure of ambiguity, or why familiarity breeds contempt. *Journal of Personality and Social Psychology, 92*(1), 97–105. doi:10.1037/0022-3514.92.1.97

Nosek, B. A., & Banaji, M. R. (2001). The Go/No-go Association Task. *Social Cognition, 19*(6), 625–666. doi:10.1521/soco.19.6.625.20886

Nosek, B. A., Hawkins, C., & Frazier, R. S. (2011). Implicit social cognition: From measures to mechanisms. *Trends in Cognitive Sciences, 15*(4), 152–159. doi:10.1016/j.tics.2011.01.005

O'Leary, K., Acevedo, B. P., Aron, A., Huddy, L., & Mashek, D. (2012). Is long-term love more than a rare phenomenon? If so, what are its correlates? *Social Psychological and Personality Science, 3*(2), 241–249. doi:10.1177/1948550611417015

Oliver, M. B., & Hyde, J. S. (1993). Gender differences in sexuality: A meta-analysis. *Psychological Bulletin, 114*(1), 29–51.

Ortigue, S., Bianchi-Demicheli, F., Patel, N., Frum, C., & Lewis, J. W. (2010). Neuroimaging of love: fMRI meta-analysis evidence toward new perspectives in sexual medicine. *Journal of Sexual Medicine, 7*(11), 3541–3552. doi:10.1111/j.1743-6109.2010.01999.x

Overall, N. C., & Hammond, M. D. (2013). Biased *and* accurate: Depressive symptoms and daily perceptions within intimate relationships. *Personality and Social Psychology Bulletin, 39*(5), 636–650.

Paulhus, D. L., & Bruce, M. (1992). The effect of acquaintanceship on the validity of personality impressions: A longitudinal study. *Journal of Personality and Social Psychology, 63*(5), 816–824. doi:10.1037/0022-3514.63.5.816

Pawlowski, B., & Jasienska, G. (2005). Women's preferences for sexual dimorphism in height depend on menstrual cycle phase and expected duration of relationship. *Biological Psychology, 70*(1), 38–43. doi:10.1016/j.biopsycho.2005.02.002

Pawlowski, B., & Koziel, S. (2002). The impact of traits offered in personal advertisements on response rates. *Evolution and Human Behavior, 23*(2), 139–149. doi:10.1016/S1090-5138(01)00092-7

Pennebaker, J., Dyer, M., Caulkins, R., Litowitz, D., Ackreman, P. L., Anderson, D. B., & McGraw, K. M. (1979). Don't the girls get prettier at closing time: A country and western application to psychology. *Personality and Social Psychology Bulletin, 5*(1), 122–125. doi:10.1177/014616727900500127

Penton-Voak, I. S., Perrett, D. I., Castles, D. L., Kobayashi, T. T., Burt, D. M., Murray, L. K., & Minamisawa, R. R. (1999). Menstrual cycle alters face preference. *Nature, 399*(6738), 741–742. doi:10.1038/21557

Peplau, L. (2003). Human sexuality: How do men and women differ? *Current Directions in Psychological Science, 12*(2), 37–40. doi:10.1111/1467-8721.01221

Perilloux, C., Easton, J. A., & Buss, D. M. (2012). The misperception of sexual interest. *Psychological Science, 23*(2), 146–151.

Perilloux, H. K., Webster, G. D., & Gaulin, S. C. (2010). Signals of genetic quality and maternal investment capacity: The dynamic effects of fluctuating asymmetry and waist-to-hip ratio on men's ratings of women's attractiveness. *Social Psychological and Personality Science*, *1*(1), 34–42. doi:10.1177/1948550609349514

Perrett, D. I., Lee, K. J., Penton-Voak, I. I., Rowland, D. D., Yoshikawa, S. S., Burt, D. M., & ... Akamatsu, S. S. (1998). Effects of sexual dimorphism on facial attractiveness. *Nature*, *394*(6696), 884–887. doi:10.1038/29772

Perrin, P. B., Heesacker, M., Tiegs, T. J., Swan, L. K., Lawrence, A. R., Smith, M. B., & ... Mejia-Millan, C. M. (2011). Aligning Mars and Venus: The social construction and instability of gender differences in romantic relationships. *Sex Roles*, *64*, 613–628. doi:10.1007/s11199-010-9804-4

Petersen, J. L., & Hyde, J. (2010). A meta-analytic review of research on gender differences in sexuality, 1993–2007. *Psychological Bulletin*, *136*(1), 21–38. doi:10.1037/a0017504

Place, S. S., Todd, P. M., Penke, L., & Asendorpf, J. B. (2009). The ability to judge the romantic interest of others. *Psychological Science*, *20*, 22–26. doi:10.1111/j.1467-9280.2008.02248.x

Place, S. S., Todd, P. M., Zhuang, J., Penke, L., & Asendorpf, J. B. (2012). Judging romantic interest of others from thin slices is a cross-cultural ability. *Evolution and Human Behavior*, *33*(5), 547–550. doi:10.1016/j.evolhumbehav.2012.02.001

Pongrácz, M. (2006). Opinions on Gender Roles: Findings of an international comparative study. In Ildikó Nagy, Marietta Pongrácz, & István György Tóth (Eds.) *Changing roles: Report on the situation of women and men in Hungary 2005*. 71–84. Budapest: TÁRKI Social Research Institute.

Prokosch, M. D., Coss, R. G., Scheib, J. E., & Blozis, S. A. (2009). Intelligence and mate choice: Intelligent men are always appealing. *Evolution and Human Behavior*, *30*(1), 11–20. doi:10.1016/j.evolhumbehav.2008.07.004

Quist, M. C., DeBruine, L. M., Little, A. C., & Jones, B. C. (2012). Integrating social knowledge and physical cues when judging the attractiveness of potential mates. *Journal of Experimental Social Psychology*, *48*(3), 770–773. doi:10.1016/j.jesp.2011.12.018

Rakowitz, S. (1995). *Instructor's manual and test-item file Sabini's Social Psychology*. New York: W. W. Norton and Company.

Ramirez, A. R., & Zhang, S. (2007). When online meets offline: The effect of modality switching on relational communication. *Communication Monographs*, *74*(3), 287–310. doi:10.1080/03637750701543493

Rao, K. V., & DeMaris, A. (1995). Coital frequency among married and cohabiting couples in the United States. *Journal of Biosocial Science*, *27*, 135–150.

Rauer, A. J., Sabey, A., & Jensen, J. F. (2013) Growing old together: Compassionate love and health in older adulthood. *Journal of Social and Personal Relationships* 0265407513503596, first published on September 24, 2013 doi:10.1177/0265407513503596

Ray, T. & Lafond, L. (Producers & Writers). (2002). *Gaydar*. (Motion Picture). USA.

Re, D. E., & Perrett, D. I. (2012). Concordant preferences for actual height and facial cues to height. *Personality and Individual Differences*, *53*(7), 901–906. doi:10.1016/j.paid.2012.07.001

Regan, P. C., Lakhanpal, S., & Anguiano, C. (2012). Relationship outcomes in Indian-American love-based and arranged marriages. *Psychological Reports*, *110*(3), 915–924. doi:10.2466/21.02.07.PR0.110.3.915-924

Reeder, H. M. (2000). "I like you ... as a friend": The role of attraction in cross-sex friendship. *Journal of Social and Personal Relationships*, *17*(3), 329–348. doi:10.1177/0265407500173002

Reeder, H. M. (1996).The subjective experience of love through adult life. *The International Journal of Aging and Human Development*, *43*, 325–340. doi:10.2190/V7J3-XQAL-2X59-M16X

Reedy, M. N., Birren, J. E., & Schaie, K. (1981). Age and sex differences in satisfying love relationships across the adult life span. *Human Development*, *24*, 52–66. doi:10.1159/000272625

Reis, H. T., Maniaci, M. R., Caprariello, P. A., Eastwick, P. W., & Finkel, E. J. (2011). Familiarity does indeed promote attraction in live interaction. *Journal of Personality and Social Psychology*, *101*(3), 557–570. doi:10.1037/a0022885

Reiss, I. L. (1964). The scaling of premarital sexual permissiveness. *Journal of Marriage and the Family*, *26*(2), 188–198. doi:10.2307/349726

Renninger, L., Wade, T., & Grammer, K. (2004). Getting that female glance: Patterns and consequences of male nonverbal behavior in courtship contexts. *Evolution and Human Behavior*, *25*(6), 416–431. doi:10.1016/j.evolhumbehav.2004.08.006

Rhodes, G. (2006). The evolutionary psychology of facial beauty. *Annual Review of Psychology*, *57*, 199–226. doi:10.1146/annurev.psych.57.102904.190208

Rhodes, G., Halberstadt, J., Jeffery, L., & Palermo, R. (2005). The attractiveness of average faces is not a generalized mere exposure effect. *Social Cognition*, *23*(3), 205–217. doi:10.1521/soco.2005.23.3.205

Rhodes, G., Morley, G., & Simmons, L. W. (2012). Women can judge sexual unfaithfulness from unfamiliar men's faces. *Biology Letters*, *9*, 20120908. http://dx.doi.org/10.1098/rsbl.2012.0908

Rhodes, G., Yoshikawa, S., Clark, A., Lee, K., McKay, R., & Akamatsu, S. (2001). Attractiveness of facial averageness and symmetry in non-Western cultures: In search of biologically based standards of beauty. *Perception*, *30*(5), 611–625. doi:10.1068/p3123

Riela, S., Rodriguez, G., Aron, A., Xu, X., & Acevedo, B. P. (2010). Experiences of falling in love: Investigating culture, ethnicity, gender, and speed. *Journal of Social and Personal Relationships*, *27*(4), 473–493. doi:10.1177/0265407510363508

Roberts, S., Kralevich, A., Ferdenzi, C., Saxton, T. K., Jones, B. C., DeBruine, L. M., & ... Havlicek, J. (2011). Body odor quality predicts behavioral attractiveness in humans. *Archives of Sexual Behavior*, *40*(6), 1111–1117. doi:10.1007/s10508-011-9803-8

Roisman, G. I., Clausell, E., Holland, A., Fortuna, K., & Elieff, C. (2008). Adult romantic relationships as contexts of human development: A multimethod comparison of same-sex couples with opposite-sex dating, engaged, and married dyads. *Developmental Psychology*, *44*(1), 91–101. doi:10.1037/0012-1649.44.1.91Rose, S., & Frieze, I. H. (1993). Young singles' contemporary dating scripts. *Sex Roles*, *28*, 499–509. doi:10.1007/BF00289677

Rose, S., & Frieze, I. H. (1989). Young singles' scripts for a first date. *Gender and Society*, *32*, 258–268.

Rosenbaum, M. (1986). The repulsion hypothesis: On the nondevelopment of relationships. *Journal of Personality and Social Psychology*, *51*(6), 1156–1166. doi:10.1037/0022-3514.51.6.1156.

Rozin, P., & Royzman, E. B. (2001). Negativity bias, negativity dominance, and contagion. *Personality and Social Psychology Review*, *5*(4), 296–320. doi:10.1207/S15327957PSPR0504_2

Rubin, L. B. (2007). The approach-avoidance dance: Men, women, and intimacy. In M. S. Kimmel & M. A. Messner (Eds.), *Men's Lives* (7th ed.) (pp. 319–324). Boston: Pearson Publishing.

Rubin, Z. (1970). Measurement of romantic love. *Journal of Personality and Social Psychology, 16*, 265–273. doi:10.1037/h0029841

Rudman, L. A., & Heppen, J. B. (2003). Implicit romantic fantasies and women's interest in personal power: A glass slipper effect? *Personality and Social Psychology Bulletin, 29*(11), 1357–1370.

Rule, N. O., Ambady, N., & Hallett, K. C. (2009). Female sexual orientation is perceived accurately, rapidly, and automatically from the face and its features. *Journal of Experimental Social Psychology, 45*(6), 1245–1251. doi:10.1016/j.jesp.2009.07.010

Rule, N. O., Rosen, K. S., Slepian, M. L., & Ambady, N. (2011). Mating interest improves women's accuracy in judging male sexual orientation. *Psychological Science, 22*(7), 881–886. doi:10.1177/0956797611412394

Salska, I., Frederick, D. A., Pawlowski, B., Reilly, A. H., Laird, K. T., & Rudd, N. A. (2008). Conditional mate preferences: Factors influencing preferences for height. *Personality and Individual Differences, 44*(1), 203–215. doi:10.1016/j.paid.2007.08.008

Saxton, T., Caryl, P., & Roberts, S. (2006). Vocal and facial attractiveness judgments of children, adolescents and adults: The ontogeny of mate choice. *Ethology, 112*(12), 1179–1185. doi:10.1111/j.1439-0310.2006.01278.x.

Saxton, T. K., Lyndon, A., Little, A. C., & Roberts, S. (2008). Evidence that androstadienone, a putative human chemosignal, modulates women's attributions of men's attractiveness. *Hormones and Behavior, 54*(5), 597–601. doi:10.1016/j.yhbeh.2008.06.001

Scheele, D., Striepens, N., Güntürkün, O., Deutschländer, S., Maier, W., Kendrick, K. M., & Hurlemann, R. (2012). Oxytocin modulates social distance between males and females. *The Journal of Neuroscience, 32*(46), 16074–16079. doi:10.1523/JNEUROSCI.2755-12.2012

Schmitt, D. P. (2005). Fundamentals of human mating strategies. In D.M. Buss (Ed.), *The handbook of evolutionary psychology* (pp. 258-291). Hoboken, New Jersey: John Wiley & Sons, Inc.

Schmitt, D. P., Alcalay, L., Allensworth, M., Allik, J., Ault, L., Austers, I., & ... ZupanÈiÈ, A. (2004). Patterns and universals of adult romantic attachment across 62 cultural regions: Are models of self and of other pancultural constructs? *Journal of Cross-Cultural Psychology, 35*(4), 367–402. doi:10.1177/0022022104266105

Schmitt, D. P., Youn, G., Bond, B., Brooks, S., Frye, H., Johnson, S., & ... Stoka, C. (2009). When will I feel love? The effects of culture, personality, and gender on the psychological tendency to love. *Journal of Research In Personality, 43*(5), 830–846. doi:10.1016/j.jrp.2009.05.008

Schneider, C. S., & Kenny, D. A. (2000). Cross-sex friends who were once romantic partners: Are they platonic friends now? *Journal of Social and Personal Relationships, 17*(3), 451–466. doi:10.1177/0265407500173007

Schneider, D., & Blankmeyer, B. (1983). Prototype salience and implicit personality theories. *Journal of Personality and Social Psychology, 44*(4), 712–722. doi:10.1037/0022-3514.44.4.712.

Schneiderman, I., Zagoory-Sharon, O., Leckman, J. F., & Feldman, R. (2012). Oxytocin during the initial stages of romantic attachment: Relations to couples' interactive reciprocity. *Psychoneuroendocrinology*, *37*(8), 1277–1285. doi:10.1016/j. psyneuen.2011.12.021

Schoenfeld, E. A., Bredow, C. A., & Huston, T. L. (2012). Do men and women show love differently in marriage? *Personality and Social Psychology Bulletin*, *38*(11), 1396–1409. doi:10.1177/0146167212450739

Schütz, A. (1999). It was your fault! Self-serving biases in autobiographical accounts of conflicts in married couples. *Journal of Social and Personal Relationships*, *16*(2), 193–208. doi:10.1177/0265407599162004

Schwarz, S., & Singer, M. (2013). Romantic red revisited: Red enhances men's attraction to young, but not menopausal women. *Journal of Experimental Social Psychology*, *49*(1), 161–164. doi:10.1016/j.jesp.2012.08.004

Sedikides, C., & Gregg, A. P. (2008). Self-enhancement: Food for thought. *Perspectives on Psychological Science*, *3*(2), 102–116. doi:10.1111/j.1745–6916.2008.00068.x

Senju, A., Vernetti, A., Kikuchi, Y., Akechi, H., Hasegawa, T., & Johnson, M. H. (2013). Cultural background modulates how we look at other persons' gaze. *International Journal of Behavioral Development*, *37*(2), 131–136. doi:10.1177/0165025412465360

Shaffer, D. R., Crepaz, N., & Sun, C. (2000). Physical attractiveness stereotyping in cross-cultural perspective: Similarities and differences between Americans and Taiwanese. *Journal of Cross-Cultural Psychology*, *31*(5), 557–582. doi:10.1177/0022022100031005002

Shaver, P., Hazan, C., & Bradshaw, D. (1988). Love as attachment. In R. J. Sternberg & M. L. Barnes (Eds.) *The Psychology of Love* (pp. 68–99). New Haven, CT: Yale University Press.

Shaw Taylor, L., Fiore, A. T., Mendelsohn, G. A., & Cheshire, C. (2011). "Out of my league": A real-world test of the matching hypothesis. *Personality and Social Psychology Bulletin*, *37*(7), 942–954. doi:10.1177/0146167211409947.

Simmons, C. H., vom Kolke, A., & Shimizu, H. (1986).Attitudes toward romantic love among American, German, and Japanese students. *The Journal of Social Psychology*, *126*, 327–336. doi:10.1080/00224545.1986.9713593

Simmons, L. W., Peters, M., & Rhodes, G. (2011). Low pitched voices are perceived as masculine and attractive but do they predict semen quality in men? *Plos ONE*, *6*(12), doi:10.1371/journal.pone.0029271

Simpson, J. A., Gangestad, S. W., & Biek, M. (1993). Personality and nonverbal social behavior: An ethological perspective of relationship initiation. *Journal of Experimental Social Psychology*, *29*(5), 434–461. doi:10.1006/jesp.1993.1020

Singh, D., Dixson, B. J., Jessop, T. S., Morgan, B. B., & Dixson, A. F. (2010). Cross-cultural consensus for waist–hip ratio and women's attractiveness. *Evolution and Human Behavior*, *31*(3), 176–181. doi:10.1016/j.evolhumbehav.2009.09.001

Slane, S., & Leak, G. (1978). Effects of self-perceived nonverbal immediacy behaviors on interpersonal attraction. *Journal of Psychology: Interdisciplinary and Applied*, *98*(2), 241–248. Retrieved from PsycINFO database.

Smith, A., Lyons, A., Ferris, J., Richters, J., Pitts, M., Shelley, J., & Simpson, J. M. (2011). Sexual and relationship satisfaction among heterosexual men and women: The importance of desired frequency of sex. *Journal of Sex and Marital Therapy*, *37*(2), 104–115. doi:10.1080/0092623X.2011.560531

Smith, J. E., Waldorf, V., & Trembath, D. L. (1990). "Single White male looking for thin, very attractive...". *Sex Roles*, *23*(11–12), 675–685. doi:10.1007/BF00289255

Smith-Lovin, L., & Brody, C. (1989). Interruptions in group discussions: The effects of gender and group composition. *American Sociological Review, 54*, 424–435. doi:10.2307/2095614

Snyder, M., Tanke, E., & Berscheid, E. (1977). Social perception and interpersonal behavior: On the self-fulfilling nature of social stereotypes. *Journal of Personality and Social Psychology, 35*(9), 656–666. doi:10.1037/0022-3514.35.9.656.

Snyder, M., & Swann, W. (1978). Hypothesis-testing processes in social interaction. *Journal of Personality and Social Psychology, 36*(11), 1202–1212. doi:10.1037/0022-3514.36.11.1202.

Soler, C., Núñez, M., Gutiérrez, R., Núñez, J., Medina, P., Sancho, M., et al. (2003). Facial attractiveness in men provides clues to semen quality. *Evolution and Human Behavior, 24*(3), 199–207. doi:10.1016/S1090-5138(03)00013-8.

Sparks, E. A., Ehrlinger, J., & Eibach, R. P. (2012). Failing to commit: Maximizers avoid commitment in a way that contributes to reduced satisfaction. *Personality and Individual Differences, 52*(1), 72–77. doi:10.1016/j.paid.2011.09.002

Spielmann, S. S., MacDonald, G., & Wilson, A. E. (2009). On the rebound: Focusing on someone new helps anxiously attached individuals let go of ex-partners. *Personality and Social Psychology Bulletin, 35*(10), 1382–1394. doi:10.1177/0146167209341580

Spielmann, S. S., Maxwell, J. A., MacDonald, G., & Baratta, P. L. (2013). Don't get your hopes up: Avoidantly attached individuals perceive lower social reward when there is potential for intimacy. *Personality and Social Psychology Bulletin, 39*(2), 219–236. doi:10.1177/0146167212472541

Sprecher, S. (2001). Equity and social exchange in dating couples: Associations with satisfaction, commitment, and stability. *Journal of Marriage and the Family, 63*(3), 599–613. doi:10.1111/j.1741-3737.2001.00599.x

Sprecher, S. (1999). "I love you more today than yesterday": Romantic partners' perceptions of changes in love and related affect over time. *Journal of Personality and Social Psychology, 76*(1), 46–53. doi:10.1037/0022-3514.76.1.46

Sprecher, S. (1989). The importance to males and females of physical attractiveness, earning potential, and expressiveness in initial attraction. *Sex Roles, 21*(9–10), 591–607. doi:10.1007/BF00289173

Sprecher, S., & Fehr, B. (2011). Dispositional attachment and relationship-specific attachment as predictors of compassionate love for a partner. *Journal of Social and Personal Relationships, 28*(4), 558–574. doi:10.1177/0265407510386190

Sprecher, S., & Fehr, B. (2005). Compassionate love for close others and humanity. *Journal of Social and Personal Relationships, 22*(5), 629–651. doi:10.1177/0265407505056439

Sprecher, S., & Hatfield, E. (1996). Premarital sexual standards among U.S. college students: Comparison with Russian and Japanese students. *Archives of Sexual Behavior, 25*(3), 261–288. doi:10.1007/BF02438165

Sprecher, S., & Metts, S. (1989). Development of the "Romantic Beliefs Scale" and examination of the effects of gender and gender-role orientation. *Journal of Social and Personal Relationships, 6*, 387–411. doi:10.1177/0265407589064001

Sprecher, S., & Toro-Morn, M. (2002). A study of men and women from different sides of earth to determine if men are from Mars and women are from Venus in their beliefs about love and romantic relationships. *Sex Roles, 46*(5–6), 131–147. doi:10.1023/A:1019780801500

Sprecher, S., Treger, S., & Sakaluk, J. K. (2013). Premarital sexual standards and sociosexuality: Gender, ethnicity, and cohort differences. *Archives of Sexual Behavior,* doi:10.1007/s10508-013-0145-6

Sprecher, S., Zimmerman, C., & Abrahams, E. M. (2010). Choosing compassionate strategies to end a relationship: Effects of compassionate love for partner and the reason for the breakup. *Social Psychology*, *41*(2), 66–75. doi:10.1027/1864-9335/a000010

Stavrova, O., Fetchenhauer, D., & Schlösser, T. (2012). Cohabitation, gender, and happiness: A cross-cultural study in thirty countries. *Journal of Cross-Cultural Psychology*, *43*(7), 1063–1081. doi:10.1177/0022022111419030

Sternberg, R. J. (1986). A triangular theory of love. *Psychological Review*, *93*(2), 119–135. doi:10.1037/0033-295X.93.2.119

Stewart, S., Stinnett, H., & Rosenfeld, L. (2000). Sex differences in desired characteristics of short-term and long-term relationship partners. *Journal of Social and Personal Relationships*, *17*(6), 843–853. doi:10.1177/0265407500176008.

Stillman, T. F., & Maner, J. K. (2009). A sharp eye for her SOI: Perception and misperception of female sociosexuality at zero acquaintance. *Evolution and Human Behavior*, *30*(2), 124–130. doi:10.1016/j.evolhumbehav.2008.09.005

Stirrat, M., & Perrett, D. (2010). Valid facial cues to cooperation and trust: Male facial width and trustworthiness. *Psychological Science*, *21*(3), 349–354. doi:10.1177/0956797610362647.

Stoessel, C., Stiller, J., Bleich, S., Boensch, D., Doerfler, A., Garcia, M., & ... Forster, C. (2011). Differences and similarities on neuronal activities of people being happily and unhappily in love: A functional magnetic resonance imaging study. *Neuropsychobiology*, *64*(1), 52–60. doi:10.1159/000325076

Stulp, G., Pollet, T. V., Verhulst, S., & Buunk, A. P. (2012). A curvilinear effect of height on reproductive success in human males. *Behavioral Ecology and Sociobiology*, *66*(3), 375–384. doi:10.1007/s00265-011-1283-2

Sümer, N., & Cozzarelli, C. (2004). The impact of adult attachment on partner and self-attributions and relationship quality. *Personal Relationships*, *11*(3), 355–371. doi:10.1111/j.1475-6811.2004.00087.x

Swaddle, J. P. (1996). Reproductive success and symmetry in zebra finches. *Animal Behaviour*, *51*, 203–210.

Swami, V., Frederick, D. A., Aavik, T., Alcalay, L., Allik, J., Anderson, D., & ... Zivcic-Becirevic, I. (2010). The attractive female body weight and female body dissatisfaction in 26 countries across 10 world regions: Results of the international body project I. *Personality and Social Psychology Bulletin*, *36*(3), 309–325. doi:10.1177/0146167209359702

Swami, V., Furnham, A., Chamorro-Premuzic, T., Akbar, K., Gordon, N., Harris, T., & ... Tovée, M. J. (2010). More than just skin deep? Personality information influences men's ratings of the attractiveness of women's body sizes. *The Journal of Social Psychology*, *150*(6), 628–647. doi:10.1080/00224540903365497

Swami, V., Henderson, G., Custance, D., & Tovée, M. J. (2011). A cross-cultural investigation of men's judgments of female body weight in Britain and Indonesia. *Journal of Cross-Cultural Psychology*, *42*(1), 140–145. doi:10.1177/0022022110383319

Swami, V., Inamdar, S., Stieger, S., Nader, I. W., Pietschnig, J., Tran, U. S., & Voracek, M. (2012). A dark side of positive illusions? Associations between the love-is-blind bias and the experience of jealousy. *Personality and Individual Differences*, *53*(6), 796–800. doi:10.1016/j.paid.2012.06.004

Swami, V., & Tovée, M. J. (2008). The muscular male: A comparison of the physical attractiveness preferences of gay and heterosexual men. *International Journal of Men's Health*, *7*(1), 59–71. doi:10.3149/jmh.0701.59

Swann, W. (1987). Identity negotiation: Where two roads meet. *Journal of Personality and Social Psychology, 53*(6), 1038–1051. doi:10.1037/0022-3514.53.6.1038

Swann, W. R., De La Ronde, C., & Hixon, J. (1994). Authenticity and positivity strivings in marriage and courtship. *Journal of Personality and Social Psychology, 66*(5), 857–869. doi:10.1037/0022-3514.66.5.857

Tannen, D. (1994). Gender and discourse. New York: Oxford University Press.

Tannen, D. (1990). *You just don't understand: Women and men in conversation.* New York: Morrow.

Tannen, D. F. (1987). Conversational style. In H. W. Dechert & M. Raupach (Eds.), *Psycholinguistic Models of Production.* (pp. 251–267). Westport, CT: Ablex Publishing.

Tennant, A. (Director). (2005). *Hitch.* (Motion Picture). USA: Columbia Pictures.

Tenney, E. R., Turkheimer, E., & Oltmanns, T. F. (2009). Being liked is more than having a good personality: The role of matching. *Journal of Research in Personality, 43*(4), 579–585. doi:10.1016/j.jrp.2009.03.004

Thao, H., Overbeek, G., & Engels, R. E. (2010). Effects of attractiveness and social status on dating desire in heterosexual adolescents: An experimental study. *Archives of Sexual Behavior, 39*(5), 1063–1071. doi:10.1007/s10508-009-9561-z

The Associated Press (2013). Suspended Eastern Conn. baseball coach retires. Retrieved from http://www.wfsb.com/story/22092945/suspended-eastern-conn-baseball-coach-retires

Thibaut, J. W., & Kelley, H. H. (1986). *The social psychology of groups.* Piscataway, NJ, US: Transaction Publishers.

Thompson, A. E., & O'Sullivan, L. F. (2012). Gender differences in associations of sexual and romantic stimuli: Do young men really prefer sex over romance? *Archives of Sexual Behavior, 41,* 949–957. doi:10.1007/s10508-011-9794-5

Thornhill, R., & Gangestad, S. W. (1999). The scent of symmetry: A human sex pheromone that signals fitness? *Evolution and Human Behavior, 20*(3), 175–201. doi:10.1016/S1090-5138(99)00005-7

Thornhill, R., Gangestad, S. W., Miller, R., Scheyd, G., McCollough, J. K., & Franklin, M. (2003). Major histocompatibility complex genes, symmetry, and body scent attractiveness in men and women. *Behavioral Ecology, 14*(5), 668–678. doi:10.1093/beheco/arg043

Todd, P. M., Penke, L., Fasolo, B., & Lenton, A. P. (2007). Different cognitive processes underlie human mate choices and mate preferences. *Proceedings of the National Academy of Sciences of The United States of America, 104*(38), 15011–15016. doi:10.1073/pnas.0705290104

Toma, C. L., Hancock, J. T., & Ellison, N. B. (2008). Separating fact from fiction: An examination of deceptive self-presentation in online dating profiles. *Personality and Social Psychology Bulletin, 34*(8), 1023–1036. doi:10.1177/0146167208318067

Trivers, R. (1972). Parental investment and sexual selection. In B. Campbell (Ed.), *Sexual selection and the descent of man: 1871–1971* (pp. 136–179). Chicago: Aldine.

Twamley, K. (2013). Love and desire amongst middle-class Gujarati Indians in the UK and India. *Culture, Health, and Sexuality, 15*(3), 327–340. doi:10.1080/13691058.2012.754945

Utne, M. K., Hatfield, E., Traupmann, J., & Greenberger, D. (1984). Equity, marital satisfaction, and stability. *Journal of Social And Personal Relationships, 1*(3), 323–332. doi:10.1177/0265407584013005

Valentova, J., Rieger, G., Havlicek, J., Linsenmeier, J. W., & Bailey, J. (2011). Judgments of sexual orientation and masculinity–femininity based on thin slices of behavior: A cross-cultural comparison. *Archives of Sexual Behavior*, *40*(6), 1145–1152. doi:10.1007/s10508-011-9818-1

Van Yperen, N. W., & Buunk, B. P. (1991). Equity theory and exchange and communal orientation from a cross-national perspective. *The Journal of Social Psychology*, *131*(1), 5–20. doi:10.1080/00224545.1991.9713820

Vazire, S., & Gosling, S. (2004). e-Perceptions: Personality impressions based on personal websites. *Journal of Personality and Social Psychology*, *87*(1), 123–132. doi:10.1037/0022-3514.87.1.123.

Wade, T., Auer, G., & Roth, T. M. (2009). What is love: Further investigation of love acts. *The Journal of Social, Evolutionary, and Cultural Psychology*, *3*(4), 290–304.

Wager, T., Atlas, L., Lindquist, M., Roy, M., Woo, C., & Kross, E. (2013). An fMRI-based neurologic signature of physical pain. *The New England Journal of Medicine*, *368*(15), 1388–1397. doi:10.1056/NEJMoa1204471

Weeden, J., & Sabini, J. (2005). Physical attractiveness and health in Western societies: A review. *Psychological Bulletin*, *131*(5), 635–653. doi:10.1037/0033-2909.131.5.635

Weege, B., Lange, B. P., & Fink, B. (2012). Women's visual attention to variation in men's dance quality. *Personality and Individual Differences*, *53*(3), 236–240. doi:10.1016/j.paid.2012.03.011

Wells, B. E., & Twenge, J. M. (2005). Changes in young people's sexual behavior and attitudes, 1943–1999: A cross-temporal meta-analysis. *Review of General Psychology*, *9*(3), 249–261. doi:10.1037/1089-2680.9.3.249

Whitchurch, E. R., Wilson, T. D., & Gilbert, D. T. (2011). "He loves me, he loves me not...": Uncertainty can increase romantic attraction. *Psychological Science*, *22*(2), 172–175. doi:10.1177/0956797610393745

White, G., Fishbein, S., & Rutsein, J. (1981). Passionate love and the misattribution of arousal. *Journal of Personality and Social Psychology*, *41*(1), 56–62. doi:10.1037/0022-3514.41.1.56

Widmer, E. D., Treas, J. & Newcomb, R. (1998). Attitudes toward nonmarital sex in 24 countries. *The Journal of Sex Research, 35*, 349–358.

Wiederman, M. W. (1997). The truth must be in here somewhere: Examining the gender discrepancy in self-reported lifetime number of sex partners. *Journal of Sex Research*, *34*(4), 375–386. doi:10.1080/00224499709551905

Wiederman, M. W. (1993). Evolved gender differences in mate preferences: Evidence from personal advertisements. *Ethology and Sociobiology, 14*, 331–351. doi:10.1016/0162-3095(93)90003-Z

Willis, J., & Todorov, A. (2006). First impressions: Making up your mind after a 100-ms exposure to a face. *Psychological Science*, *17*(7), 592–598. Retrieved from SPORTDiscus with Full Text database.

Winquist, L. A., Mohr, C. D., & Kenny, D. A. (1998). The female positivity effect in the perception of others. *Journal of Research in Personality*, *32*(3), 370–388. doi:10.1006/jrpe.1998.2221

Wlodarski, R., & Dunbar, R. M. (2013). Menstrual cycle effects on attitudes toward romantic kissing. *Human Nature*, *24*(4), 402–413. doi:10.1007/s12110-013-9176-x

Wright, R., Wadley, V., Danner, M., & Phillips, P. (1992). Persuasion, reactance, and judgments of interpersonal appeal. *European Journal of Social Psychology*, *22*(1), 85–91. doi:10.1002/ejsp.2420220109.

Xiaohe, X., & Whyte, M. (1990). Love matches and arranged marriages: A Chinese replication. *Journal of Marriage and The Family, 52*(3), 709–722. doi:10.2307/352936

Xu, X., Aron, A., Brown, L., Cao, G., Feng, T., & Weng, X. (2011). Reward and motivation systems: A brain mapping study of early-stage intense romantic love in Chinese participants. *Human Brain Mapping, 32*(2), 249–257. doi:10.1002/hbm.21017

Yabiku, S. T., & Gager, C. T. (2009).Sexual frequency and the stability of marital and cohabiting unions. *Journal of Marriage and Family, 71*(4), 983–1000. doi:10.1111/j.1741-3737.2009.00648.x

Yanover, T., & Thompson, J. (2010). Perceptions of health and attractiveness: The effects of body fat, muscularity, gender, and ethnicity. *Journal of Health Psychology, 15*(7), 1039–1048. doi:10.1177/1359105309360426

Yelsma, P., & Athappilly, K. (1988). Marital satisfaction and communication practices: Comparisons among Indian and American couples. *Journal of Comparative Family Studies, 19*(1), 37–54.

Yong, J. C. & Li, N. P. (2012). Cash in hand, want better looking mate: Significant resource cues raise men's mating standards. *Personality and Individual Differences, 52*, 53–58.

Yum, Y., & Canary, D. J. (2009). Cultural differences in equity theory predictions of relational maintenance strategies. *Human Communication Research, 35*(3), 384–406. doi:10.1111/j.1468-2958.2009.01356.x

Zajonc, R. (1968). Attitudinal effects of mere exposure. *Journal of Personality and Social Psychology, 9*(2, Pt.2), 1–27. doi:10.1037/h0025848.

Zajonc, R., Adelmann, P., Murphy, S., & Niedenthal, P. (1987). Convergence in the physical appearance of spouses. *Motivation and Emotion, 11*(4), 335–346. doi:10.1007/BF00992848.

Zayas, V., & Shoda, Y. (2005). Do automatic reactions elicited by thoughts of romantic partner, mother, and self relate to adult romantic attachment? *Personality and Social Psychology Bulletin, 31*(8), 1011–1025. doi:10.1177/0146167204274100

Zebrowitz, L. A., Franklin, R. R., Hillman, S., & Boc, H. (2013). Older and younger adults' first impressions from faces: Similar in agreement but different in positivity. *Psychology and Aging, 28*(1), 202–212. doi:10.1037/a0030927

Zebrowitz, L. A., Hall, J. A., Murphy, N. A., & Rhodes, G. (2002). Looking smart and looking good: Facial cues to intelligence and their origins. *Personality and Social Psychology Bulletin, 28*(2), 238–249. doi:10.1177/0146167202282009

Zebrowitz, L. A., Wang, R., Bronstad, P., Eisenberg, D., Undurraga, E., Reyes-García, V., & Godoy, R. (2012). First impressions from faces among U.S. and culturally isolated Tsimane' people in the Bolivian rainforest. *Journal of Cross-Cultural Psychology, 43*(1), 119–134. doi:10.1177/0022022111411386

Zuckerman, M., Hodgins, H., & Miyake, K. (1990). The vocal attractiveness stereotype: Replication and elaboration. *Journal of Nonverbal Behavior, 14*(2), 97–112. doi:10.1007/BF01670437.

Zuckerman, M., Miyake, K., & Hodgins, H. (1991). Cross-channel effects of vocal and physical attractiveness and their implications for interpersonal perception. *Journal of Personality and Social Psychology, 60*(4), 545–554. doi:10.1037/0022-3514.60.4.545.

Index

Printed by Printforce, the Netherlands